The Testimony of the Spirit

The Testimony of the Spirit

New Essays

Edited by

R. DOUGLAS GEIVETT
AND PAUL K. MOSER

OXFORD
UNIVERSITY PRESS

OXFORD
UNIVERSITY PRESS

Oxford University Press is a department of the University of Oxford. It furthers
the University's objective of excellence in research, scholarship, and education
by publishing worldwide. Oxford is a registered trade mark of Oxford University
Press in the UK and certain other countries.

Published in the United States of America by Oxford University Press
198 Madison Avenue, New York, NY 10016, United States of America.

© Oxford University Press 2017

Library of Congress Cataloging-in-Publication Data
Names: Geivett, R. Douglas and Paul, K. Moser, editors.
Title: The testimony of the Spirit : new essays /
edited by R. Douglas Geivett and Paul K. Moser.
Description: 1 [edition]. | New York : Oxford University Press, 2017. |
Includes bibliographical references and index.
Identifiers: LCCN 2016032129 (print) | LCCN 2017005622 (ebook) |
ISBN 9780190225391 (hbk: alk. paper) | ISBN 9780190225407 (pbk: alk. paper) |
ISBN 9780190225414 | ISBN 9780190225421
Subjects: LCSH: Holy Spirit.
Classification: LCC BT122 .T47 2017 (print) | LCC BT122 (ebook) |
DDC 231/.3—dc23 LC record available at https://lccn.loc.gov/2016032129

1 3 5 7 9 8 6 4 2
Paperback printed by Webcom Inc., Canada
Hardback printed by Bridgeport National Bindery, Inc., United States of America

Contents

Preface

THE TOPIC OF the testimony of the Spirit of God emerges from various biblical writings, but it has suffered from a lack of due attention in recent work in theology, biblical studies, and the philosophy of religion. This book aims to correct this deficiency to some extent. It does so from an interdisciplinary perspective, including theology, biblical studies, philosophy of religion, ethics, psychology, aesthetics, and apologetics.

The book includes new work on the topic of the testimony of the Spirit in relation to its role in biblical literature (Craig A. Evans and Jeremiah J. Johnston), an ontology of the Spirit (Stephen T. Davis), conscience and the voice of God (Paul Gooch), moral knowledge (C. Stephen Evans), religious diversity and spiritual testimony (Roger Trigg), psychology and neuroscience (Malcolm Jeeves), community and language (Oliver Davies), art and beauty (Steven R. Guthrie), desire and gender (Elizabeth T. Groppe), apologetics (Kevin Kinghorn and Jerry L. Walls), and the church and discernment (Angus Ritchie). The book offers an Introduction that covers some key theological and philosophical topics, and concludes with a bibliography on the testimony of the Spirit. It takes up its topics in a manner accessible to a wide range of readers from various disciplines, including college students, educated non-academics, and researchers.

We thank three anonymous referees for their helpful suggestions, the book's contributors for their cooperation with a number of deadlines, and Abby Thigpen for her work on the index. We especially thank Cynthia Read, Senior Editor at Oxford University Press, for her guidance on the project.

R.D.G. and P.K.M.
La Mirada and Chicago
Pentecost, May 15, 2016

Contributors

OLIVER DAVIES is Professor of Christian Doctrine at King's College, London, where he is coordinator of the Transformation Theology project. He has taught at the University of Cologne, the University of Wales, the University of Virginia, and the Pontifical Gregorian University at Rome. He is a past President of the Society for the Study of Theology, and is the author of *The Creativity of God* and *Theology of Transformation* (Oxford University Press).

STEPHEN T. DAVIS is the Russel K. Pitzer Professor of Philosophy at Claremont McKenna College. Writing mainly in the philosophy of religion and analytic theology, he is the author of some 80 academic essays and author and/or editor of 17 books, including *After We Die: Theology, Philosophy, and the Question of Life After Death*, *Christian Philosophical Theology* (Oxford University Press), and *Encountering Evil: Live Options in Theodicy*.

CRAIG A. EVANS currently serves as the John Bisagno Distinguished Professor of Christian Origins at Houston Baptist University. He has written numerous books on Jesus and Christian origins and is a scholar of the Dead Sea Scrolls. Some of his recent books include *Jesus and His World*, *From Jesus to the Church*, and *Jesus and the Remains of His Day*.

C. STEPHEN EVANS is University Professor of Philosophy and Humanities at Baylor University and a Professorial Fellow at Australian Catholic University. His most recent books include *Why Christianity Still Makes Sense*, *God and Moral Obligation* (Oxford University Press), *Natural Signs and Knowledge of God* (Oxford University Press), and *Kierkegaard: An Introduction*. Evans has received numerous awards and fellowships, including two fellowships

from the National Endowment for the Humanities and the C. S. Lewis prize for best book in philosophy of religion.

R. Douglas Geivett is Professor of Philosophy in the Talbot School of Theology at Biola University. He is the author of *Evil and the Evidence for God* and co-editor of *Contemporary Perspectives on Religious Epistemology* (Oxford University Press), *In Defense of Miracles, Being Good: Christian Virtues for Everyday Life*, and *Christian Apologists and Their Critics*.

Paul W. Gooch is Professor of Philosophy and President Emeritus, Victoria University in the University of Toronto. His many years of academic administration have been balanced by research and publication, including *Partial Knowledge: Philosophical Studies in Paul* and *Reflections on Jesus and Socrates: Word and Silence*, along with many articles and chapters on Greek philosophy and philosophical issues in the New Testament.

Elizabeth T. Groppe is Associate Professor of Theology at Xavier University in Cincinnati, Ohio. She is the author of *Yves Congar's Theology of the Holy Spirit* (Oxford University Press) and *Eating and Drinking*. Her articles in such areas as Trinitarian theology, Christian–Jewish relations, and theological responses to the ecological crisis appear in various journals, including *Theological Studies, Horizons*, and *Modern Theology*.

Steven R. Guthrie is Professor of Theology, Religion, and the Arts at Belmont University in Nashville, Tennessee, and is the founding Director of Belmont's programs in Religion and the Arts and in Worship Studies. He was Lecturer in Theology at the University of St. Andrews and was a Postdoctoral Research Fellow there in the Institute for Theology, Imagination, and the Arts. He performs and records in the Nashville area. His publications include *Creator Spirit: The Holy Spirit and the Art of Becoming Human, Resonant Witness: Conversations between Music and Theology* (ed. with Jeremy Begbie), and *Faithful Performances: Enacting Christian Tradition* (ed. with Trevor Hart).

Malcolm Jeeves, C.B.E., a past president of the Royal Society of Edinburgh, and former Editor of *Neuropsychologia*, is professor emeritus of psychology at the University of St. Andrews. He was Foundation Professor of Psychology there, and established the psychology department. The author of 16 books, including nine related to science and faith, his most recent books are *Human Nature at the Millennium* (with R. J. Berry), *Science, Life, and Christian Belief* (with Warren Brown), *Neuroscience, Psychology, and Religion: Illusions, Delusions, and Realities about Human Nature*, and *Minds, Brains, Souls, and Gods: A Conversation on Faith, Psychology, and Neuroscience*, along with two edited volumes, *From Cells to Souls—and Beyond: Changing Portraits of Human Nature* and *Rethinking Human Nature*.

JEREMIAH J. JOHNSTON is Associate Professor of Early Christianity at Houston Baptist University and founder of the Christian Thinkers Society. Johnston's specialty is in Jesus and the Gospels, New Testament manuscripts (their number, nature, and reliability), extra-canonical Gospels and Gospel-like writings, and apologetics.

KEVIN KINGHORN is Professor of Philosophy and Religion at Asbury Theological Seminary, having taught at Wycliffe Hall, University of Oxford. He has published over 30 articles in moral philosophy and philosophy of religion. He is the author of *The Decision of Faith: Can Christian Beliefs Be Freely Chosen?* and *A Framework for the Good*.

PAUL K. MOSER is Professor of Philosophy at Loyola University Chicago. He is the author of *Philosophy after Objectivity* (Oxford University Press), *Knowledge and Evidence*, *The Elusive God*, *The Evidence for God*, *The Severity of God*, and *The God Relationship*; co-author of *The Theory of Knowledge* (Oxford University Press); editor of *The Oxford Handbook of Epistemology* (Oxford University Press) and *A Priori Knowledge* (Oxford University Press); and co-editor of *Human Knowledge*, 3d ed. (Oxford University Press). He is the General Editor of *The Oxford Handbooks of Philosophy*, and past Editor of the *American Philosophical Quarterly*.

ANGUS RITCHIE is Director for the Centre of Theology and Community in east London and Priest in Charge at St. George-in-the-East. His publications include *From Morality to Metaphysics: The Theistic Implications of our Ethical Commitments* (Oxford University Press) and (with Paul Hackwood) *Just Love: Personal and Social Transformation in Christ*.

ROGER TRIGG is Emeritus Professor of Philosophy, University of Warwick and Senior Research Fellow at the Ian Ramsey Centre, University of Oxford. He is the author of many books in philosophy, the latest being *Religious Diversity: Philosophical and Political Implications* and *Beyond Matter: Why*

Science Needs Metaphysics. He was the Founding President of the British Society for Philosophy of Religion and is a past President of the European Society for Philosophy of Religion.

JERRY L. WALLS is Scholar in Residence and Professor of Philosophy at Houston Baptist University. His books include a trilogy on the afterlife, and more recently two volumes on moral philosophy co-authored with David Baggett: *Good God: The Theistic Foundations of Morality* and *God and Cosmos: Human Truth and Human Meaning* (both with Oxford University Press).

The Testimony of the Spirit

Introduction

WITHIN THEOLOGICAL CIRCLES, controversy about the Spirit of God has centered mainly on two things: (a) the Filioque, or the procession of the Spirit from God, and (b) the gifts or manifestations of the Spirit. We may distinguish between "manifestations" as *effects of the Spirit's activity*, regardless of whether these are seen to be manifestations, and "manifestations" as *revelations of the Spirit* in some fashion or other. Many theologians and philosophers of religion speak of "the testimony of the Spirit" of God to identify some kind of divine revelation in human experience, and this book focuses on that topic.

Testimony and Witness

Typical talk of the testimony of the Spirit assumes that the Spirit is a personal agent, regardless of whether one assumes a Trinitarian understanding of God. The Spirit's interest in the world and in humanity is, we thus might say, "personal," involving a personal will. In particular, the Spirit of God has desires and intentions for the world, and takes seriously the plight of humans, including their moral shortcomings and (impending) death. On a traditional understanding, the Spirit of God has a loving will to bring about fellowship between humans and God, and this includes a resolve to challenge the aspirations of humans who refuse the divine–human fellowship they need.

Some writers of the Jewish and Christian scriptures speak of the Spirit (*ruach* in Hebrew, *pneuma* in Greek) of God with special emphasis on this Spirit's interventions in human experience. They do not offer a detailed metaphysics, or ontology, of the Spirit, but they often characterize this

Spirit functionally, as *God in action*, with distinctive power. The kinds of power characteristic of the Spirit of God are diverse and sometimes subtle, but they share the feature of serving God's creative and redemptive purposes in action. Some of these divine purposes include witnessing to humans regarding who God is and what God expects of humans.

Some of the Jewish and Christian scriptures represent God's Spirit as the source of created life, as the unique power (and even the breath) of God, and as the origin of the human reflection of God's righteousness. Our interest, however, is now in the testimony or witness of the Spirit of God. Something is a witness only if it is a witness *to something*—that is, only if it indicates, perhaps fallibly, the reality of something. Talk of "testimony" may suggest something akin to a verbal report, but a "witness" need not be verbal.[1]

God's Spirit might witness *to* a feature of God's moral character by presenting divine *agapē* (or righteous love) to a person, perhaps in that person's conscience. This witness would not be reducible to the Spirit's witnessing *that* God manifests *agapē*. The latter witness (*that* something is the case) would be *de dicto* in virtue of its propositional content, whereas the former witness would be *de re* in virtue of its presenting the reality in question, with no required propositional content. Similarly, I could present you with the blue ticket in my pocket without presenting any propositional content, or, alternatively, I could witness to you *that* I have a blue ticket in my pocket. I also could do both, of course, but this does not challenge the conceptual distinction at hand. Witnessing *to* something need not be witnessing *that* something is the case. Otherwise, the familiar distinction between *showing* (or, manifesting) and *telling* (or, describing) would collapse, and simple experiential witnessing would be lost. We do well to preserve that distinction, including in connection with a witness from God's Spirit.

Witness to Divine Agapē

We should ask what the main intended point of the Spirit's witness is. A hint may be found in Jesus's filial use of the term *"Abba"* ("Father") for God and in the subsequent use of this Aramaic term in the Greek writings

---

1. See R. Douglas Geivett, "Can and Would God Speak to Us? A Dialogue on Divine Speaking," in Steven B. Cowan and Terry L. Wilder (eds.), *In Defense of the Bible* (Nashville, TN: Broadman & Holman, 2013), pp. 13–46.

of the apostle Paul and in the Greek Gospel of Mark (Mark 14:36). We do well to consider Paul's perspective on the witness of the Spirit.

Paul introduces the filial theme to the Galatian Christians by using the Aramaic language of Jesus, as follows: "when the fullness of time had come, God sent his Son, born of a woman, born under the law, in order to redeem those who were under the law, so that we might receive adoption as children. And because you are children, God has sent the Spirit of his Son into our hearts, crying, 'Abba! Father!'" (Gal. 4:4–6, NRSV, here and in subsequent biblical translations). The Spirit of the risen Jesus, in Paul's account, confirms one's being a child of God with the cry "Abba! Father!" Paul makes a closely related point to the Roman Christians, as follows: "you did not receive a spirit of slavery to fall back into fear, but you have received a spirit of adoption. When we cry, 'Abba! Father!' it is that very Spirit bearing witness with (*summarturei*) our spirit that we are children of God" (Rom. 8:15–16). This filial language of Paul, in the wake of Jesus, indicates that the Spirit of God seeks to witness not only to God's reality and faithfulness, but also to one's having become (or, at least, one's becoming) a cooperative child of the living God, in filial relationship with God. We may think of the "witness" identified by Paul as part of the "testimony" of God's Spirit.

Paul thinks of the human reception of the Spirit of God as God's way of now providing a guarantee, or a down payment, for the future realization of God's redemptive promises. He writes to the Corinthian Christians: "It is God who establishes us with you in Christ and has anointed us, by putting his seal on us and giving us his Spirit in our hearts as a first installment" (2 Cor. 1:22; see 2 Cor. 5:5, Eph. 1:13–14). This view suggests that the witness of the Spirit is eschatological, because the presence of the Spirit, like the kingdom of God, has not fully arrived yet. As a result, the Spirit points to the fullness of God's future, for which one can hope, even hope on the basis of a distinctive ground in one's experience (as we shall see).

We do not (yet) apprehend the full perfection of God's presence among humans. We can experience, however, the "first fruits of the Spirit," according to Paul: "We ourselves, who have the first fruits of the Spirit, groan inwardly while we wait for adoption, the redemption of our bodies" (Rom. 8:23, NRSV). Paul states a related eschatological point as follows: "through the Spirit, by faith, we eagerly wait for the hope of righteousness" (Gal. 5:5, NRSV). Paul holds that the disciples of Jesus have already received as a gracious gift righteousness from God, reconciliation with God, and adoption into God's family (see Rom. 3:21–26, 5:11, 8:14–16; Gal. 3:7, 4:4–7).

Even so, Paul acknowledges that redemption is *now realized in part* but *not yet fully realized*, owing in part to the future redemption of human bodies. As a result, Paul emphasizes eschatological hope in God that awaits the completion of God's redemption for humans (see Rom. 8:24–25). The witness of God's Spirit is partly eschatological, then, owing to its pointing to God's future completion of redemptive promises.

Paul, among other New Testament writers, characterizes the reception of God's Spirit (and of the accompanying witness of the Spirit to becoming God's child) as requiring a human response to God's intervention. Paul remarks on this matter directly to the Galatian Christians: "Did you receive the Spirit by doing the works of the law or [instead] by believing what you heard? Are you so foolish? Having started with the Spirit, are you now ending with the flesh? . . . [I]n Christ Jesus the blessing of Abraham [would] come to the Gentiles, so that we might receive the promise of the Spirit through faith" (Gal. 3:2–4, 14, NRSV). Paul, then, holds that one receives God's Spirit by responding in faith, including trust, in God to God's redemptive intervention in Christ.

Some distinctive features mark the filial relation that emerges from the human reception of God's Spirit via faith in God (not to be confused with belief that God exists). We may understand this relation in terms of a goal regarding moral character: namely, "like parent, like child." On the assumption that Christ is "the image of God" (2 Cor. 4:4, Col. 1:15), Paul identifies God's goal that humans "be conformed to the image of his Son, in order that he might be the firstborn within a large family" (Rom. 8:29, NRSV). Writing to the Corinthian Christians, Paul makes a closely related point in terms of "the Lord, the Spirit": "all of us, with unveiled faces, seeing the glory of the Lord as though reflected in a mirror, are being transformed into the same image from one degree of glory to another; for this comes from the Lord, the Spirit" (2 Cor. 3:18, NRSV). We need not digress to ontological questions about the exact relation between "the Lord" and "the Spirit" in Paul's thought. The point now is that the work of God's Spirit includes the transformation of humans into the image of Christ, who is the "the image of God."

The image of God in Christ has distinctive moral and spiritual features. A central feature is exemplified in the self-sacrificial *agapē* of the crucified Jesus. Paul highlights this feature not only in his seminal chapter on *agapē* (1 Cor. 13) but also in his letter to the Roman Christians. A centrally important passage on the witness of God's Spirit is the following: "we also boast in our sufferings, knowing that suffering produces endurance, and endurance produces character, and character produces hope, and hope does not disappoint us, because God's love has been poured into our hearts through the Holy Spirit that has been given to us" (Rom. 5:3–5, NRSV, cf. 2 Cor. 5:14). This passage captures a key feature of the "inner witness" of God's Spirit, because it identifies the work of God's Spirit in relaying a central feature of God's moral character to the volitional and affective center of humans (their "hearts"). This is an "inner" work, but it is not a matter of merely subjective opinion; nor is it beyond describing (Paul just described it). (This inner work has an awareness component, awareness *by* the person and *of* an objective reality.)

Paul does not relinquish a central role for God's witness through the crucified Christ. The passage just cited is followed by this remark: "God proves his love for us in that while we still were sinners Christ died for us" (Rom. 5:8, NRSV). God's witness to his *agapē* for humans in the cross of Christ does not depend on any mere human receiving an inner witness from God. Instead, the inner witness manifests in a human's "heart" the kind of *agapē* that motivated Christ to obey God's call to the cross, in order to "prove" God's love for humans.[2]

We might think of the cross of Christ as a divine witness that is "outer" in that it is not itself, as a spatiotemporal historical event, relayed to a human heart. Historical events that are spatiotemporally finite or bounded are not themselves relayed, strictly speaking, to any other spatiotemporal situation, even if *descriptions* of them are. In any case, the witness of the historical cross of Christ, as a spatiotemporal historical event, was not inner to any mere human, even if the *message* of the cross and (more basic than a message) the divine *agapē* conveyed by the cross can become inner, in virtue of being relayed to a human heart.

We can distinguish two kinds of inner witness of the Spirit, with regard to two kinds of "being relayed" of the message and the *agapē* of the cross of Christ: *cooperatively* relayed, and *uncooperatively* relayed. The message and the *agapē* of the cross are cooperatively relayed if and only if they are relayed to an intended recipient in a manner whereby that recipient *cooperatively receives* them. By contrast, they are uncooperatively relayed to an intended recipient if and only if they are relayed to an intended recipient in a manner whereby that recipient does not cooperatively receive them. So, an inner witness of the Spirit to an intended

---

2. On the role of obedience in Christ's undergoing crucifixion, see Phil. 2:8.

recipient need not be cooperatively received by that intended recipient. In particular, humans can reject the Spirit's inner witness to the message and the *agapē* of the cross of Christ.

Humans can have varying degrees of cooperatively receiving the message and the *agapē* of the cross of Christ. Some people may cooperate more than others in receiving the Spirit's, for various reasons. This fact allows, however, for there being a definite threshold of volitional cooperation for one's cooperatively receiving the message and the *agapē* of the cross of Christ. The threshold, as suggested by Paul's account, includes one's committing oneself *as a priority* to cooperation with God's message and *agapē*.[3] So, people can be responsible to God for how they respond to the inner witness of the Spirit. As agents, they can exercise their will to cooperate with, reject, or withhold judgment on the inner witness from God's Spirit.

Although widely neglected, Paul's suggestion of the distinctive cognitive, or evidential, role of the Spirit's witness can clarify the nature of the Spirit's inner witness. Concerning people who respond in faith to God, Paul says that God's *agapē* is poured out into their hearts through the Spirit. In addition, Paul says that hope in God does not disappoint these people because this *agapē* has been poured out into their hearts. Paul would say the same of *faith* in God, given that he began Romans 5 with the importance of faith in God, and he regards faith and hope as very closely interconnected, so much so that he remarks that "in hope we were saved" (Rom. 8:24). Paul holds, then, that neither hope nor faith in God disappoints the Roman Christians, because they have received God's supporting *agapē* in their hearts, courtesy of the Spirit of God.

Paul's idea in Romans 5:5 includes a notion of psychological disappointment, but not just of psychological disappointment. Paul is saying more than that the Roman Christians are not psychologically disappointed by their hope in God. Given their experience of God's powerful *agapē* in their hearts, the Roman Christians had received inner *evidence* of God's reality, and therefore they are not *cognitively*, or *evidentially*, disappointed. The Spirit witnesses to God's reality and moral character via divine *agapē* poured into a cooperative human's heart, and this witness includes distinctive experiential evidence received by such a human. The directly experienced *agapē* from God, in Paul's view, saves one from cognitive disappointment in hope and faith in God, because

---

3. We need not settle the details of the nature of such commitment here.

one thereby has a cognitive base, or foundation, from God for one's hope and faith in God.[4]

The divine *agapē* in question is God's *compassionate will* to bring about what is morally and spiritually best for cooperative humans. Humans who refuse to cooperate block the power of this *agapē* for themselves, because it is not coercive of human wills. When humans cooperatively receive divine *agapē*, however, they are transformed toward the moral and spiritual character of God in Christ. Specifically, in cooperatively responding to God's intervention, one finds God's will within oneself (if imperfectly), particularly God's will to love others, even one's enemies. In addition, one can be surprised by this new reality of *agapē* within oneself, given that it marks a discernible change from one's previous inclinations, especially toward one's enemies.

The evidence from the relevant divine *agapē* is inner, given its presentation directly to the heart, or will, of humans. It is not, however, purely subjective, because it does not depend just on human desires, intentions, beliefs, hopes, or feelings. In addition, this *agapē*, when cooperatively received, yields and involves a distinctive life direction, a Christ-ward direction, we might say. A human life with this direction is a Christ-shaped life, given its being formed by the Spirit of Christ. Accordingly, Paul speaks to the Galatian Christians in these terms: "My little children, for whom I am again in the pain of childbirth until Christ is formed in you . . ." (Gal. 4:19, NRSV). Paul thinks of this formation as empowered by the Spirit of God and Christ. One can see, from a suitably well-positioned perspective, the salient reality of Christ-shaped lives in such disciples as the apostle Paul, Francis of Assisi, and Mother Teresa. It would be a mistake to call the reality of these lives purely subjective or illusory. The disciples in question have become life-size evidence of the reality of God and God's empowering Spirit. In addition, this opportunity to become such living evidence is available to all disciples of Christ, even if its realization demands considerable human resolve and obedience toward God.

The Johannine writings in the New Testament agree with Paul's emphasis on the role of *agapē* in the Spirit's witness. For instance, the writer of 1 John states: "No one has ever seen God; if we love one another, God lives

---

4. For a helpful description of the experience in question, see P. T. Forsyth, *The Person and Place of Jesus Christ* (London: Hodder and Stoughton, 1909), pp. 195–205. See also Paul Moser, "Divine Hiddenness, Agape Conviction, and Spiritual Discernment," in *Sensing Things Divine*, eds. Frederick Aquino and Paul Gavrilyuk (Oxford: Oxford University Press, forthcoming 2017).

in us, and his love is perfected in us. By this we know that we abide in him and he in us, because he has given us of his Spirit" (1 John 4:12–13, NRSV). The key idea is that God's *agapē* is being realized and perfected in humans cooperative with this *agapē*, and the Spirit of God empowers such change. The author of 1 John links this idea to knowing God, as follows: "Beloved, let us love one another, because love is from God; everyone who loves is born of God and knows God. Whoever does not love does not know God, for God is love" (1 John 4:7–8, NRSV).

Agapē, according to 1 John, has its source in God, not in humans, and human cooperative participation in it is necessary for knowing God, given God's inherently loving character. The writer of 1 John also sounds a note similar to Paul's on confident hope in God: "Love has been perfected among us in this: that we may have boldness on the day of judgement, because as he is, so are we in this world" (1 John 4:17, NRSV). We may read this remark to agree with Paul's idea that inner *agapē* from God grounds a disciple's confident hope in God's future completion of redemption.

Convicting and Groaning

An important theme in John's Gospel is that the witness of God's Spirit includes the convicting of humans regarding their waywardness from God's character of perfect *agapē*. For instance, that author attributes the following remark to Jesus: "It is to your advantage that I go away, for if I do not go away, the advocate (*paraklētos*) will not come to you; but if I go, I will send him to you. And when he comes, he will prove the world wrong about sin and righteousness and judgement" (John 16:7–8, NRSV). This convicting work, according to John's Gospel, aims to witness to God's character of *agapē* and to invite humans to cooperate with it, in faithful obedience. Because this *agapē* is inherently unselfish and servant-like, it is self-sacrificial and, in that regard, kenotic. 1 John 3:16 connects *agapē* with self-sacrifice directly: "We know love by this, that he [Jesus] laid down his life for us—and we ought to lay down our lives for one another." The Spirit's witness, then, points to and manifests divine *agapē* and thereby involves the kind of self-sacrifice found in the cross of Christ.

Paul acknowledges that God's Spirit empowers a robust moral life for cooperative humans. For instance, Paul remarks: "The law of the Spirit of life in Christ Jesus has set you free from the law of sin and of death. For God has done what the law, weakened by the flesh, could not do: by sending his own Son in the likeness of sinful flesh, and to deal with sin, he condemned sin in the flesh, so that the just requirement of the law might be fulfilled in us, who walk not according to the flesh but according to the Spirit" (Rom. 8:2–4, NRSV). Paul thinks of "the Spirit of life in Christ" as the Spirit of righteous life in Christ.

Paul opposes any human means for supposedly earning, or meriting, God's approval or righteousness, such as by the Mosaic law or any other law (see Rom. 4:2, 9:31–32). He holds, however, that an aim of the cross of Christ and the guiding Spirit of God in Christ is that "the just requirement of the law might be fulfilled in us." We may understand this as a call to be conformed to God's moral character as represented in the law of God as fulfilled by the obedient Christ. This reading fits not only with Paul's emphasis on human righteousness via Christ and his Spirit (see Rom. 5:21, 2 Cor. 5:21, 1 Cor. 3:16) but also with a central lesson on righteousness in the Gospel of Matthew (Matt. 5:17–18, 20). It also fits with Paul's view that divine grace works "through righteousness" (Rom. 5:21). The witness of the Spirit, then, is inseparable from a witness to God's righteousness available to humans without their earning it. That is, it is inseparable from a witness to the gift of divine grace.

Paul thinks of the inner witness of the Spirit as including the inner intercession of the Spirit in prayer to God. He states: "Likewise the Spirit helps us in our weakness; for we do not know how to pray as we ought, but that very Spirit intercedes with sighs too deep for words. And God, who searches the heart, knows what is the mind of the Spirit, because the Spirit intercedes for the saints according to the will of God" (Rom. 8:26–27, NRSV). Paul understands this intercession as experiential for cooperative humans. The "sighs too deep for words" are within a person who has received God's Spirit, and are thus part of the inner witness of the Spirit. These sighs witness to God's profound redemptive intervention in a person's experience, even if they are too deep for words. They qualify as experiential evidence of God's intervention for a recipient, as they are not produced just by that recipient.

The sighs in question include eschatological groanings originating from God's Spirit. So, as noted, Paul remarks: "not only the creation, but we ourselves, who have the first fruits of the Spirit, groan inwardly while we wait for adoption, the redemption of our bodies" (Rom. 8:23; cf. Gal. 4:19). We may think of this inward groaning as co-groaning with the Spirit of God, who witnesses through the depth of this groaning for the fullness of redemption. This inner witness is to God's character of faithful redemption toward humans.

The eschatological theme in question emerges also from Paul's understanding of the Spirit's relation to the resurrection of humans. Paul writes: "If the Spirit of him who raised Jesus from the dead dwells in you, he who raised Christ from the dead will give life to your mortal bodies also through his Spirit that dwells in you" (Rom. 8:11, NRSV). The Spirit, then, empowers God's resurrection of humans, including Jesus. Paul acknowledges a sense in which Christians already have been "raised with Christ" (see Col. 3:1; Rom. 6:4, 11; Eph. 2:5, 6). We might call this "spiritual resurrection" by the Spirit to new life with Christ now; it precedes the bodily resurrection promised to disciples of Christ. The Spirit witnesses to the present reality of this new spiritual life for Christians. Even so, the fullness of new life awaits bodily resurrection, and this calls for an eschatological witness from the Spirit and for human hope in God as faithful to complete the redemptive promises.

Self-Manifesting and Self-Authenticating Spirit

The Spirit's witness supplies God's way of authenticating God's reality and character for humans. This way is *self*-authentication, because it includes God's Spirit *self*-manifesting the divine moral character to cooperative humans, perhaps in their conscience. It also includes God's producing traits of this divine character, such as divine *agapē*, in the experiences and lives of cooperative recipients. God, then, can be self-evidencing and self-authenticating toward humans, given God's Spirit who self-manifests God's unique, morally perfect character. This view does not entail the implausible view that a subjective human experience, such as a vision, or a literary document, such as the Bible, is self-authenticating regarding God's existence. It entails instead that *God* is an independent moral agent who is self-authenticating toward humans as the ultimate source of *agapē* in human lives. Neither such a God nor such *agapē* is a subjective human experience.

According to various New Testament writers, God ultimately testifies to Godself, including God's reality and moral character, via the Spirit of the risen Christ, God's own image. We should not expect mere claims or mere subjective experiences to be self-attesting about objective reality. God, however, is an intentional causal agent who can be self-authenticating in being self-manifesting and self-witnessing regarding God's own reality and moral character. Accordingly, Paul attributes the following statement to God: "I have *shown myself* [*emphanēs egenomēn*] to those who did not ask for me" (Rom. 10:20, NRSV).

John's Gospel likewise portrays Jesus as being self-manifesting: "Those who love me will be loved by my Father, and I will love them and reveal myself to them" (John 14:21). This kind of self-authenticating via self-manifestation fits with the biblical theme of God's confirming God's own reality. The underlying rationale is that God inherently has a self-sufficient morally perfect character and cannot find anyone or anything else to serve the purpose of adequate authentication for God's reality and moral character. So, the prophet Isaiah attributes the following announcement to God: "I am God, and there is no other. By myself I have sworn" (Isa. 45:22–23; see also Gen. 22:16–17, Heb. 6:13–14).

The reality of divine self-authentication via God's Spirit has important consequences for human knowledge of God. James S. Stewart called this reality *the divine self-verification of Christ in conscience*. He identified a key feature of this form of divine self-authentication, as follows: "This is a very wonderful thing which happens: you begin exploring the fact of Christ, perhaps merely intellectually and theologically—and before you know where you are, the fact is exploring *you,* spiritually and morally. . . . You set out to see what you can find in Christ, and sooner or later God in Christ finds you. That is the self-verification of Jesus."[5] More specifically, we may think of this phenomenon as God's self-authentication of God and Christ via the inner witness of the Spirit of God.[6] Inquirers about God can benefit from examining this kind of religious experience, which does not reduce to a philosophical argument about the existence of God. In fact, philosophical arguments about God's existence can divert attention from this distinctive kind of religious experience.[7]

In Paul's pneumatic epistemology, as noted, God self-manifests the divine character of *agapē* in the experience of cooperative humans, pouring out God's enemy-love in their hearts, through the Spirit (Rom. 5:5). Mere humans and counterfeit gods lack the needed power and moral character

---

5. James S. Stewart, "Who is this Jesus? (2)," in Stewart, *The Strong Name* (Edinburgh: T & T Clark, 1940), pp. 87–88; cf. Paul K. Moser, *The Severity of God* (Cambridge: Cambridge University Press, 2013), Chapter 3.

6. See H. R. Mackintosh, *The Doctrine of the Person of Jesus Christ* (Edinburgh: T & T Clark, 1912), pp. 317–20.

7. For a discussion of non-inferential, experience-based justification for belief in God, see R. Douglas Geivett, "The Evidential Value of Religious Experience," in Paul Copan and Paul K. Moser (eds.), *The Rationality of Theism* (London: Routledge, 2003), pp. 175–203; and Paul K. Moser, *The God Relationship: Ethics for Inquiry about God* (Cambridge: Cambridge University Press, 2017), Chapter 3.

to self-manifest in this manner. Only a God of perfect love can self-manifest in this way, because only such a God has the needed power and moral character. Given that God is *sui generis* in this regard, we should expect God to be self-manifesting, self-witnessing, and self-authenticating. Only God has the self-sufficient *agapē* character of enemy-love needed for the task; no other agent, then, is worthy of worship or divinely self-manifesting, even if there are counterfeits. God's self-authentication via self-manifestation challenges humans to cooperate with enemy-love and forgiveness, in opposition to destructive selfishness and pride. In this perspective of divine self-authentication, mere humans do not convince people regarding God. *God* alone can do this, and humans may contribute by being in cooperation with God in Christ, thereby manifesting the power of God's own *agapē*.

As self-authenticating, God would want people to know God directly, in a cooperative acquaintance relationship. So, God would want the self-commitment of human agents to *God*, not ultimately to an inference or a conclusion of an argument. A recurring theme among biblical writers is thus that God alone is our foundation, rock, and anchor, and this includes our cognitive foundation regarding God's reality (see, for instance, Ps. 18:2,31, 28:1, 31:3; Isa. 44:8; cf. 1 Cor. 2:9–13). This theme implies that God wants to be one's sole evidential foundation for believing in God and for believing that God exists, and hence no argument is to assume this foundational role. The evidential foundation, more precisely, is *God in God's self-manifesting interventions through the Spirit* in one's life, including in one's conscience. This foundation upholds *God's* vital existential and cognitive significance for human inquirers. Humans can put themselves in a position to apprehend the witness from divine self-manifestations by becoming willingly open to receive and to cooperate with redemptive self-sacrifice, the trademark of God's perfect moral character.

A *Nondiscursive Witness*

Inquirers about God often neglect the importance of a *nondiscursive* manifestational witness in human experience to God's reality. This neglect may result from their overemphasizing the role of discursive, intellectual reasons for beliefs regarding God. Perhaps this neglect comes from a dubious kind of epistemic belief-coherentism that lacks the needed resources of an experience-oriented foundationalism. It also may stem from a confusion of the conditions for one's having or manifesting evidence and the conditions for one's giving an argument. It is a mistake, however, to confuse evidence and an argument. If all evidence is an argument, we face a devastating epistemic regress problem.[8]

Evidence is *discursive* if and only if it uses assertive language to express a state of affairs, or a situation. The New Testament category of "witness" (*marturia*), however, is more inclusive than that of discursive evidence. A witness to God's reality and redemption can include discursive evidence, but it need not do so. For instance, a *nondiscursive* mode of human existing or relating can be a witness to God's redemptive character in virtue of manifesting *de re* some distinctive features of God's character, such as divine *agapē*, without making an assertion. The inner witness of the Spirit of God can manifest in the same way, without loss of distinctive nonpropositional content. This lesson bears directly on an aim to manifest one's reasons for acknowledging God, including an aim to manifest a reason for the hope in God within one (1 Pet. 3:15). The desired manifestation and witness need not be discursive. Even when a witness to God's reality includes a discursive component, that component need not be an argument. It could be a descriptive testimony to what God has done in one's life.

Foundational reasons or evidence need not be discursive or propositional, but can be nonpropositional character traits supplied by God's self-manifesting Spirit: love, joy, peace, patience, kindness, gentleness, and so on (see Gal. 5:22–23). In the same vein, John's Gospel portrays Jesus as stating that his disciples will be *known* by their *agapē* for others (John 13:35). The Jesus of the Gospels did not mention or use any philosophical arguments in this connection, or in any other connection, with regard to God's reality and intervention. The same is true of his followers represented in the New Testament, and this fact does not entail a defect in their actual reasons or evidence. Many inquirers rightly wonder whether an argument has support from a corresponding nondiscursive witness, which can have power and cogency irreducible to statements and arguments.[9]

Cases of a nondiscursive witness to God need not be accompanied by a judgment that something is the case regarding God. A dual witness, however, will include both a nondiscursive and a discursive witness, with the discursive witness elucidating the nondiscursive manifestation. The inner witness of the Spirit, accordingly, need not come with a propositional

8. See Paul K. Moser, *Knowledge and Evidence* (Cambridge: Cambridge University Press, 1989).

9. On a nondiscursive witness in *personifying evidence* of God, see Paul K. Moser, *The Evidence for God* (Cambridge: Cambridge University Press, 2010), Chapter 4.

affirmation that elucidates the Spirit's nondiscursive witness. The Spirit's presentation of God's *agapē* to a person can be free of any discursive characterization. It follows that the witness of the Spirit need not be limited to the propositional content of the Old and New Testaments. One can argue plausibly that the witness of the Spirit will not conflict with the person and the message of Christ, but it would be unduly restrictive to limit the Spirit's witness to the propositional content of the biblical writings. Paul had in mind the Spirit's nondiscursive witness when he remarked: "My speech and my proclamation were not with plausible words of wisdom, but with a demonstration of the Spirit and of power, so that your faith might rest not on human wisdom but on the power of God" (1 Cor. 2:4–5, NRSV). This power includes at least the self-manifested *agapē* of God, courtesy of the Spirit's inner witness.

The Spirit's inner witness of divine *agapē* can bridge the historical chasm between the first-century cross of Christ and contemporary people. It can do this not by relaying the historical, first-century event of the cross itself (nothing could do that for a past event-*token*), but by relaying the divine *agapē* that motivated the cross and the crucified Christ. This kind of witness yields an alternative to the kind of historicism that limits evidence of God's redemptive work to past history. It offers evidence regarding the historic Christ that is not itself evidence just from the past. The witness of the Spirit, we might say, transcends the limitations of historical events, and thereby provides a distinctive kind of evidence of God's reality and character. In this respect, not all evidence regarding God is limited to past events. History is important as evidence, but it does not exhaust the evidence given by the witness of the Spirit.[10]

The fact that God is self-authenticating via self-manifestation allows for one's using abductive, or explanatory, considerations to present evidence for God. *Presenting* evidence, however, goes beyond *having* evidence, and the two should not be confused. One might argue that the power of self-sacrificial love in a disciple of Jesus is explained best, at least so far as our available evidence indicates, by the good news that God's Spirit has genuinely intervened with *agapē* in the disciple's life. This power yields a salient kind of evidence for the reality and the moral character of God, at least for the recipient of this power. One's recognition of such divine

---

10. See H. R. Mackintosh, *The Doctrine of the Person of Jesus Christ*, pp. 306–20; Emil Brunner, *Truth as Encounter*, trans. A. W. Loos and David Cairns (Philadelphia: Westminster Press, 1964).

power and evidence depends on one's willingness to acknowledge these as not of our own, human making. Arguably, they are received as a gift from God or not at all.

The human cooperative reception of God's Spirit, as suggested, is no merely subjective matter, because it yields one's becoming loving and forgiving (to some discernible degree) as God is loving and forgiving.[11] It yields salient fruit of God's Spirit, such as love, joy, peace, patience, kindness, goodness, faithfulness, humility, and self-control (see Gal. 5:22–23). These are not merely subjective phenomena. On the contrary, they are discernible by anyone attentive to them and open to the redemptive power of God.[12] Even so, people are free to resist the relevant presentation of evidence, and they can do so consistently if they maintain certain standards for evidence and belief. In the latter case, one's presentation of evidence for God on the basis of explanatory considerations will fail to produce a non–question-begging argument for the people who resist. This does not challenge, however, the person who has the relevant evidence for God.

The writer of 1 John advises people to "test the spirits to see whether they are of God" rather than to believe every spirit (1 John 4:1). Otherwise, people can be led away from truth and into serious error by false teachers. Jesus offers similar advice: "Beware of false prophets, who come to you in sheep's clothing but inwardly are ravenous wolves. You will know them by their fruits. . . . Every good tree bears good fruit, but the bad tree bears bad fruit" (Matt. 7:15–17, NRSV). We can know the reality of the presence of God's Spirit by means of the fruits yielded by the Spirit. God's Spirit makes one loving (to some discernible degree) as God is loving. This is the primary fruit of the Spirit, and it is identifiable and testable in a person's life. The presence of God's Spirit thus comes with salient evidence observable by any suitably receptive person.

The salience of the evidence for God's Spirit does not exclude its elusiveness or even its hiddenness at times for some people. Paul remarks: "Those who are unspiritual do not receive the [things] of God's Spirit, for they are foolishness to them, and they are unable to understand them because they

---

11. On forgiveness as a Christian virtue, to be patterned after God's own forgiving nature, see R. Douglas Geivett, "Forgiveness," in Michael W. Austin and R. Douglas Geivett (eds.), *Being Good: Christian Virtues for Everyday Life* (Grand Rapids, MI: Eerdmans, 2011), pp. 204–41.

12. For discussion of the nature and concrete expression of these traits, see Michael W. Austin and R. Douglas Geivett (eds.), *Being Good: Christian Virtues for Everyday Life* (Grand Rapids, MI: Eerdmans, 2011).

are discerned spiritually" (1 Cor.2:14, NRSV; cf. John 14:22–24). The underlying idea is that God can hide the witness of the Spirit from people who
are unwilling to engage it with due seriousness and sincerity. Their unwillingness may be understood as a refusal to face a Gethsemane crisis with
the obedient attitude of Jesus toward God. The divine hiding would save
some people from self-harming by treating as trivial something that is vital
for them. In this respect, at least, the witness of God's Spirit is elusive and
even hidden at times.[13]

Modes of Divine Testimony

We need not hold that all people have an explicit awareness of the presence
of God's Spirit. As perfectly good, however, this Spirit would desire and
seek meaningful relationships between humans and God. In particular,
the Spirit would work uncoercively toward divine–human reconciliation
and fellowship. Perhaps, however, some humans face obstacles in perceiving God's presence. This prompts the question what the modes of divine
witness or testimony to humans would be.

Perhaps the Spirit's testimony is characteristically mediated or conveyed
via impressions—that is, impressions made on or within the consciousness of human persons, more or less directly. Accordingly, some people
invoke the language of feeling to denote the experience of divine testimony.
For instance, we sometimes hear: "I feel that God is speaking to me," or
"I feel led by the Spirit to do this or that." We suspect, however, that there
is a better way to describe what is happening when one feels directed by
God's Spirit.

The apostle Paul, we have indicated, stresses the role of the Spirit
in personal transformation, particularly in the shaping of moral character, where the goal is conformity to the image of Christ in cooperative
relationship with God. This teaching is summarily captured in Paul's
aforementioned description of the "fruit of the Spirit" (Gal. 5:22–23).
The one in whom the Spirit dwells (that is, the one who is "filled with
the Spirit") is empowered to move through the world at the leading of the
Spirit. The Spirit-filled person's discernment is so trained that she is able

---

13. See Paul K. Moser, *The Elusive God* (Cambridge: Cambridge University Press, 2008);
Moser, "Divine Hiddenness and Self-Sacrifice," in Adam Green and Eleonore Stump (eds.),
Hidden Divinity and Religious Belief (Cambridge: Cambridge University Press, 2016), pp. 71–88;
and Moser, *The God Relationship*.

to discern good and evil, to know where she stands in relation to God, and to conduct herself wisely in service to God's purposes and for God's good pleasure. To conceive this as fundamentally mystical confuses the work of the Spirit in and through an obedient child of God with something less morally robust. Mystical experience, as treated typically in the philosophy of religion, completely misses the robust moral side of being led by God's Spirit.

We should expect that, owing to God's moral superiority to humans, the conditions for human fellowship with God would be set by God and would call for the submission of human persons to the morally perfect will of God. The opportunity for such fellowship would be good news for human persons, and this news would need to be communicated to humans in an authoritative and gracious way. Such a communication, we should expect, would be initiated by God in self-revelation, including self-expression of God's will. This self-revelation would be part of a *testimony of the Spirit* to God's offer of fellowship to humans, and it would bring about a unique means of divine–human contact. Jewish and Christian monotheism has identified this testimony in a number of areas.

Israel and the Testimony of the Spirit

The testimony of the Spirit through Israel was mediated through select individuals within the nation of Israel, whether kings (e.g., David), prophets (e.g., Isaiah), or priests (e.g., Ezekiel), and through the national influence of Israel in the world. This testimony focused on the people of Israel and God's will for them, but this testimony also was intended to benefit Israel's neighbors. In historical Israel, the testimony of the Spirit was, according to a Christian understanding following the book of Isaiah, indicative of what was to come in the broader revelation of God to the Gentiles. In particular, the redemptive love to be shown in the Messiah would be intended for all and would give full expression to the Spirit's testimony begun in historical Israel.

Jesus and the Testimony of the Spirit

According to the Jesus movement that came to be called "Christianity," Jesus Christ as God's risen representative is still present among his human followers. His presence is no longer in his earthly body, but is instead in his Spirit abiding in the hearts, the volitional and affective centers, of his disciples. This Spirit, the "Holy Spirit," is the Spirit of Jesus and of his divine Father. As a result, many New Testament writers elucidate pneumatology with Christology, given that God's Spirit is to be understood in terms of the crucified and risen Christ. New Testament Christology, including the character of Christ, gives some definite contours to the understanding of God's Spirit.

A recurring theme of the New Testament is that Jesus as God's unique representative would baptize his followers with the Spirit of God (see Mark 1:8; Luke 3:16; Matt. 3:11; John 1:33; Acts 1:4–5, 11:16). In doing so, Jesus would bring people into reconciliation and fellowship with God, in God's kingdom family. The apostle Peter finds the prophecy of Joel 2:28 to be fulfilled in the Pentecost experience of Acts 2, and he credits the risen Jesus as the source of the fulfillment: "This Jesus God raised up, and of that all of us are witnesses. Being therefore exalted at the right hand of God, and having received from the Father the promise of the Holy Spirit, he has poured out this that you both see and hear" (Acts 2:32–33, NRSV). According to the four canonical Gospels and Acts, then, the risen Jesus has the authority and the power to give people the Spirit of God and thereby to make them renewed members of God's kingdom. The book of Acts clarifies, with due amazement, that this gift of the Spirit was not limited to Jewish believers but extended also to Gentiles who believe in Christ as Lord (Acts 10:44–48, 11:15–18).

The Gospel of Luke (Luke 4:18–19, NRSV) portrays Jesus as announcing the fulfillment of Isaiah 61:1–2 in his own ministry:

> The Spirit of the Lord is upon me
> because he has anointed me
> to bring good news to the poor.
> He has sent me to proclaim release to the captives
> and recovery of sight to the blind,
> to let the oppressed go free, to proclaim the year of the Lord's favor.

God's Spirit anoints Jesus to bring good news to the poor along with the power of freedom to live cooperatively with God (see also Acts 10:38). In this way, God's Spirit witnesses to God's reality and character through Jesus as God's beloved son (see Mark 1:9–11, Luke 3:21–22, Matt. 3:16–17). This is a divine witness through a historical human being, and it thereby replaces abstract talk of "divine spirit" with concrete talk of a particular human life that exemplifies the Spirit of God. The contours for the witness of God's Spirit thus become more definite and identifiable in the person and life of Jesus.[14]

We can clarify the nature of the Spirit's witness through Jesus by attending to some remarks from Paul and John. Paul uses the following language interchangeably at times: "the Spirit of God," "the Spirit of Christ," and "Christ." For instance, he writes as follows to Christians in Rome: "You are in the Spirit, since the Spirit of God dwells in you. Anyone who does not have the Spirit of Christ does not belong to him. But if Christ is in you, though the body is dead because of sin, the Spirit is life because of righteousness. If the Spirit of him who raised Jesus from the dead dwells in you, he who raised Christ from the dead will give life to your mortal bodies also through his Spirit that dwells in you" (Rom. 8:9–11, NRSV). In keeping with this usage, Paul thinks of Jesus as having become at his resurrection a "life-giving Spirit" (1 Cor. 15:45). Paul also connects the life of God's Spirit with "righteousness," thereby linking it to God's moral character as exemplified in Jesus (see Rom. 8:2, 4, 10; cf. Rom. 5:18, 21).

In agreement with some of Paul's remarks, John's Gospel represents the coming of God's Spirit as the coming of the risen Jesus. It also represents Jesus as being in an authoritative position to control the sending of God's Spirit to humans. For instance, John's Jesus remarks to his disciples: "If you love me, you will keep my commandments. And I will ask the Father, and he will give you another advocate, to be with you forever. This is the Spirit of truth, whom the world cannot receive, because it neither sees him nor knows him. You know him, because he abides with you, and he will be in you. I will not leave you orphaned; I am coming to you" (John 14:15–18, NRSV). In the coming of God's Spirit to people, then, Jesus himself comes. In addition, this Spirit witnesses for Jesus: "When the advocate comes, whom I will send to you from the Father, the Spirit of truth who comes from the Father, he will testify [i.e., witness, *marturēsei*] on my behalf" (John 15:26, NRSV; cf. 1 John 5:9, 11).

The Spirit of God, according to John and Paul, is as much the Spirit of Jesus as the Spirit of his Father. This suggests that the power of God's Spirit is inherently the power of self-sacrificial *agapē* exemplified in the obedient crucified Jesus. Given this lesson, we should not separate the character of God's Spirit from the self-sacrificial character of the crucified

---

14. For further discussion, see James D. G. Dunn, *Jesus and the Spirit* (London: SCM Press, 1975); James D. G. Dunn, *The Christ and the Spirit, vol. 2: Pneumatology* (Grand Rapids, MI: Eerdmans, 1998).

Jesus, as Paul emphasizes in various contexts (see Gal. 3:10–14; 1 Cor. 2:2–5, 13:1–13).

Further Testimony of the Disciples

According to John's Gospel, Jesus testified that the Spirit would be present in an unprecedented way through the future activity of his disciples (see John 8:39). His disciples would be his emissaries, authorized by Jesus to continue proclaiming the message that Jesus had received from God (see John 17). They would be empowered, as Jesus was, to be God's witnesses, and this power would be the same Spirit-power that energized Jesus's own life and ministry (see Acts 1:8). The dramatic outpouring of the Spirit for this task is recounted in Acts 2, and Peter's sermon to the nations gathered in Jerusalem on that occasion is a paradigm of the testimony of the Spirit (Acts 2:14–36). Some three thousand repented (Acts 2:41), and to this number was added a host of others, day after day (Acts 2:47). The Christian church has grown exponentially from generation to generation for two thousand years, owing to the faithful witness of the disciples.

The first disciples included the "apostles of Christ" (1 Thess. 2:6; 2 Cor. 11:13; Eph. 2:20), who were specially commissioned to launch the Good News movement. Jesus had said to his disciples, "whoever believes in me will also do the works that I do; and greater works than these will he do, because I am going to the Father" (John 14:12). In addition, Jesus had prayed for "all those who believe on me through their word" (John 17:20). This ingathering of believers, through the outpouring of the Spirit and the preaching of the apostles, exceeded the breadth of Jesus's own activity.

The apostles were fallible interpreters of what they had heard and witnessed when Jesus was with them. Even their memories could not be trusted, however sincere their reports might be. Indeed, they hardly knew what role they were to play in Jesus's absence. So, as suggested, Jesus would send the Spirit (another "advocate," *paraklēton*) to empower them for authoritative witness to the truths central to Jesus's mission (John 14:16). This is dramatically accomplished and displayed on the day of Pentecost when, as the apostles preached the coming of God's kingdom, their audience heard the apostolic speakers in the appropriate language. Some of the preaching and teaching of some of the earliest disciples contributed to various later documents in the Christian New Testament. Some Christians regard the New Testament as part of the Spirit's witness to humans. This topic is too complex for an adequate treatment here, and the relevant literature is extensive.[15]

Among the many ways the Spirit acted as advocate, four are noteworthy. First, the Spirit produced morally significant fruit in the disciples' lives, thus nurturing them in fellowship with God and each other. Second, in partnership with the Spirit, they formed a new spiritual community, acting with unprecedented purpose and success in offering profound moral transformation to the world. Third, the disciples witnessed the conversion of many individuals across all walks of life (see the book of Acts). Fourth, they were filled with the hope of eternal life with God, which stimulated them to obedience to God's commands and strengthened them in the midst of persecution and suffering.

Whereas historical Israel had been the Spirit-enabled witness to the surrounding nations, the Spirit-indwelt disciples (the "church") would be a witness to the whole world (Matt. 28:18–20; Acts 1:8). As Paul noted, without shame, this witness attests to the "power of God" for salvation that extends to Jews and Gentiles alike (Rom. 1:16). Israel, according to Paul, was in need of the same Gospel (i.e., the "good news") that must reach the Gentiles as well. The witness of the Spirit would be confirmed in personal and corporate experience, chiefly in the radical transformation of cooperative recipients towards God's moral character and the creation of a corresponding community of people "led by the Spirit" (Rom. 8:14). The community would consist of those who stand in proper relationship with God through "the obedience of faith," which includes cooperative submission to God's morally perfect Spirit and will.

Tests of Divine Testimony

A familiar question is whether to believe one who gives testimony. In particular, is a person justified in accepting a testimony offered, that is, in believing what is communicated, particularly when the alleged source is the Spirit of God? It is possible, of course, to believe that I have received some testimony of the Spirit when I have not. Perhaps I could even be justified in believing that I have received some testimony from the Spirit when

---

15. See, for instance, Emil Brunner, *Revelation and Reason*, trans. Olive Wyon (Philadelphia: Westminster Press, 1946), pp. 273–93; G. C. Berkouwer, *Holy Scripture*, trans. Jack B. Rogers (Grand Rapids: Eerdmans, 1975); and James D. G. Dunn, *The Living Word*, 2nd ed. (Minneapolis: Fortress Press, 2009).

I have not. If God is indeed self-authenticating for humans, as various biblical writers suggest, then God can and will supply the needed justifying evidence, perhaps in *de re* self-manifestation. The Biblical theophanies may illustrate this point. We have noted the role of *agapē* in that evidence, in connection with Paul's view in Romans 5:5. Even so, further evidence could arise from historical and other experiential factors.

Someone might propose that evidence from sources other than the Spirit must be added to the testimony of the Spirit for any belief based on such testimony to be justified. This proposal would imply that the Spirit's testimony cannot stand on its own as a source of justified belief. Likewise, one might propose that there must be added evidence—lying in the background, as it were—for justified belief that the Spirit of God has given testimony to a human. In this connection, we would need to examine the conditions for justified belief in general, and this would take us beyond our present topic. We think it wise, however, not to offer an epistemology that precludes God's being self-authenticating to humans in virtue of divine self-manifestation. We humans seem not to be in a cognitive position to block that alternative, or, at least, we have not found any way to block it. So, we recommend leaving this topic for careful exploration by theologians and philosophers of religion.

Chapter Summaries

In Chapter 1, "The Testimony of the Spirit in Biblical Literature," Craig A. Evans and Jeremiah J. Johnston examine the roles and functions of the Holy Spirit in the canonical scriptures of Judaism and Christianity. They survey the material from the Old and New Testaments and the books of the Apocrypha, with some reference to the Pseudepigrapha and the Dead Sea Scrolls. In the Old Testament, the Spirit of God is involved in the creation, inspires leadership and various skills, and reveals the will of God to leaders of Israel. During the inter-testamental period, the Spirit functions much as it does in the older literature of Israel. Sources from this period focus especially on the creative power of the Spirit and the Spirit's provision of wisdom, inculcation of moral character, and readiness to purify the repentant sinner. In the New Testament gospels, the Holy Spirit is personally active in the life of Jesus: Jesus is conceived by the Spirit, empowered by the Spirit at his baptism, and filled with the Spirit at the inauguration of his ministry. This same Spirit continues the ministry of Jesus in founding and strengthening the primitive church. Filled with the Spirit, the disciples proclaim the good news of God's saving work in Jesus, and witness genuine and lasting conversion in response.

The apostle Paul stresses the role of the Spirit in the resurrection of Jesus and in the transformation of the believer. In addition, the Spirit equips the church with gifted persons so that the church may fulfill its ministry. The General Letters of the New Testament underscore the Spirit's role in divine revelation. The Spirit is particularly active in the experience of the seer John in the book of Revelation, where a heavenly throne room and future events are revealed. Having gathered extensive data about the Spirit from the full range of canonical sources, Evans and Johnston find that the Old and New Testaments offer a coherent approach to the testimony of the Spirit of God. In both Testaments the Spirit of God is a power that transcends human power and all powers of creation. The Spirit is the source of revelation, making known the mind and will of God, and the regenerative power that transforms the lives of believers.

In Chapter 2, "An Ontology of the Spirit," Stephen T. Davis addresses the question, "Who or what sort of thing is the Holy Spirit?" His initial observation is that our sources are limited, and much of what we wish to know is beyond our ken. Cognizant of this constraint, Davis approaches the ontological question through an exploration of the way the Spirit works or acts. He then considers some implications of his exploration for understanding human personhood. Among the actions of the Spirit are some that are unique to persons. While the Spirit's acts in nature are of interest, Davis focuses on the Spirit's action in relation to human persons, for it is here where talk of the testimony of the Spirit is especially apt.

Davis divides the "person-to-person" works of the Spirit into five categories: convicting, teaching, inspiring, guiding, and bestowing. These find support in the scriptures and are affirmed in the traditions of the church. In direct consideration of the *testimony* of the Spirit, Davis describes ways the Spirit witnesses to certain truths and the sorts of truths to which the Spirit testifies. He argues that the Spirit's witness can be resisted by humans, and that one must discern between the witness of the true Spirit of God and other spirits. In due course he is led to define the testimony of the Spirit as "that influence of the Holy Spirit on the minds of believers that causes them to believe firmly that the Christian message, or some aspect of it, is true." He frankly confesses that we do not know how the Spirit does this. The ontology of the Spirit as a person whose testimony works in varied ways yields insight into the nature of human persons. Davis singles out four distinct lessons to be learned about ourselves from

consideration of the Spirit's work, and attends to special difficulties that
arise in this light.

In Chapter 3, "Conscience and the Voice of God: Faithful Discernment,"
Paul Gooch takes up the question of whether and how the faithful can,
on the basis of conscience, discern the "voice" of God. He examines the
concept of conscience in search of a clean definition that would clarify
what it means to discern the voice of God. His investigation begins with
observations about how conscience is supposed to work in human moral
psychology. The result of this investigation is admittedly meager, however, depending heavily as it does on a metaphor when talking about conscience. Characteristic ways of talking about conscience suggest that it is a
special person-like faculty that involves the person in making moral judgments and feeling sentiments with moral import. Greater clarity than this
is hard to come by. Still, Gooch presses for what detailed phenomenology
may be found.

Gooch argues against the claim that conscience is the voice of God. He
sees in scripture and tradition support for this negative assessment. One
might initially suppose that biblical language lines up with customary talk
of conscience. After all, the law is said to be "written on the heart," but
this easy supposition is insensitive to "the ways in which biblical writers
apprehend operations of the Spirit." The *interiority* of the Spirit's action
does not denote the play of conscience as we generally think of it. Gooch
qualifies his verdict, however, with a discussion of "faithful discernment"
of "the voice of God." Developmental psychology by itself leaves us with a
truncated view of conscience. Whereas conscience cannot be strictly identified with the voice of God, the testimony of the Spirit is responsive to the
conditions of a person's "heart," and acts to form the person into someone with moral insight and spiritual alertness. The Spirit may act upon
the conscience of a person; alternatively, the Spirit may need to override
the play of conscience within a person. As the Spirit produces the fruit of
virtuous character within a person, the person becomes better equipped
to discern the Spirit's testimony, and to resist undue dependence on conscience to hear the voice of God.

In Chapter 4, "The Testimony of the Spirit and Moral Knowledge,"
C. Stephen Evans explores the multiple roles the Spirit plays in giving
humans moral knowledge—more precisely, how the Spirit makes possible
an understanding of God's requirements for his human creatures. Evans
works with a "divine command theory" of moral *obligations*, according to
which our moral duties are grounded in God's will, insofar as that will

has been communicated. He recounts several significant theological and philosophical advantages of this perspective. He argues that this divine command theory is no rival to natural law accounts of the good or to virtue ethics; the three approaches, he contends, are complementary aspects of a Christian ethic.

A divine command theory needs an account of how God's will for humans is communicated. For this, the activity of the Spirit, who is often associated in scripture with giving knowledge or insight, is crucial. Evans discusses three ways God communicates his will to humans: conscience, scripture, and special revelatory experiences. He defends the importance of conscience as a form of general revelation. Though conscience is fallible and requires human nurture to function properly, this does not mean that no moral knowledge is possible. Regarding scripture, the Spirit plays multiple roles. The Spirit inspires human authors to write what God intends, but also, through the "internal testimony of the Spirit," enables humans to understand the message and recognize it as coming from God. Nevertheless, the finitude and the sinfulness of humans entail that the relevant moral judgments, though arrived at through Scripture, are fallible. Finally, the Spirit provides moral guidance to individuals through special experiences: dreams, visions, voices, and simply convictions that seem to come from God. Evans acknowledges obvious epistemological problems lurking here, but he concludes that these experiences can be a source of moral guidance. He delineates several criteria for discerning between genuine and counterfeit messages, and argues that a concern whether a particular message really is from God is not an expression of unfaithfulness or unbelief, but a proper manifestation of the desire to obey God.

If the Spirit of God attests to what is true, and God desires good relationships with human persons, why is the world of human experience so filled with divergent perspectives? How are we to understand the nature, operation, and value of the testimony of the Spirit in light of profound disagreement about religious reality? These questions are pursued by Roger Trigg in Chapter 5, "Diversity and Spiritual Testimony." Latent within every religious tradition is a notion of spiritual testimony. On the human side, reception of such testimony is irreducibly subjective, but what is attested can be objective truth communicated via spiritual testimony. Religious traditions, however, can be distinguished by incompatible judgments about what is true under conditions of spiritual enlightenment. In addition, testimony can intimate the existence of some source of revelation about what is objectively true. Among revelation claims, however, which are authentic and which not?

The Christian theological tradition recognizes two forms of revelation, namely general revelation and special revelation. Both the fact and the problem of religious diversity can be explained in terms of these categories. General revelation is generously supplied to all through a variety of modalities, providing access to the knowledge that a personal Creator God exists. This lies in the background of a proper expectation that God would provide more ample and specific (i.e., *special*) revelation. Arguably, this God has done, chiefly through the testimony of the Spirit. If objective truth is revealed by these means, belief is by no means coerced. God would wish more than mere knowledge of revealed truths for humans; God would desire "to enter our hearts and minds." Even so, humans can resist the testimony of the Spirit to objective truth. In particular, religious experience will often be an unreliable guide in the knowledge of divine truths; it risks lending undue weight to the subjective side of spiritual testimony. Trigg attends to difficulties in discerning the testimony of the Spirit, but he argues against a convenient pluralism that levels competing religions to what is common to them all.

In Chapter 6,"The Testimony of the Spirit: Insights from Psychology and Neuroscience," Malcolm Jeeves turns to issues of human nature and personality. He ties his discussion of the testimony of the Spirit to how spirituality is manifested as both "embodied in our physical make-up and embedded in our social and cultural groups." He pays special attention to advances in psychology and neuroscience. These cast light on what it means to be human, and therefore on how the spirituality of human persons is to be understood. If the Spirit is at work in the lives of human persons, then the Spirit must be at work in ways consistent with our nature. Jeeves identifies some developments in mind and brain studies, and draws special attention to ever-tightening mind–brain links. This is crucial for his understanding of spirituality. The emerging picture of the mind–brain relation suggests that our spiritual formation intimately involves our physicality. This is reinforced by the behavioral implications of the emerging picture. Some scientific studies indicate that morally censured behavior is sometimes modified when damage to the brain has been repaired. The apparent lesson: Moral dispositions can somehow be embodied in our physical constitution, or at least, subjectivity can be conditioned by neurological states.

Some scientific studies indicate connections between religious experience and brain function. They prompt questions about how religious beliefs and practices correlate with unique brain states, and what this can mean for the likelihood that these beliefs are true. The science is so far inconclusive, and perhaps it must remain so. In addition, social and cultural factors are profoundly formative religiously. Jeeves suggests that this empirically supported conviction is supported within the biblical theology of persons as creatures in the image of God. The chapter concludes with pastoral reflections, delving specifically into issues of aging and degeneration at the level of brain function, and of their significance for human spirituality. Jeeves wonders whether someone's supposed spirituality "may be reduced, masked, or, at times, in the experience of extreme suffering, obliterated." The testimony of the Spirit may be very real and ongoing, but not obvious to some people.

In Chapter 7, "Freedom, Community, and Language: Outline of a 'Neuroanthropological' Pneumatology," Oliver Davies finds that an understanding of the Spirit of God often suffers from lack of clarity concerning the relation between the material world and immateriality, including such things as *nous, pneuma*, and consciousness. He proposes that an adequate understanding of the human reception of the Spirit of God requires an understanding of how a cultural re-presentation of the Spirit has occurred in the Western tradition. Davies seeks to identify a deep change in understanding of mind and matter that bears on our self-understanding. In particular, he finds that the rise of the scientific method has led to a new understanding of matter and mind.

Davies contends that part of the new understanding from science acknowledges an "intimate relation between how we are in the world as body and mind and how we conceive of the relation between body and mind, in terms of both explicit and tacit knowledge." Indeed, he finds that the transition to modern science has reconfigured our living experience of being human. Having drawn from Paul Ricouer, Davies looks to the apostle Paul for the idea that our seeing the work of God's Spirit may involve our willingness to turn our focus to other people. In this scenario, a basic human freedom is in our power to choose rather than to resist relations with others. In addition, this perspective suggests that our social biology contributes to our being instinctively drawn to the presence of our neighbor, and the Spirit of God has shaped us in that way as part of creation. Davies holds, then, the reception of our neighbor is our acceptance of the work of the Spirit in us and between us, and it grounds our hope in God for the future.

In Chapter 8, "Art, Beauty, and the Testimony of the Spirit," Steven R. Guthrie asks whether the Spirit of God is distinctively active in the creative arts. In particular, he asks what sort of testimony the Spirit offers in the creative arts. He examines a number of answers that have been offered, inside and outside Christian traditions. Guthrie aims to preserve the insight that the Spirit of God can be active in human creativity without precluding the genuine agency and activity of human artists. He finds that Jesus's life makes actual in history the prospect that divine and human agency can coexist, including in human artistry. Guthrie identifies four dimensions of the Spirit's work in human art and beauty: restoring sight, creating community, sanctifying or perfecting something, and bringing freedom.

In Guthrie's perspective, human love can be "spiritual" in virtue of pointing toward the Spirit's work of creating community. In creating community founded on love, the Spirit can give testimony to the kind of world God has created, including to the new creation God is creating. The creative arts likewise can point to the creative work of God's Spirit. When creative art is "spiritual," a Christian theology can offer an explanation in terms of the creative work of God's Spirit, in creating freedom and community founded on love. Guthrie suggests that when Socrates, Plato, Shelley, Schiller, and others link human creativity and aesthetic delight with spirit, they offer their own testimony to the Spirit of God in action. In attending to their witness, he proposes, we can find the testimony of God's Spirit in art and beauty.

Gendered language has recently brought sociological and psychological changes that generate new questions about naming God. These changes have spurred new critiques of the language "Father, Son, and Spirit" to name God. They also have prompted constructive proposals for alternative formulations, where feminine terms are used to name the Holy Spirit, or even each divine *hypostasis* within the Trinity. In Chapter 9, "'Sighs Too Deep for Words': The Holy Spirit, Desire, and the Name of the Incomprehensible God," Elizabeth T. Groppe charts the relevant developments and theologically motivated responses. She draws on Sarah Coakley's systematic theology in search of understanding the Spirit's work. Coakley traces the origins of pneumatology to the prayer in the Spirit of Christ found in Romans 8:15–16 and adopted later by Origen, Athanasius, and others. This prayer experience manifests the *hypostasis* of the Holy

Spirit, the *eros* or desire of God, and the incomprehensibility of God whom we "see in not seeing" and "know in not knowing" (Gregory of Nyssa).

A contemplative realization of God's "proto-erotic" desire for us is, according to Coakley, foundational to moving constructively through questions about gender now confronting Christian churches. Since the meaning of desire has been individualized and physicalized in our hypersexualized secular culture, it is imperative, according to Groppe, that we retrieve the theological meaning and *telos* of desire. This, in turn, requires a renewed theology and practice of asceticism, a discipline that can enable us to purify our desires, to discriminate between holy desires and misdirected desires, and to intensify our desire for God. The "kneeling work" promoted by Coakley reveals that desire is theologically more fundamental than gender. This insight can reframe in constructive ways discussions about using gendered language for God. There can be no satisfactory solution to the problem of gender and naming God without asking first: What is the ultimate meaning and purpose of desire? How are sexual desire and desire for God related? How can desire sometimes be manifest as domination, power, control, subservience, and violence? In addition, how can we open our hearts to the healing of corrupted desire made possible through the Spirit of Christ?

In Chapter 10, "The Spirit and the Bride Say, 'Come': Apologetics and the Witness of the Holy Spirit," Kevin Kinghorn and Jerry L. Walls conceive of Christian apologetics in terms of "God's plan for helping people form beliefs about Jesus Christ." They seek to develop a biblical model of Christian apologetics that accommodates a "dual witness": that of human testimony and that of the Holy Spirit's testimony. While these witnesses are complementary, and though God is pleased to involve people in the transmission of the faith to others, the witness of the Spirit is essential and basic. Sometimes it is sufficient in the sense that nothing more is needed. Some have even suggested that the work of the Spirit is sufficient in the stronger sense, where belief is bound to result under the causal influence of the Spirit. All of this could be true whether or not human persons recognize the action of the Spirit in persuading them of the Christian message.

Kinghorn and Walls explore how the Spirit can provide *testimony*. They hold that the cognitive, rational aspect of apologetics serves the relational goal of drawing a prospective believer into fellowship with God. In particular, they identify "mitigating" works and "positive" works of the Spirit. First, the Spirit orients the individual toward the good, turning the person away from what hinders and toward what is excellent. Second, the Spirit cultivates a desire for the truth of the Gospel, by frustrating desires that impede conversion and by promoting imagination, dreams, and the faithful witness of the church to supplant those desires with what is intrinsically more desirable. Third, the Spirit persuades the unbeliever thus prepared to receive the truth, acting through human witnesses to break down the unbeliever's defenses against the truth and to marshal reasons to believe. They conclude with a brief discussion of the operation of grace in the testimony of the Spirit.

In Chapter 11, "The Role of the Church in Discerning the Testimony of the Spirit," Angus Ritchie explores the extent to which there needs to be a social aspect in the discernment of revealed truths of the Spirit of God. He denies that the testimony of the Spirit is simply a matter of God's implanting propositional truths in the mind of an individual believer. His case for a social aspect stems from his wider understanding of the work of the Spirit in the life of the individual believer and the community of the church. In particular, he contends that even if one holds the highest possible doctrine of the authority of the Bible, one still has reason to hold that the church has an authoritative role in discerning the testimony of the Spirit.

Ritchie holds that discernment of the testimony of the Spirit is social, and not purely individualistic, at several stages. First, the biblical writers were themselves engaged in a communal dialogue about their message and theology. Second, the community of the church discerned the extent and authority of the scriptures, from a range of available options. Third, given the plural nature of the biblical texts and their socially important role, the church today has an ongoing role in interpreting them for its social purposes. In addition, Ritchie contends that the use of reason, often in a social setting, must be included as an important supplement to scripture for identifying what a text of scripture is actually saying. He observes that "if someone thought that rational argument had no role in the interpretation of Scripture, then he or she would have removed all constraints on what could be deemed to be a legitimate interpretation of Scripture." Given a social role for scripture, we should expect reason to figure in the social deliberations on scripture.

Conclusion

According to the New Testament, the Spirit of God is the Spirit of Jesus Christ and thus is seen most clearly (but not exclusively) in his life, death, and resurrection. The witness of this Spirit relays God's redemptive love and the message of this love to cooperative people. Humans will apprehend aright this Spirit's reality only if they are willing, in the words of Jesus, to have "eyes to see and ears to hear" what God intends for humans. The intended recipients of the witness must open themselves to be attuned to the moral character of God, including divine *agapē* toward others, even enemies.

In the case of humans knowing God, God would seek to move their wills toward cooperative obedience to God's perfect will, just as Jesus obeyed in Gethsemane. Being perfectly loving, God would seek to have humans learn to love and to obey as Jesus loves and obeys. So, the witness of God's Spirit aims for the reconciliation of humans to God, in cooperative fellowship. A final issue remains: Are we willing cooperatively to receive the challenging witness on offer, for the sake of moral transformation toward God's character? With this issue, the role for sincere human decision in response becomes clear and vital. If this is so, the topic of the testimony of the Spirit has existential value irreducible to intellectual problem solving.

I

The Testimony of the Spirit in Biblical Literature

Craig A. Evans and Jeremiah J. Johnston

THE IMPORTANCE OF spirit, or the Spirit, in biblical literature can hardly be exaggerated. It is closely linked with God and in fact often the Spirit is qualified as the "Spirit of God," "Spirit of the Lord," or "Holy Spirit." (The last occurs but three times in the Old Testament, but more than 90 times in the New Testament.) The Spirit functions in a variety of ways in the literature of the Old Testament and in the literature of the intertestamental period. Its function narrows somewhat in the writings of the New Testament and early Christianity.

The Spirit of God in the Old Testament

The word "spirit" (*ruah* in Hebrew) occurs more than 400 times in the Old Testament. It can mean wind but most of the time it is in reference to spirit, usually the Spirit of God. (It is sometimes in reference to the spirit of a human or a malignant spirit.) In the Greek Old Testament (i.e., the Septuagint) *pneuma*, occurring some 350 times, translates most of these occurrences.

In Old Testament literature spirit is linked primarily to prophecy, though spirit is also linked to creation and other acts of God's direct engagement with humanity or the created order.

Creation

The spirit is referenced in the opening verses of Genesis: "In the beginning God created the heavens and the earth. The earth was without form and void, and darkness was upon the face of the deep; and the Spirit of God was moving over the face of the waters" (Gen. 1:1–2). It is not stated explicitly, but the implication is that the Spirit of God is the agency by which creation is achieved. God creates the heaven and earth (Gen. 1:1), and then God commands, "Let there be light" (Gen. 1:3). But it is the Spirit of God that is in close proximity of the primordial waters, out of which creation will be fashioned and given form. One is left with the impression that without the Spirit creation could not have taken place.

It is the Spirit that constitutes the very power of God, that power that impacts the created order. This is the implication of the words of the prophet who declares that the will of God is accomplished through God's Spirit, not through human strength: "Not by might, nor by power, but by my Spirit, says the LORD of hosts" (Zech. 4:6; cf. Isa. 31:3: "The Egyptians are men, and not God; and their horses are flesh, and not spirit").

The high point of Genesis 1–2 is the creation of humankind. Although it would be assumed that it is the Spirit of God that gives life to all living creatures (as in Ps. 104:30: "When thou sendest forth thy Spirit, they are created"; Isa. 42:5: "Thus says God, the LORD, who created the heavens and stretched them out, who spread forth the earth and what comes from it, who gives breath to the people upon it and spirit to those who walk in it"), it is the human in the creation story who is said specifically have been given life through the Spirit of God: "[T]he LORD God formed man of dust from the ground, and breathed into his nostrils the breath of life; and man became a living being" (Gen. 2:7).

The breath of God was closely associated with God's Spirit. We see this in Job, where the famous sufferer says, "[A]s long as my breath is in me, and the spirit of God is in my nostrils" (Job 27:3). God has breathed into Adam's nostrils not simply his breath, but his Spirit. This idea is made explicit elsewhere in Job: "The spirit of God has made me, and the breath of the Almighty gives me life" (Job 34:4; see also 32:8). Similarly, the prophet Isaiah declares the word of the Lord: "from me proceeds the spirit, and I have made the breath of life" (Isa. 57:16; see also Mal. 2:15: "Has not the one God made and sustained for us the spirit of life?").

The Spirit of God not only constitutes the very power of God, as seen in creation and in the giving of life, it is also the agency by which God communicates. It is through his Spirit that God discloses his will to humanity. For Israel this usually meant leadership and/or prophecy.

The Spirit and Leadership

Of Joshua, the successor of Moses, it is said: "And Joshua the son of Nun was full of the spirit of wisdom, for Moses had laid his hands upon him; so the people of Israel obeyed him" (Deut. 34:9). Although it is not stated, it would have been assumed that the "spirit of wisdom" given Joshua was ultimately sourced in God. Thus, to have the spirit of wisdom is to have the Spirit of God, the author of all wisdom (cf. 1 Kings 3:28, 4:29, 10:24; Dan. 1:17, 2:23). Elsewhere in Old Testament narratives the Spirit of God plays a prominent role in the leaders of the tribes of Israel.

Israel's leaders (called "judges"), empowered by the Spirit, are a commonplace in the book of Judges. The Spirit of the Lord "came upon" Othniel, the nephew of Caleb (cf. Num. 13:30; Josh.14:6), "and he judged Israel; he went out to war, and the LORD gave" Israel's enemies into his hands (Judg. 3:9–10). Later we are told that "the Spirit of the LORD took possession of Gideon; and he sounded the trumpet" (6:34). Gideon, guided by God, routed the Midianites (7:19–22). The "Spirit of the LORD came upon Jephthah" (11:29), enabling Israel's judge to defeat the Ammonites (11:32–33). The Spirit of the Lord strengthened Samson (13:24–25), enabling him to achieve astonishing feats of strength (14:6, 19; 15:14, 19).

The power of the Holy Spirit comes into play in the history of Israel's kings. During the civil war between Saul and David, numbers of fighting men joined the latter (1 Sam. 22:1–2). Although the much older Samuel narrative says nothing about men prompted or guided by the Spirit of God, the later Chronicler, who rewrites the ancient stories, makes a point of it: "Then the Spirit came upon Amasai, chief of the thirty, and he said, 'We are yours, O David; and with you, O son of Jesse! Peace, peace to you, and peace to your helpers! For your God helps you'" (1 Chron. 12:18). We should probably understand the words of Amasai as an example of prophetic utterance.

The Spirit of God plays a conspicuous role in the lives and activities of Elijah and Elisha, two of the best-known prophets of the northern kingdom. King Ahab's frightened servant says to the prophet Elijah, "[A]s soon as I have gone from you, the Spirit of the LORD will carry you whither I know not; and so, when I come and tell Ahab and he cannot find you, he will kill me" (1 Kings 18:12). The king's servant has alluded to Elijah's mysterious ability to elude capture by Israel's wicked king. He assumes that it is the Spirit of God that is responsible.

Elijah's successor, Elisha, requests of a "double share" of his master's spirit. Although the prophet has not explicitly requested the Spirit of God, it would have been assumed that the spirit of Elijah, especially a double share of his spirit, would have included the Spirit of God. In any event, we are told that "when the sons of the prophets who were at Jericho saw him over against them, they said, 'The spirit of Elijah rests on Elisha'" (2 Kings 2:15). Something about the manner and being of Elisha convinced the prophets of Jericho that the prophet of the north must be in possession of the spirit of Elijah his master. They are willing to search for Elijah, assuming that "the Spirit of the LORD has caught him up and cast him upon some mountain or into some valley" (2:16; cf. Ezek. 3:14: "the Spirit lifted me up and took me away"; 11:1; "the Spirit lifted me up and brought me to the east gate of the house of the LORD").

An Evil, Lying Spirit

Perhaps the most surprising aspect of the work of the Spirit is seen in the sending of an evil or lying spirit. Because of his disobedience "the Spirit of the Lord departed from Saul, and an evil spirit from the Lord tormented him" (1 Sam. 16:14). The king's servants believe if someone played the lyre, the king would find relief from the evil spirit (16:15–16). As it turns out, young David, the king's rival, is the very man for the job (16:23). David serves Saul in this capacity successfully, even though the king twice tries to murder him (1 Sam. 18:10–11, 19:9–10). Evidently, the "evil spirit" resulted in raving and acts of violence. It should also be observed that the departure of the Spirit of the Lord from Saul may provide the backdrop to David's petition in Psalm 51, where after his affair with Bathsheba and his murder of her husband he begs of God, "Do not take your Holy Spirit from me." King David may have feared suffering the same fate that had overtaken his predecessor.

One of the most instructive episodes of a "lying spirit" involves the conflict between the prophet Micaiah and rival prophets who habitually prophesied what the king wanted to hear. The king of Israel had invited the king of Judah to join him in waging war against Syria, to reclaim some disputed territory. With the exception of Micaiah, all of the prophets of the king of Israel predict victory over Syria. When pressed, Micaiah offers a very different "word of the Lord." He says to the kings of Israel and Judah:

I saw the LORD sitting on his throne, and all the host of heaven standing beside him on his right hand and on his left; and the LORD said, "Who will entice Ahab, that he may go up and fall at Ramoth-gilead?" And one said one thing, and another said another. Then a spirit came forward and stood before the LORD, saying, "I will entice him." And the LORD said to him, "By what means?" And he said, "I will go forth, and will be a lying spirit in the mouth of all his prophets." And he said, "You are to entice him, and you shall succeed; go forth and do so." Now therefore behold, the LORD has put a lying spirit in the mouth of all these your prophets; the LORD has spoken evil concerning you. (1 Kings 22:19b–23 = 2 Chron. 18:21–22)

Zedekiah, one of the king's prophets, confronts Micaiah, demanding to know, "How did the Spirit of the LORD go from me to speak to you?" (22:24). The challenge is more than rhetorical; evidently it was believed that the Spirit of God sometimes *did* move from one prophet to another. Perhaps Elisha's request for a double share of Elijah's spirit is related in some way. In any event, Micaiah's prophetic word explains why it is that all of the king's prophets continue to proclaim the thing that the king wants to hear. They say what they say, not because they are moved by the Spirit of God, but because they are prompted by a lying spirit. Placing a "lying spirit in the mouth" of these prophets again reflects the belief that all spiritual power, whether good or evil, ultimately functions under the authority of God. The Spirit of God is holy and is a source of truth, but this does not mean that God cannot send evil, lying spirits to do his bidding.

Similarly, Isaiah, addressing the leaders of Judah, declares that the "the LORD has poured out upon you a spirit of deep sleep, and has closed your eyes, the prophets, and covered your heads, the seers" (Isa. 29:10). Because of their rebellion against God, the Lord has rendered the political and spiritual leaders of Judah obdurate.

This idea is seen again in the deliverance of the kingdom of Judah from the threat of Sennacherib, the king of Assyria (2 Kings 18:13–19:37). Sennacherib has invaded Judah and laid siege to Jerusalem, mocking God and demanding that Hezekiah, Judah's king, capitulate. In response to the king's tearful prayers, Isaiah the prophet prophesies: "Thus says the LORD: Do not be afraid because of the words that you have heard, with which the servants of the king of Assyria have reviled me. Behold, I will put a spirit in him, so that he shall hear a rumor and return to his own land" (19:6–7; cf. Isa. 37:6–7). We are not told that this "spirit" is a lying spirit, but it is nonetheless a spirit that prompts Sennacherib to break off the siege and return to his own land.

The Spirit and Prophecy

The Spirit is very closely linked to prophecy in the Old Testament. This is primarily because the Spirit gives the word that is to be spoken, as we hear in the song of David, near the end of the famous king's life: "The Spirit of the LORD speaks by me, his word is upon my tongue" (2 Sam. 23:2). The idea that the words of David, the "sweet psalmist of Israel" (2 Sam. 23:1), were given by the Spirit of God led to the widely held view, presumed in the Scrolls of Qumran, in the New Testament, and in rabbinic literature, that David was a prophet and that many of the Psalms are prophetic. The Spirit is closely linked to speech. God speaks and his Spirit acts (cf. Isa. 34:16). To put the Spirit in a person is to put God's words in him (59:21).

On occasion the Spirit manifests itself in forms of prophetic ecstasy. An early example of this is seen in Numbers 11, in a context in which the wandering Israelites express doubt about the power of God. In response, the Lord asks Moses: "Is the LORD's hand shortened? Now you shall see whether my word will come true for you or not" (Num. 11:23). Moses and the elders of Israel gather around the sacred tent and "the LORD came down in the cloud and spoke to him, and took some of the spirit that was upon him and put it upon the seventy elders; and when the spirit rested upon them, they prophesied" (11:25). This passage could be understood to imply that the divine Spirit has, in a sense, quantity. Not long after the spirit rested upon two men, Eldad and Medad, who had been near the tent, "so they prophesied in the camp" (11:26). The link between the Spirit of God and prophecy is quite clear. What is also clear is that the Spirit of God is hardly limited, whatever the precise meaning of Numbers 11:25, an idea to which Jesus many centuries later gives expression: "[I]t is not by measure that he gives the Spirit" (John 3:34).

The point of this interesting story is that the power of God is such that he can bestow his Spirit on many, not on only one (such as Moses) or on a few. Rather, the Spirit of God is without limit and so can be bestowed on many. Moses understood this, so that when Joshua asked Moses to stop Eldad and Medad (Num. 11:28), because they were not among the group that had been specifically gathered, he retorted: "Would that all the LORD's people were prophets, that the LORD would put his spirit upon them!" (11:29).

We encounter another interesting incident at the time of the anointing of Saul, son of Kish, as Israel's first king. To allay Saul's doubts, Samuel the priest and prophet tells Saul that when he meets a band of prophets "the spirit of the LORD will come mightily upon you, and you shall prophesy with them and be turned into another man" (1 Sam. 10:6). Not only will this ecstatic experience convince the hesitant Saul that he really is the Lord's anointed and that with God's help has what it takes to be an effective king, the spirit of prophecy that will come upon him will provide a link, as it were, with his predecessor Samuel, the last of Israel's judges, who was himself a prophet and possessed the Spirit.

Samuel's prophecy soon comes to pass. At Gibeah Saul encounters a band of prophets "and the Spirit of God came mightily upon him, and he prophesied among them. And when all who knew him before saw how he prophesied with the prophets, the people said to one another, 'What has come over the son of Kish? Is Saul also among the prophets?'" (1 Sam. 10:10–11). Because ecstatic speech was closely associated with prophecy, Saul's prophesying, which likely manifested itself as ecstatic speech, led to the assumption that perhaps he too was now a prophet. Later during his rule this strange event occurs again.

When Saul turns against David, slayer of Goliath and the new hero in the eyes of the people of Israel, he sends messengers to take David into custody. But "when they saw the company of the prophets prophesying, and Samuel standing as head over them, the Spirit of God came upon the messengers of Saul, and they also prophesied" (1 Sam. 19:20). When told this, Saul sends more messengers, but the same thing happens. He sends for David a third time and again the Spirit of God comes upon Saul's men and they prophesy (19:21–22). So Saul goes himself to the place where David was hiding "and the Spirit of God came upon him also, and as he went he prophesied, until he came to Naioth in Ramah" (19:23). The prophetic ecstasy was such that Saul "stripped off his clothes, and he too prophesied before Samuel, and lay naked all that day and all that night. Hence it is said, 'Is Saul also among the prophets?'" (19:24).

After Saul fell out of favor with God, the Spirit was no longer with him. This meant that when he "inquired of the LORD, the LORD did not answer him, either by dreams, or by Urim, or by prophets" (1 Sam. 28:6). Estranged from God and his Spirit, Saul no longer received prophetic counsel. In desperation the king sought out a medium, who could call up from the grave the spirit of Samuel, the late prophet (28:8–13). The medium succeeds, but the message Saul receives from the awakened Samuel is not what he wanted to hear: The king will lose his kingdom to David and he will lose his life on the field of battle (28:15–19). Samuel may be dead, "asleep" in Sheol, but he still possesses his prophetic power. Even in death it seems a prophet can access the Spirit of God and disclose the divine will.

Frequently in Hebrew narrative we hear of the Spirit of God coming upon this prophet or that person. This is especially seen in the later, post-exilic literature. For example, the "Spirit of God came upon Azariah the son of Oded" (2 Chron. 15:1); "the Spirit of the LORD came upon Jahaziel the son of Zechariah, son of Benaiah, son of Jeiel, son of Mattaniah, a Levite of the sons of Asaph, in the midst of the assembly" (20:14); "the Spirit of God took possession of Zechariah the son of Jehoiada the priest; and he stood above the people" (24:20a). In all of these cases, the persons on whom the Spirit of God came or rested spoke words of prophecy (cf. 15:2–7, 20:15–17, 24:20b). Having returned to Jerusalem, after the exile, the people pray to God, rehearsing their history, acknowledging that God had given Israel his "good Spirit to instruct" them (Neh. 9:20) and had warned them by his "Spirit through the prophets" (9:30). Stubborn Israel "rebelled and grieved [God's] holy Spirit" (Isa. 63:10). The restoration of Israel was itself seen as fulfillment of "the word of the LORD by the mouth of Jeremiah" (Ezra 1:1; cf. 2 Chron. 36:22).

The so-called Writing Prophets provide us with important data relating to the testimony of the Spirit, in revealing the will or word of God to humans. The Spirit of God is not always explicitly referenced. Often there is reference to "vision" (*hazōn*) or "word" (*dabar*), as we find in the Major Prophets. The book of Isaiah begins, "The vision of Isaiah the son of Amoz, which he saw concerning Judah and Jerusalem" (Isa. 1:1). Jeremiah begins, "The words of Jeremiah, the son of Hilkiah . . . to whom the word of the LORD came" (Jer. 1:1–2). Ezekiel begins, "In the thirtieth year . . . the heavens were opened, and I saw visions of God" (Ezek. 1:1). Several of the Minor Prophets begin with "the word of the Lord came to" the prophet (Hos. 1:1; Joel 1:1; Jon. 1:1; Mic. 1:1; Zeph. 1:1; Hag. 1:1; Zech. 1:1). Amos begins, "The words of Amos . . . which he saw concerning Israel" (Amos 1:1), while Obadiah begins, "The vision of Obadiah" (Obad. 1). The remaining Minor Prophets reference "oracle" (Nah. 1:1 "An oracle concerning Nineveh. The book of the vision of Nahum"; cf. Hab. 1:1; Mal. 1:1).

Although the Spirit is not mentioned in these opening lines, it would have been universally assumed that underlying the oracles, words, and visions of these prophets was the Spirit of God (note the implied equation in the parallelism of Hosea 9:7 "the prophet . . . the man of the Spirit"). Of course, some of the prophets do make explicit reference to the Spirit. In the book of Isaiah the prophet says, "[T]he Lord GOD has sent me and his Spirit" (Isa. 48:16). Ezekiel states, "And when he spoke to me, the Spirit entered into me and set me upon my feet; and I heard him speaking to me" (Ezek. 2:2). Later the prophet says, "And the Spirit of the LORD fell upon me" (11:5). Micah asserts, "I am filled with power, with the Spirit of the LORD, and with justice and might, to declare to Jacob his transgression and to Israel his sin" (Mic. 3:8). Looking back on Israel's history of stubborn resistance to the will of God, Zechariah states: "They made their hearts like adamant lest they should hear the law and the words which the LORD of hosts had sent by his Spirit through the former prophets" (Zech. 7:12). Several times the prophet and wise man Daniel is recognized as a man—expressed in pagan language—in whom the "spirit of the holy gods" resides (Dan. 4:8, 18; 5:14).

Eschatology and the Messianic Hope

The Spirit of God plays an important role in eschatology and the messianic hope. It is prophesied of the branch of David that "the Spirit of the LORD shall rest upon him (and) the spirit of wisdom and understanding" (Isa. 11:2). In reference to his servant, through whom Israel will be redeemed, God says: "Behold my servant, whom I uphold, my chosen, in whom my soul delights; I have put my Spirit upon him, he will bring forth justice to the nations" (42:1). The Spirit of God will anoint him who will proclaim the good news of redemption: "The Spirit of the Lord GOD is upon me, because the LORD has anointed [mashah] me to bring good tidings to the afflicted; he has sent me to bind up the brokenhearted, to proclaim liberty to the captives ..." (61:1). The awaited Messiah [meshiah] will be anointed by the Spirit of God. Anointing by the Spirit could lead to many things: wisdom, skill, prophetic speech, super strength (as in Samson). In Isaiah 61:1 the anointing of the Spirit leads to the proclamation of the good news of God's reign.

In the eschatological time God promises to pour out his Spirit on his people: "For I will pour water on the thirsty land, and streams on the dry ground; I will pour my Spirit upon your descendants, and my blessing on your offspring" (Isa. 44:3; cf. Ezek. 39:29). Through God's Spirit his people will receive life: "I will put my Spirit within you, and you shall live, and I will place you in your own land" (Ezek. 37:14). In the last days God will pour out his Spirit on all flesh, with the result that God's people will prophesy and see visions (Joel 2:28). Though God's Spirit his people will acquire a deep knowledge of God's word, which they will never forget (Isa. 59:21).

The Spirit of God in the Intertestamental Period

Much of the Jewish literature produced during the intertestamental period (roughly 300 BC to the beginning of the first century AD) reflects the ideas found in Old Testament scripture. There are developments, to be sure. The Spirit of God is referenced more frequently, often in contexts concerned with eschatology. The Holy Spirit is a revealer of God's truth. It is also the agency of renewal. When actions of the Spirit are referenced, they are almost always in reference to what God did in the Old Testament period and serve as an inspiration to the righteous in the intertestamental period. The texts considered here are traditionally classified as belonging to the Apocrypha, the Pseudepigrapha, and the Dead Sea Scrolls.

The Spirit of God is viewed as the agent of creation. The author of Judith gives expression to this idea: "Let all thy creatures serve thee, for thou didst speak, and they were made. Thou didst send forth thy Spirit, and it formed them; there is none that can resist thy voice" (Jth. 16:14). The spoken word of God created life (cf. Gen. 1:20, 24), but the Spirit of God gave them form. It is the Spirit of God that fills the word and "holds all things together" (Wisd. of Sol. 1:7; 4Q422 1:7–8).

The Spirit of God reveals truth and enables Ezra the faithful scribe to write Scripture. "[S]end the Holy Spirit into me," Ezra petitions God, "and I will write everything that has happened in the world from the beginning, the things which were written in thy law, that men may be able to find the path, and that those who wish to live in the last days may live" (4 Ezra 14:22; cf. 1Q34bis frag. 3, col. ii, lines 6–7: "You renewed Your covenant for them in a vision of your glory and words of Your Holy Spirit").

The Holy Spirit gives wisdom and knowledge to the faithful (Wisd. of Sol. 7:7; 9:17: "Who has learned thy counsel, unless thou hast given wisdom and sent thy holy Spirit from on high?"; 1QS 9:4 "guided by the instruction of his holy Spirit"; *Prayer of Levi* 8: "Let the Holy Spirit, Master, be shown to me, and give to me counsel and wisdom and knowledge"; 1QH^a 20:14–15 = 4Q427 frag. 8, col. ii, lines 17–18: "I have listened faithfully to Your wondrous counsel by your Holy Spirit"). "We know these things," say the pious of Qumran, "because you have graciously granted us your Holy Spirit" (4Q506 frags. 131–132, lines 10–11 = 4Q504 frag. 4, line 5).

The Holy Spirit keeps the faithful morally pure (*T. Benj.* 8:2; 1QS 3:6–7, 4:20–22, 9:4: "cleanse me by your Holy Spirit"). Joseph the patriarch "was a good man," we are told, because he "had the Spirit of God within him" (*T. Sim.* 4:4). Bereft of the Holy Spirit Solomon turned to vanity and idolatry (*T. Sol.* 26:6). Because of the Holy Spirit, the faithful remnant have returned to God, earnestly petitioning him in prayer (4Q504 frags. 1–2, col. v, lines 12–17).

The Holy Spirit inspires the prophets. They are called the "anointed by the Holy Spirit, the seers of truth" (CD 2:12–13 = 4Q266 frag. 2, col. ii, line 12). The Holy Spirit spoke through Moses and through the prophets, the anointed (CD 5:21–6:1 = 4Q267 frag. 2, lines 5–6).

The Holy Spirit renews the community of the faithful, especially in preparation for the Last Days: "For only through the spirit pervading God's true society can there be atonement for a man's ways, all of his iniquities; thus only can he gaze upon the light of life and so be joined to His truth by His holy spirit, purified from all iniquity" (1QS 3:6–8 = 4Q255 frag. 2, line 1). "Over the humble his Spirit hovers," the author of an eschatological scroll assures his readers, "and he renews the faithful in his strength" (4Q521 frag. 2, col. ii, line 6). This will be the time when God's Messiah, whom heaven and earth will obey, will make his appearance (4Q521 frag. 2, col. ii, lines 1–2).

The Spirit of God in the Life and Activities of Jesus

The Spirit of God plays an important, even essential, role in the life and public activities of Jesus of Nazareth. Although more than two dozen Gospels were produced in the first and second centuries of the Common Era, critical scholars almost exclusively depend on the four that the early Church received into its canon of Scripture, viz., Matthew, Mark, Luke, and John. These were the Gospels widely recognized as composed in the first century, probably within the lifetime of persons acquainted with Jesus and his closest disciples. Scholars make use of the New Testament Gospels, not only because of their greater antiquity but because they—in marked contrast to the second-century sources—exhibit verisimilitude, reflecting the realities of pre-70 Jewish Palestine.

According to the New Testament Gospels Jesus is conceived by the Holy Spirit (Matt. 1:18, 20; Luke 1:35). This is an unusual testimony, in that there was no expectation that the awaited Messiah would be conceived and born in such a fashion. (Until the appearance of the Christian movement there was no expectation of a virginal conception and birth of the Messiah. Jewish interpreters did not understand Isa. 7:14 in that sense. The birth narratives of Matthew and Luke can hardly be seen as fictions that were generated by an expectation of a virginal conception of the Messiah. The passage from Isaiah was viewed as a prophecy that clarified but did not generate the unusual story of the birth of Jesus.) Moreover, to claim that Jesus was conceived by the Spirit of God would readily bring to the pagan mind stories of Greco-Roman gods birthing children through mortal women. The stories of the virginal conception of Jesus, found in independent traditions in Matthew and Luke, are early and deeply entrenched in the tradition. As it turns out, the Holy Spirit is at the very center of Jesus's being and activities, from his birth to his death and resurrection.

The Holy Spirit's actions are not limited to Jesus at the time of his birth and early years. The parents of John, who will become the "Baptist" and forerunner of Jesus, are told that their son will be empowered by the Spirit (Luke 1:15). Indeed, the Holy Spirit prompts John's elderly father to speak (Luke 1:67). When the righteous Simeon sees the infant Jesus, the Holy Spirit comes upon him, prompting him to prophesy (Luke 2:25–27). Later as an adult and engaged in his own ministry, John speaks of Jesus, telling the crowds that the one who soon comes will baptize them with the "Holy Spirit" (Matt. 3:11, Mark 1:8, Luke 3:16, Acts 1:5).

The Holy Spirit comes upon Jesus at his baptism (Matt. 3:16, Mark 1:10, John 1:32–33), with Luke noting that it descended upon him "in bodily form" (Luke 3:22), probably underscoring the power and substance of the Spirit. The Spirit then drives or leads Jesus into the wilderness, where he confronts Satan (Matt. 4:1, Mark 1:12, Luke 4:1). Filled with the Holy Spirit, Jesus bests Satan in the wilderness temptations (Matt. 4:1–11, Mark 1:12–13, Luke 4:1–13).

Because he begins his public ministry "in the power of the Spirit" (Luke 4:14), Jesus may quote the words of Isaiah 61:1, "The Spirit of the Lord is upon me," and claim that they are fulfilled (Luke 4:18–21). Jesus teaches that people must be "born of the Spirit" (John 3:8). Jesus rejoices "in the Holy Spirit" and prays (Luke 10:21). Jesus's ministry is such that the evangelist Matthew feels justified to cite Isaiah 42:1–4 (especially "I will put my Spirit upon him"), claiming it is fulfilled in Jesus's ministry (Matt. 12:18).

Jesus promises his followers that God will give his Holy Spirit to those who ask for it (Luke 11:13) and that God will give his Spirit generously (John 3:34). Jesus replies to skeptics and critics, "[I]f it is by the Spirit of God that

I cast out demons, then the kingdom of God has come upon you" (Matt. 12:28, Luke 11:19). He also warns his critics to take care, lest by calling the works of Jesus works of the devil they blaspheme against the Holy Spirit (Matt. 12:31–32, Mark 3:28–30, Luke 12:10). Jesus's success in casting out evil spirits, as well as his claim to have bound Satan himself (Mark 3:27), would have been understood by his contemporaries as clear evidence of Jesus's empowerment by the Spirit of God. Only the Spirit of God has the power to defeat Satan.

Jesus teaches the people that the Spirit inspired David to speak of his messianic son (Matt. 22:43, Mark 12:36). Likewise he assures his disciples that the Holy Spirit will speak through them (Matt. 10:20, Mark 13:11, Luke 12:12) and that the Holy Spirit, as a comforter or counselor, will guide them into all truth (John 14:17, 26; 15:26; 16:13).

After his resurrection, Jesus breathes into his disciples the Holy Spirit (John 20:22), in anticipation of the day of Pentecost, when the Holy Spirit will be poured out on his followers (cf. Acts 1:8; 2:4, 17–18). Prior to his ascension the risen Jesus commands his disciples: "Go therefore and make disciples of all nations, baptizing them in the name of the Father and of the Son and of the Holy Spirit" (Matt. 28:19).

The Spirit in the Book of Acts

The Holy Spirit plays a prominent role in the book of Acts, the narrative that describes the birth and growth of the early Church. The Spirit empowers the disciples of Jesus, prompting them to proclaim the good news and enabling them to perform works of power.

Pentecost and the Giving of the Spirit

The risen Jesus commanded his disciples to wait in Jerusalem until the Holy Spirit came upon them in power. Then they would bear testimony to what God had done in his Son (Acts 1:6–8). On the day of Pentecost ("fifty"—that is, fifty days after Easter) the apostles of Jesus "were all filled with the Holy Spirit and began to speak in other tongues, as the Spirit gave them utterance" (Acts 2:4).

Peter, Jesus's chief disciple and now leader of the apostles, explains the meaning of this strange phenomenon by appeal to the prophecy of Joel: "And in the last days it shall be, God declares, that I will pour out my Spirit upon all flesh, and your sons and your daughters shall prophesy, and your young men shall see visions, and your old men shall dream dreams; yea, and on my menservants and my maidservants in those days I will pour out my Spirit; and they shall prophesy" (Acts 2:17–18; cf. Joel 2:28–29). The pouring out of the Spirit of God was seen not only as the fulfillment of the prophecy of Joel but as unmistakable evidence of the dawning of a new era, the beginning of the "last days."

Peter and the other apostles proclaim the resurrection of Jesus and urge their fellow Jews to respond in repentance and faith. Peter commands his hearers: "Repent, and be baptized every one of you in the name of Jesus Christ for the forgiveness of your sins; and you shall receive the gift of the Holy Spirit" (Acts 2:38). Some three thousand respond to the preaching of the apostles and are baptized (Acts 2:37–42). The early Christian Church has been launched.

The Apostles Speak in the Power of the Holy Spirit

A theme that runs throughout the book of Acts is the role of the Holy Spirit in prompting the apostles to speak, either in the proclamation of the good news of the resurrection or in defending the faith against challenges and criticism. Often the author of Acts speaks of the apostles being "filled with" the Holy Spirit.

When threatened and ordered to desist from this proclamation, Peter is "filled with the Holy Spirit" and then speaks boldly to the Jewish leadership in Jerusalem (Acts 4:8). Later, the apostles and other disciples gathered to pray. While praying, "the place in which they were gathered together was shaken; and they were all filled with the Holy Spirit and spoke the word of God with boldness" (Acts 4:31).

The Holy Spirit not only emboldened the apostles and other leaders to speak but also gave them wisdom. This is illustrated in the remarkable story of Stephen, a Greek-speaking Jew who along with several others was appointed as a deacon. Stephen began to proclaim the new Christian message and soon found himself challenged by a number of men from a synagogue in Jerusalem. They disputed with Stephen "but could not withstand the wisdom and the Spirit with which he spoke" (Acts 6:10). When martyred, the author of Acts states that Stephen was "full of the Holy Spirit" and had a vision of heaven, in which he "saw the glory of God, and Jesus standing at the right of God" (Acts 7:55).

The Holy Spirit also empowered the followers of Jesus to heal and restore. One notable example is seen in the conversion of Saul of Tarsus, who becomes the influential apostle Paul. When Saul saw the risen Jesus on the road to Damascus, he lost his sight. Arriving in the city one Ananias came to Saul and laid hands on him, with the result that he regained his sight and was filled with the Holy Spirit (Acts 9:17). This filling with the Holy Spirit is seen in Saul (Paul) later in the Acts narrative. During his first missionary journey (Acts 13–14) Saul encountered a Jewish magician who spoke against the Christian movement (Acts 13:6–8). We are told that Saul, "filled with the Holy Spirit," rebuked the magician, with the result that he suffered temporary blindness. The ironic reversal seen in the narrative about Saul who through the Holy Spirit regained his sight and the magician who through the Holy Spirit lost his sight would not have been lost on ancient readers.

The Holy Spirit Is Proof of the Genuine Conversion of Gentiles

A major function of the Holy Spirit in the early Church, as narrated in the book of Acts, is in its confirmation of the reality of conversion. Those who embrace the Christian message are filled with the Holy Spirit, and this filling almost always exhibits itself in speech. In any event, it is the Holy Spirit that is proof that the conversion is genuine. This was especially important in the conversion of non-Jews.

There are two noteworthy examples of the filling of the Holy Spirit in Acts as evidence that conversion of non-Jews is genuine. The first occurs in Samaria, the region that lies between Judea in the south and Galilee in the north. In the time of Jesus and the early Church Samaria was linked to Judea, and both were administered by a Roman governor. Many Samaritans responded to the preaching of Philip the evangelist. The apostles in Jerusalem sent Peter and John to investigate. Although the Samaritans were believers and had been baptized, the Holy Spirit had not come upon them (Acts 8:14–16). Peter and John lay hands on the Samaritan believers "that they might receive the Holy Spirit" (Acts 8:15, 17).

The second example involves the conversion of a Roman centurion in Caesarea Maritima, Israel's most important port city. A believer in the God of Israel, the centurion summoned Peter. As Peter proclaims the good news, the Holy Spirit "fell on all who heard the word" (Acts 10:44). The Jewish Christians "were amazed, because the gift of the Holy Spirit had been poured out even on the Gentiles" (Acts 10:45). They knew that the

Holy Spirit had come upon the centurion and others of his household because they spoke in tongues and praised God (Acts 10:46).

The qualifying phrase "even on the Gentiles" makes clear the importance of the testimony of the Spirit, in what was a crucial and at times controversial issue in the early Church: Could Gentiles become true members of the new messianic movement? Reception of the Spirit of God in a sense ratifies the conversion. Not only could Samaritans, who were of partial Jewish descent, receive the Spirit, so could Gentiles. The Holy Spirit was proof that the redemptive message of the apostles of Jesus had universal application. Convinced that this was so, the apostles permitted the centurion and his family to be baptized (Acts 10:47–48).

The Spirit and Rival Spirits

On occasion the Holy Spirit comes into conflict with other spirits or with those who have contempt for the Spirit. An example of the latter is seen in the case of Ananias and Sapphira, members of the new Church who deceptively and hypocritically presented a gift to the apostles. Peter responds to the man, accusing him of lying to the Holy Spirit, and later responds to his wife, accusing her of tempting the Spirit (Acts 5:3, 9). Both suddenly die and "great fear came upon the whole church" (Acts 5:11).

A second example is seen in the story of Simon the Samaritan magician. When Simon observes that the Spirit of God was given to new believers "through the laying on of the apostles' hands," he offers the apostles money, hoping to acquire this perceived apostolic power (Acts 8:18–19). Simon is rebuked for thinking that the Spirit of God is something that can be purchased (Acts 8:20–24). This encounter between Simon Peter and Simon the Samaritan magician gave rise to a long and colorful tradition in the memory of the early Church.

In another example we have a case in which the apostles receive an unwelcome endorsement. In Philippi of Macedonia Paul and his companions encounter a slave girl who was possessed of a "spirit of divination," or more literally the "python" spirit, usually associated with the god Apollo (Acts 16:16). This spirit prompts the girl to prophesy—accurately from the point of view of the author of the book of Acts: "These men are servants of the Most High God, who proclaim to you the way of salvation" (Acts 16:17). The prophetic utterance may have been accurate, but it was not prompted by the Holy Spirit. After several days of this, Paul became annoyed and said to the spirit: "I charge you in the name of Jesus Christ to come out of her" (Acts 16:18). The spirit departed from the girl, with the result that she lost of powers of divination. Ancient readers would have assumed that it was through the agency of the Holy Spirit that the python spirit was driven out.

The last example offers another case of spiritual misadventure, involving the misuse of the name of Jesus. While Paul is in Ephesus seven sons of a Jewish ruling priest, who are professional, itinerant exorcists, learn of the apostle's ability to heal and cast out evil spirits by invoking the name of Jesus. Impressed by Paul's success, the seven brothers make use of the name of Jesus in what apparently was a particularly difficult case: "[We] adjure you by the Jesus whom Paul preaches" (Acts 19:13). The result is a disaster for the brothers. The evil spirit responds, "Jesus I know, and Paul I know; but who are you?" (Acts 19:15). The evil spirit then attacked the men, overpowered them, "so that they fled out of that house naked and wounded" (Acts 29:16). Readers of this story would likely assume that the seven brothers had been stripped of their garments, which would have included their protective symbols and amulets. At the same time the story implies that this powerful, evil spirit knows of Jesus, whom Paul preaches, and respects him. But the spirit has no respect for the men who without authorization and without the assistance of the Holy Spirit invoke the name of Jesus. This extraordinary episode results in public respect for the name of Jesus (Acts 19:17–20).

The Spirit of God in the Teaching
of the Apostle Paul

The Spirit of God figures prominently in Paul's teaching. There are many parallels with contemporary Jewish literature, especially as seen in the Dead Sea Scrolls. But there are distinctive features, which are rooted in the Spirit's work in Jesus and, especially, in his resurrection.

The role of the Holy Spirit in the resurrection of Jesus is affirmed by Paul in his letter to the Christians of Rome, where he speaks of "the gospel concerning his Son, who was descended from David according to the flesh and designated Son of God in power according to the Spirit of holiness by his resurrection from the dead, Jesus Christ our Lord" (Rom. 1:3–4). Later in his letter Paul alludes to this act of the Holy Spirit when he tells his readers that "the Spirit of him who raised Jesus from the dead dwells in you" and that God "who raised Christ Jesus from the dead will give life to your mortal bodies also through his Spirit" (Rom. 8:11).

For Paul the Spirit of God plays a prominent, empowering role in the lives of all believers. The Spirit gives new life, something that the Law of Moses could not do (Rom. 7:6). The Spirit, not the flesh (i.e., human will and power), enables believers to fulfill the just requirements of the Law (Rom. 8:4). To set one's mind on the Spirit results in living "according to the Spirit," not the flesh, which leads to death (Rom. 8:5–6).

Consistent with what was observed in the book of Acts, possessing the Spirit of God is proof that the believer in fact belongs to Jesus the Messiah (Rom. 8:9). It is the Spirit that bears witness with the human spirit that one truly is a child of God (Rom. 8:16). If one is "led by the Spirit of God," one is in fact a son of God (Rom. 8:13). Because of the Spirit of God believers are adopted as sons, who cry, "Abba! Father!" (Rom. 8:14–15).

The Holy Spirit, moreover, helps believers pray as they should, interceding for believers according to the will of God (Rom. 8:26–27). In addition to that, the Holy Spirit reveals the will of God to the believer, for the Holy Spirit knows the very mind of God (1 Cor. 2:10–12). Consequently, the apostle of Jesus is able to teach spiritual truths, which the spiritually inclined will receive because both the apostle and the believer who is taught possess the Spirit (1 Cor. 2:13).

The Holy Spirit also equips believers and the Church with spiritual gifts, whereby the work of evangelism and other aspects of the Church's work may be carried out. There may be many gifts, but there is only one Spirit (1 Cor. 12:4). The Spirit of God prompts believers to proclaim the lordship of Jesus but never to utter a word of blasphemy (1 Cor. 12:3).

The presence of the Spirit in the life of the believer manifests itself in attitudes and behaviors and offers further evidence of the reality of the Spirit's indwelling presence. Consequently the apostle commands believers to "walk by the Spirit, and do not gratify the desires of the flesh" (Gal. 5:16), reminding them that "the desires of the flesh are against the Spirit, and the desires of the Spirit are against the flesh; for these are opposed to each other" (Gal. 5:17). If one walks by the Spirit, then one's life will exhibit the "fruit of the Spirit," which includes "love, joy, peace, patience, kindness, goodness, faithfulness," and the like (Gal. 5:22–23).

In another context Paul exhorts believers not to "grieve the Holy Spirit of God" (Eph. 4:30). He also warns believers not to be "drunk with wine," which leads to destruction, but to be "filled with the Spirit, addressing one another in psalms and hymns and spiritual songs, singing and making melody to the Lord with all your heart, always and for everything giving thanks in the name of our Lord Jesus Christ to God the Father" (Eph. 5:18–20).

The contrast between drunkenness and being filled with the Spirit clearly alludes to the cult of Dionysius and related mysteries, in which it was believed that adherents acquired the spirit of a deity through imbibing alcohol and other intoxicants. The result of this pagan activity was speaking, singing, and visions (or hallucinations), which often resulted in injury, illness, or other forms of negative experience. For Paul, the filling of the Holy Spirit results in positive, beneficial results, not the destructive excesses that result from intoxication.

The Spirit of God in the Theology of Hebrews

As in Paul, the author of the book of Hebrews speaks of "gifts of the Holy Spirit" that are distributed among believers (Heb. 2:4). Also similar to Pauline thought, Hebrews speaks of believers as "partakers of the Holy Spirit" and reception of the "heavenly gift" (6:4), which may refer to the Holy Spirit. And just as Paul exhorted believers not to "grieve the Holy Spirit of God" (Eph. 4:30), so the author of Hebrews warns his readers and hearers not to offend the Holy Spirit: "How much worse punishment do you think will be deserved by the man who has spurned the Son of God, and profaned the blood of the covenant by which he was sanctified, and outraged the Spirit of grace?" (Heb. 10:29).

In Hebrews the Holy Spirit is understood as the very voice behind Scripture. In quoting Psalm 95 the author of Hebrews does not say, "David says," or something to that effect; rather, "the Holy Spirit says, 'Today, when you hear his voice . . .'" (Heb. 3:7). Similarly, when the author of Hebrews appeals to the New Covenant promise of Jeremiah 31, it is again the Holy Spirit who "bears witness" through the words of the ancient prophet: "And the Holy Spirit also bears witness to us; for after saying, 'This is the covenant that I will make with them after those days, says the Lord: I will put my laws on their hearts . . .'" (Heb. 10:15–17; cf. Jer. 31:33–34).

Indeed, the Holy Spirit speaks through the ancient narratives of Scripture. After recalling the Tabernacle in the wilderness, its lampstand, table of the Presence, curtains, and altar, the author of Hebrews states, "By this the Holy Spirit indicates that the way into the sanctuary is not yet opened as long as the outer tent is still standing . . ." (Heb. 9:8). The Holy Spirit is thus speaker and teacher in the sacred Scripture.

Recalling the role of the sacrificial system, the author of Hebrews declares that "the blood of Christ, who through the eternal Spirit offered himself without blemish to God, [will] purify your conscience from dead works to serve the living God" (Heb. 9:14). The blood of the crucified Jesus possesses cleansing power far greater than the blood of sacrificial animals because he offered himself "through the eternal Spirit."

The Spirit in the Petrine and Johannine Letters

The author of 1 Peter alludes to the early apostolic preaching, if not Pentecost itself, when he speaks of the good news preached "through the Holy Spirit sent from heaven" (1 Pet. 1:12; cf. Acts 1:8, 2:1–4). Having embraced the good news, believers are "sanctified by the Spirit for obedience to Jesus Christ" (1 Pet. 1:2; cf. Acts 26:18, Rom. 15:16, 1 Cor. 1:2). Similar to what was observed in Hebrews, the author of 2 Peter says that "no prophecy ever came by the impulse of man, but men moved by the Holy Spirit spoke from God" (2 Pet. 1:21).

The author of 1 John speaks of the indwelling Spirit (1 John 3:24, 4:13), a prominent theme in the Farewell Discourse of the Fourth Gospel (cf. John 14:17, 15:7). The Spirit of God assists the believer in "testing the spirits" and discerning truth (1 John 4:1–3, 6; 5:7), which again echoes the Farewell Discourse (cf. John 15:26, 16:13).

The Spirit in the Book of Revelation

The Spirit of God plays an important role in the book of Revelation (or the Apocalypse), a role that is similar to what is observed in the Old Testament prophets. The seer, who calls himself John (Rev. 1:9), says he was "in the Spirit on the Lord's day" (i.e., Sunday, as opposed to Shabbat [Saturday]) and heard "a loud voice like a trumpet saying, 'Write what you see in a book and send it to the seven churches . . .'" (Rev. 1:10–11). By being "in the Spirit" the seer is able to receive divine revelation. Later the seer says he is "in the Spirit" and is able to see into heaven itself, to see the very throne on which God sits (Rev. 4:2). By being "in the Spirit" the seer can be transported, into heaven (Rev. 4:2) or into the wilderness (Rev. 17:3), or to a high mountain (Rev. 21:10).

The seer is told that the "testimony of Jesus is the spirit of prophecy" (Rev. 19:10). The passage is ambiguous, perhaps meaning that the spirit of prophecy prompts speaking or testifying of Jesus. But it may mean that behind the spirit of prophecy is what Jesus says or testifies to. It is probably the latter (Rev. 1:1–2), for the seven letters written to the seven churches are dictated by the Spirit; they are what "the Spirit says to the churches"

(Rev. 2:7). Yet it is the risen Jesus who utters the words that Spirit speaks to the churches (Rev. 1:17–20).

At the end of the book the author invites readers and hearers to join the community of faith: "The Spirit and the Bride say, 'Come.' And let him who hears say, 'Come.' And let him who is thirsty come, let him who desires take the water of life without price" (Rev. 22:17). Reference to thirst and water of life recalls themes from the Fourth Gospel (John 4:13–15, 6:35, 7:37), while the qualifier "without price" alludes to the eschatological vision of the book of Isaiah, where the thirsty one is invited: "Ho, every one who thirsts, come to the waters; and he who has no money, come, buy and eat! Come, buy wine and milk without money and without price" (Isa. 55:1, cf. 25:6).

Conclusion

The Old and New Testaments offer a coherent approach to the testimony of the Spirit of God. In both Testaments the Spirit of God is a power that transcends human power and all powers of creation. In both Testaments, for example, the Spirit is contrasted with the flesh. The Spirit of God is the source of revelation, making known the mind and will of God, usually to selected individuals (such as the prophets).

There are, however, two significant differences. First, in the New Testament the testimony of the Spirit centers on the word *of* Jesus and the word (or Gospel) *about* Jesus. This christological focus, which in some sense seems to have been anticipated in some of the prophetic literature of the Old Testament, is clearly a distinctive feature in the literature of the New Testament.

Second, the testimony of the spirit becomes universal among the New Testament people of God. Whereas in Old Testament literature the testimony of the Spirit appears to be limited to prophets and other key individuals, in the experience of the early Church, beginning with Pentecost, the testimony of the Spirit appears to have been widely experienced. Here it is suggested that in contrast to the exceptional nature of the activities of the Holy Spirit in the Old Testament, in which the Spirit rests upon certain individuals, from Pentecost on, the Spirit rests upon all believers.

In the Gospels and Acts this new dimension of the testimony of the Spirit is hinted at, even foretold, but in the letters of Paul it is explicitly affirmed and clarified. The Spirit brings about changes in the believer that bear witness to the reality of the believer's redemption. The Spirit, moreover, equips believers with gifts whereby the church may fulfill its role and purpose.

In the final analysis it is not too much to say that the testimony of the Spirit is in evidence everywhere in biblical literature. The Spirit of God is the creative force in the cosmos, in nature, and in the human sphere. With respect to the latter, the Spirit transforms, energizes, gives life, reveals the mind of God, and redeems. Without the work and witness of the Spirit biblical literature would be greatly reduced both in content and in meaning.

Bibliography

C. K. Barrett, *The Holy Spirit and the Gospel Tradition* (London: SPCK; New York: Macmillan, 1947).

T. G. Brown, *Spirit in the Writings of John* (JSNTSup 253; London and New York: T & T Clark International, 2003).

B. Charette, *Restoring Presence: The Spirit in Matthew's Gospel* (JPTSup 18; Sheffield: Sheffield Academic Press, 2000).

J. D. G. Dunn, *Baptism in the Holy Spirit* (London: SCM Press, 1970).

G. D. Fee, *God's Empowering Presence: The Holy Spirit in the Letters of Paul* (Peabody, MA: Hendrickson, 1994).

G. D. Fee, *Paul, the Spirit, and the People of God* (Peabody, MA: Hendrickson, 1996).

G. F. Hawthorne, *The Presence & the Power: The Significance of the Holy Spirit in the Life of Jesus* (Dallas: Word, 1991).

J. Hur, *A Dynamic Reading of the Holy Spirit in Luke–Acts* (JSNTSup 211; Sheffield: Sheffield Academic Press, 2001).

G. W. H. Lampe, *The Seal of the Spirit* (London: SPCK, 1951).

J. R. Levison, *Filled with the Spirit* (Grand Rapids, MI: Eerdmans, 2009).

J. R. Levison, *The Spirit in First-Century Judaism* (AGJU 29; Leiden: Brill, 1997).

G. N. Stanton, B. W. Longenecker, and S. C. Barton (eds.), *The Holy Spirit and Christian Origins: Essays in Honor of James D. G. Dunn* (Grand Rapids, MI: Eerdmans, 2004).

M. Turner, *The Holy Spirit and Spiritual Gifts* (Carlisle, UK: Paternoster, 1996; Peabody, MA: Hendrickson, 1998).

G. von Rad, *The Message of the Prophets* (New York: Harper & Row, 1962).

L. Wood, *The Holy Spirit in the Old Testament* (Grand Rapids, MI: Zondervan, 1976).

2

An Ontology of the Spirit

Stephen T. Davis

And the Holy Spirit also testifies to us.

HEBREWS 10:15

I

Who or what is the Holy Spirit?[1] Christians affirm that the Holy Spirit is the third person of the Holy Trinity. Accordingly, the Holy Spirit is a person, is divine, and like the other two divine persons is omnipotent (Ps. 104:30; Rom. 15:18–19), omniscient (1 Cor. 2:10–12), everlasting (Heb. 9:14), omnipresent (Ps. 139:7–10), holy (Rom. 1:4), and perfectly morally good. Unlike the Son, the Holy Spirit is a spirit (i.e., is not embodied). The Holy Spirit is the agent of God's personal and powerful interactions with the world. God's actions in the world are of course incredibly multiple in number and various in type, but they are all taken to be works of the Holy Spirit.[2]

This chapter is primarily concerned with the ontology of the Holy Spirit. That is, we will ask what sort of thing or person the Holy Spirit is. But our direct information on that subject is extraordinarily limited. Indeed, in itself, the Holy Spirit is, like the Father and the Son, beyond our human

---

1. In this chapter, I will use the terms "Holy Spirit," "Spirit of God," "Spirit of Christ," and "the Spirit" synonymously.

2. Perhaps I should say that *virtually* all actions of God in the world are acts of the Holy Spirit. I add this caveat because it is not clear whether theophanies, appearances of angels, or acts of the incarnate Jesus during his ministry were direct acts of the Holy Spirit, although of course all were under the influence of the Holy Spirit. Of course, it is an important part of the theological tradition to affirm that all of God's *ad extra* works (i.e., outside the Trinity itself) are equally the work of all three Persons.

ken.[3] The Holy Spirit is like the wind: "You do not know where it comes from or where it goes" (John 3:8). Accordingly, we will have to approach the ontological question via questions about the work of the Holy Spirit. The chapter is secondarily concerned with human beings. Our findings on the Holy Spirit will have some implications for our view of human nature. We will have to ask what those implications are.

When the church fathers arrived at the Trinitarian formula of three persons (Father, Son, and Holy Spirit) in one Godhead, they were using the word "person" in a slightly different way than contemporary philosophers use the term. Still, there is enough commonality of meaning for us to hold that the Holy Spirit, as a person, has intelligence, will, desire, knowledge, feeling, memory, intentions, and the ability to act to achieve those intentions. As a person, the Holy Spirit naturally has the ability to interact with other persons, including human beings.

Although some thinkers have wanted to understand the Holy Spirit impersonally, as a power or force or influence, the notion that the Holy Spirit is a person is far too clear in scripture and embedded in the tradition for us to take the impersonal idea seriously. Indeed, the Holy Spirit is a "you" (or, in Buber's terms, a "thou") rather than an "it." We human beings are to have a personal relationship with the Spirit. And you cannot relate personally to a rock, a principle, an idea, an ideal, a number, a set, or a power. To anticipate a bit, the Holy Spirit is our counselor, helper, guide, advocate, teacher, and leader. These are roles of persons.

II

It might be helpful to divide the work of the Holy Spirit into two categories. The first involves what we might broadly call work in nature rather than work with human beings, although all such works certainly affect human beings. These would be items like causing Mary to be pregnant with Jesus (Luke 1:35) or enabling the miracles of Jesus (Mark 2:22–30; Matt. 12:28), for example the casting out of demons (Matt. 12:28). The Spirit's work in

---

3. Thus Karl Barth: "It is strange but true that fundamentally and in general practice we cannot say more of the Holy Spirit and His work than that He is the power in which Jesus Christ attests Himself, attests Himself effectively, creating in man response and obedience. We describe Him as His awakening power." In G. W. Bromiley and T. F. Torrance (eds.), *Church Dogmatics* (Edinburgh: T & T Clark, 1936–1962), IV/1, p. 648.

creating the church at Pentecost might also fit here, at least so far as the wind and the tongues of fire were concerned (Acts 2:1–47).

But in this chapter I am most interested in the Spirit's direct work with human beings. These actions are, as we might say, person-to-person works. All of them presuppose the biblical notion that in some sense the Holy Spirit indwells believers (John 14:17; Eph. 2:22). But they too are of various sorts. In a rough and crude way, let us say that there are five main sorts of person-to-person works of the Holy Spirit: convicting, teaching, inspiring, guiding, and bestowing.[4]

First, the Bible makes it clear that the Holy Spirit is the agent that convicts or convinces people of their own sinfulness (John 16:8–11). Since this is a clear prerequisite to receiving the Christian gospel of grace through Christ—people will hardly be interested in receiving God's mercy unless they recognize their need for it—this is an important work. But the Spirit's actions in this area do not cease here. Indeed, the Spirit is at work throughout the whole process of salvation. This would include both the bringing about of rebirth (John 3:1–16; Rom. 8:16) and of sanctification (Rom. 5:1–5).

Second, teaching and revealing are cognitive aspects of the Spirit's work (1 Cor. 2:9–10). Thus Jesus says to the disciples, "But the Advocate, the Holy Spirit, whom the Father will send in my name, will teach you everything" (John 14:26). In the birth story in Luke, we are told that it was revealed to Simeon that "... he would not see death before he had seen the Lord's Messiah" (Luke 2:26). And it is the Holy Spirit who makes known the person and works of Jesus Christ. Thus, at Jesus's baptism, the Spirit says, "You are my Son, the Beloved, with you I am well pleased" (Luke 3:22).

But equally important is the Spirit's third role—in inspiring believers. Sometimes this means allowing them to know what to say in perilous situations (Mark 13:11; Luke 12:11–12). Moreover, it has always been a common Christian teaching that the Holy Spirit inspires the writers of scripture: "All scripture is inspired by God and is useful for teaching, for reproof, for correction, and for training in righteousness" (2 Tim. 3:16; see

---

4. Obviously, this is not meant to be an exhaustive list. Indeed, there are many important works of the Holy Spirit that I will not discuss in this chapter, such as interceding for us (Rom. 8:26), binding together the church in unity (I Cor. 12; Eph. 4:1–7), and interpreting scripture for us (1 Pet. 1:10–13). Moreover, I will not discuss the question of how much human beings must or do cooperate with the Spirit in its works with human beings (e.g., in regeneration or sanctification). This point is skillfully considered in William P. Alston, "The Indwelling of the Holy Spirit," in Thomas V. Morris (ed.), *Philosophy and the Christian Faith* (Notre Dame, IN: University of Notre Dame Press, 1988).

also 2 Pet. 1:21). In 1 Corinthians 2:9–15, Paul quotes an Old Testament text and then says, "These things God has revealed to us through the Spirit." What biblical inspiration actually amounts to has been much disputed, of course.[5] I will define it minimally as that influence of the Holy Spirit on the writers of the Bible so that what they wrote was the word of God and was accordingly accurate, revelatory, and normative.

Fourth, the Holy Spirit guides and leads. Jesus was led by the Spirit into the wilderness to be tempted by the devil (Luke 4:1–2). The Holy Spirit guides believers, too. Thus, Paul says, "All who are led by the Spirit of God are children of God" (Rom. 8:14). And the Spirit at times leads and guides in company with human leaders. Thus the Apostles at the Council of Jerusalem prefaced their decision with the words, "It has seemed good to the Holy Spirit and to us ..." (Acts 15:28). The guidance of the Holy Spirit can come, so to speak, directly, via a voice, dream, vision, or inner conviction. But it can also come indirectly, through the words of a fellow believer, the example of a fellow believer, a historical event, or, most importantly, a text of scripture.

Fifth, the Holy Spirit is the great bestower of gifts and powers, especially for the work of the church (Rom. 12:3–8). The Spirit calls and commissions people for certain tasks and responsibilities in the church (Acts 13:2; 20:28). People are called to serve in certain roles, such as apostles, prophets, evangelists, pastors, and teachers (Eph. 4:7–16). And the Spirit distributes various gifts to believers, such as wisdom, knowledge, faith, healing, miracles, prophecy, discernment, tongues, and interpretation of tongues (1 Cor. 12:1–31). Verse 11 is particularly important here: The Holy Spirit, it says, "allots to each one individually just as the Spirit chooses."

It is clear, then, that there is a huge range of ways in which the Holy Spirit does the work of God in the world. But in the experience of Christians, it seems that God's Spirit works with persons primarily through prayer, the voice of conscience, the influence of fellow believers, and, preeminently, scripture.

III

What is meant by "the testimony of the Spirit"? Here I can do no better than to quote John Wesley: "By the testimony of the Spirit, I mean, an

---

5. For my own views on this matter, see my "Revelation and Inspiration," in Thomas F. Flint and Michael C. Rae (eds.), *The Oxford Handbook of Philosophical Theology* (Oxford: Oxford University Press, 2009).

inward impression of the soul, whereby the Spirit of God immediately and directly witnesses to my spirit, that I am a child of God; that Jesus Christ hath loved me, and given Himself for me; that all my sins are blotted out, and I, even I, am reconciled to God."[6] He goes on to say that the testimony can be received from an audible voice, an inward voice, or a passage of scripture. The only point I would add (and with which I suspect Wesley would agree) is that there are many other items that the Spirit can and does testify to than the ones he mentions. I am thinking primary of cognitive items here (although the Spirit's testimony naturally can be broader than that)—that is, cases where the Spirit testifies to the truth of some claim or statement.

An example: In chapter 7 of I Corinthians, Paul was addressing himself to such questions as marriage, divorce, celibacy, and sexual relations. In so doing, he was careful to make a distinction between his own teachings and those of Jesus. When Paul turned in verses 30 to 40 to the topic of the freedom of widows to remarry, he noted that what he was saying constituted his own teaching rather than the Lord's ("in my judgment"), but he then added, "I think that I too have the Spirit of God." Paul seems to have been claiming, then, that he was teaching the Corinthians what the Holy Spirit would have him teach. He was claiming that the Spirit stood behind or validated his own teaching (see also Rom. 9:1; 1 Cor. 7:25, 14:37). And it is clear that the Spirit testifies not just to Paul and the Apostles, but also to believers throughout history.

This point raises epistemological and criteriological issues that will be addressed in other chapters in this volume. Suffice it to say that some people are more attuned to the guidance of the Spirit than others. And the Bible makes it clear that the Holy Spirit can be resisted (Acts 7:51), grieved (Eph. 4:30), quenched (1 Thess. 5:19), and even blasphemed (Matt. 12:31). In Christian history, there has been no end of misguided or ill-intentioned folk who claim to have been led by the Holy Spirit. Even in biblical times, this issue of discernment was being worried about: "Beloved do not believe every spirit, but test the spirits to see whether they are from God; for many false prophets have gone out into the world" (1 John 4:1).

John Calvin spoke of what he called "the inward testimony of the Holy Spirit" as a path toward certainty. He was convinced that believers need to be persuaded beyond doubt of Christian truth. But he thought that

---

6. Edward H. Sugden (ed.), *Wesley's Standard Sermons* (London: Epworth Press, 1951), II, p. 343.

apologetic arguments and proofs in favor of Christian claims had only limited value, and as a Reformer he was suspicious of the Catholic claim that the locus of certainty for Christians was the Holy Mother Church. Thus he said, "The word of God will not find acceptance in man's heart before it is sealed by the inward testimony of the Holy Spirit."[7] This testimony, he said, produces a certainty that each believer experiences; it is an illumination that opens the sinful heart to the word of God and gives assurance of its truth. Apart from this testimony, the word of God cannot penetrate into our minds.

Let us define the inward testimony of the Holy Spirit as follows: It is *that influence of the Holy Spirit on the minds of believers that causes them to believe firmly that the Christian message, or some aspect of it, is true.* This is the origin of the certainty that believers feel. The inward testimony is a species of persuasion, not of evidence. It is an illumination that opens eyes that are closed to the truth. Thus we read: "The Spirit is the one that testifies, for the Spirit is the truth" (1 John 5:7).

As we all know, many people are not moved by the Christian Gospel. Even Paul recognized this fact: "Those who are unspiritual do not receive the gifts of God's spirit, for they are foolishness to them, and they are unable to understand them because they are spiritually discerned" (1 Cor. 2:14; cf. also 2:10). The Spirit's testimony does not supply new evidence of the truth of the Gospel; rather, it illumines or shows to be convincing evidence that is already there. It is not a question of brainwashing or propaganda or making feeble evidence appear strong. It is a question of removing blinders and helping people to grasp the epistemic situation correctly. It is not a process of reasoning or weighing evidence, but a direct intuition of truth. It is like the opening of blind eyes, the unplugging of deaf ears, the removal of a veil. "And by this we know that [Christ] abides in us, by the Spirit that he has given us" (1 John 3:24; cf. 4:13; Eph. 1:13).

How does the testimony of the Holy Spirit work phenomenologically? We do not know. Bernard Ramm says that it is

No audible voice; no sudden exclamation that "the Bible is the word of God"; no miracle removing us out of our normal routine of creaturely existence; no revelation with flashing lights and new ideas;

---

7. John Calvin, *The Institutes of the Christian Religion*, ed. John T. McNeil, 2 vols. (Philadelphia: Westminster Press, 1960), I, vii, 4.

no religious experience as such; no creation of some new or special organ of spiritual vision; but rather, it is the touch of the Holy Spirit upon native and resident powers of the soul which had been rendered ineffective through sin.[8]

Notice that the inward testimony is private or secret. The assurance that it provides cannot be proved or even passed on via communication. This is why nonbelievers typically take the Christian message to be sheer foolishness and the Bible to be a book like any other book.

Those of us who teach at secular institutions of higher learning and who have friends in departments of religious studies can speak with some authority on this matter. We know people who have spent their professional careers teaching and writing about the Bible, but who do not believe what it says. Since the inward testimony is essentially private, it is not (so to speak) directly communicable. Just because you claim that the Spirit has told *you* that p is true, that does not mean that *I* must accept p. Of course, if you are a person whom I respect, especially in religious matters, your testimony will doubtless impress me and may cause me to look at p in a new light. I may even become convinced that you are correct. But the point is that your testimony will not constitute for me the inner witness of the Holy Spirit. It will not be normative for me. On any topic, a mere appeal to the Spirit is insufficient to carry conviction; as noted, the Bible itself recognizes that many who are in error will try to validate their claims by appealing to the Spirit (1 John 4:1; 1 Cor. 12:10).

It might be objected that the inward testimony is too subjective to warrant any religious beliefs at all. Muslims can claim what might be called the inward testimony of Allah on behalf of the claim that the words of the Koran are from God. Mormons often ask non-Mormons to read the Book of Mormon and see how it makes them feel. But surely the mere fact that people disagree with one of my beliefs does not *by itself* cast doubt on that belief. More importantly, as I have emphasized, the inward testimony is not to be understood as an argument, and certainly not as an argument directed at those who deny or doubt the Christian message. The inward testimony constitutes the central reason why I (and presumably other believers) accept the Christian message. It is not meant as an apologetic vehicle for convincing others.

---

8. Bernard Ramm, *The Witness of the Spirit* (Grand Rapids, MI: Eerdmans, 1959), p. 84.

It is important to note that the inward testimony is not a source of new truths or revelation. It is not an "inner light" or mystical oracle or private vision that provides extra-biblical answers to theological questions. It is a witness to the truth of scripture and of the Christian message. As Jesus said, "When the Advocate comes, whom I will send you from the Father, he will testify on my behalf" (John 15:26; cf. also 1 Cor. 2:10). If this were not so—if the inward testimony provided new truths—the shape of the Christian gospel would be perennially dependent on private visions and revelations. Moreover, it goes without saying that the inward testimony is not a vehicle for solving scholarly problems (e.g., about the biblical text, canon, authority, geography, archaeology, or history).

In an article entitled "Is Faith Infused into Man by God?," Aquinas argued that the assent or belief aspect of faith is not adequately explained by external inducements, such as being persuaded by someone or seeing a miracle. Such influences obviously do not constitute sufficient explanation, because some people are exposed to the same sermon or even observe the same miracle, yet do not believe. There must, then, be an external cause of assent. Aquinas rejected the suggestion that our own free will is the cause; he thought that idea smacked of Pelagianism. Thus, he concluded, the cause must be "some supernatural principle" that moves us inwardly by grace, and that (he says) is God.

Aquinas did not use any expression like "the inward testimony of the Holy Spirit," but his central point was similar to Calvin's. A properly disposed heart (or, if you will, an illuminated mind) is necessary to weigh the evidence properly. Those who have not been illuminated by the Spirit are in an inferior epistemic position. They do not see everything that must be seen.

IV

We have been discussing the ontology of the Holy Spirit. We have been trying to ask what sort of thing the Holy Spirit is, although, as noted, of necessity we have had to approach this question by asking about the Holy Spirit's work. But are there any implications here for our understanding of what sort of thing a human being is? What does the Holy Spirit teach us about human nature? I would have thought that we already knew certain facts about human beings, for example, that they are persons (in roughly the ways described above), that they (unlike the Holy Spirit) are embodied persons, that they are contingent, that they are sinful, and so forth. But perhaps study of the Holy Spirit teaches us other, perhaps less obvious, things about human beings. I will speak of four such characteristics of human beings.

First, human beings were designed to be related to God in loving intimacy. We were created to be in communication with God, in fellowship with God, and under the constant influence of God. And since that relationship has been damaged by our disobedience and self-centeredness, we are now living much reduced and damaged lives because we are improperly related to God. Amoebas and coyotes are not in need of redemption (although, of course, the whole physical universe needs restoration—Romans 8:19–21); human beings are.

Second, all living organisms, including amoebas and coyotes, have certain needs that must be met in order for them to survive and thrive—food, shelter, a method of reproduction, and so forth. But human beings are special among all the creatures in that we have an additional need, a need for words, particularly *words from God*. Thus, in Deuteronomy 8:3, Moses (speaking for God) says to the children of Israel, "One does not live by bread alone, but by every word that comes from the mouth of the Lord." We might express this point by saying that it is part of human nature that we are verbivores.[9] In order to thrive as human beings, we need the Holy Spirit to speak to us. On our own initiative, so to speak, we can know very little about God. We need God to reveal himself and his purposes to us, and to do so is the office of the Holy Spirit. That is, we human beings were designed to be receivers of the Holy Spirit's testimony. But because of the pervasive effects of sin in our lives, our receptor faculty has been damaged. Someday, in the kingdom of God, it will be fully restored.

Third, human beings were designed to be receptacles, so to speak, for the Holy Spirit. To be a believer in Christ is to have received the Holy Spirit. Thus Paul writes, "But you are not in the flesh; you are in the Spirit, since the Spirit of God dwells in you. Anyone who does not have the Spirit of Christ does not belong to him" (Rom. 8:9). Amoebas and coyotes are not receivers of the Spirit in this sense, but the Holy Spirit indwells those human beings who are believers. This is not the same as being "filled with the Holy Spirit," which is an empowering and enabling by the Spirit that can happen to individual believers on special occasions.

---

9. I did not invent this term; so far as I know it was coined by Robert C. Roberts, "Parameters of a Christian Psychology," in Robert C. Roberts (ed.), *Limning the Psyche: Explanations in Christian Psychology* (Grand Rapids, MI: Eerdmans, 1998).

The fourth point (which I am going to spend more time on) is this: Human beings were made to be like God. The idea is called divinization or theosis. This is a notion that always has been strongly emphasized in Eastern Orthodox traditions. It is present but not strongly emphasized in Roman Catholic thought; Protestant thinkers do not usually explicitly deny theosis, but they hardly mention it.

Does the idea that the blessed will become godlike, or even (in some sense) God, have a biblical basis? Yes, it does. In the Fourth Gospel, Jesus was defending himself against the charge of blasphemy; his enemies accused him of making himself God. To this Jesus replied, "Is it not written in your law, 'I said, you are gods'?" (John 10:31–34; here Jesus was quoting Psalm 82:6). Moreover, in Romans, Paul wrote that we will be "conformed to the image of [God's] Son" (Rom. 8:29). And in the second epistle of Peter, it declares that God, by his divine power, has given us everything we need for life and goodness so that we "may become participants of the divine nature" (2 Pet. 1:4). And in 1 John it says, "When he [God] is revealed, we will be like him, for we will see him as he is" (1 John 3:2).

But in what sense will we be like God or be gods? Theosis is affirmed by several of the church fathers. Irenaeus, for example, wrote that God "became what we are, that he might bring us to be even what he is himself."[10] Similarly, Clement of Alexandria wrote, "If one knows himself, he will know God, and knowing God he will become like God."[11] And Athanasius declared that "The Word was made flesh in order that we might be made gods" and "He, indeed, assumed humanity that we might become God."[12]

What should we think about theosis? Let me make a distinction between (1) *becoming like God* (what I will call the weak sense of theosis) and (2) *becoming God* (the strong sense). The first seems to me to be entirely defensible and appropriate from a Christian theological perspective. The Bible affirms that we were initially created "in the image of God" (Gen. 1:26–27), and although that image is greatly marred by the entry of sin into our lives, the idea that the image will be perfectly restored in

---

10. Irenaeus, *Against Heresies*, Book V, Preface. *The Ante-Nicene Fathers*, Vol. I (Edinburgh: T & T Clark, 1989), p. 526.

11. Clement of Alexandria, *Stromata*, 23 (The Instructor 3.1), *The Ante-Nicene Fathers*, p. 271.

12. Athanasius, *Against the Arians*, I, 39.3.34. *The Nicene and Post-Nicene Fathers*, Vol. I (Edinburgh: T & T Clark, 1989); *Saint Athanasius on the Incarnation* (Crestwood, NY: St. Vladimir's Orthodox Theological Seminary, 1989), p. 93.

heaven is correct. We will have mystical fellowship with God; we will know God in ways far more intimate than we now know God; we will love God for God's own sake and not for the sake of what God can do for us[13]; and we will achieve a kind of union with God. Indeed, we will become holy. We will be like God as much as it is possible for a created, contingent, limited thing to be like God.

But theosis is not the Greek and Roman idea of apotheosis—the idea that humans can become exalted to the rank of God. The Jewish and Christian emphasis on (indeed, insistence on) the essential oneness of God rules out any idea like that. The union with God that we will then know has nothing to do with penetrating into or sharing God's essence. There will be no merging or comingling with God. We will not become God or even lesser gods.

Criticizing the strong sense of theosis is not an empty exercise. Divinization in this sense is an important part of the Latter-day Saints' concept of "eternal progression." Indeed, I believe that Mormon scholars often refer to the Church Fathers and Eastern Orthodox theologians on theosis in an attempt to normalize their own theory in the eyes of mainstream Christians. That is, it is used as a way of deflecting the criticism that the LDS theory of eternal progression is heretical or unorthodox. Believing as Mormons do in the uncreatedness of human spirits and the sameness of species between God and human beings, Mormons hold that human beings can progress to the point of becoming divine. Indeed, the God whom they worship—so Latter-day Saints believe—was once a man and grew to divinity.

But I believe that the Church Fathers, as well as Orthodox theologians today, would be shocked and horrified at the suggestion that human beings can ontologically become God or even gods. Moreover, nowhere in the mainstream Christian tradition is there any hint of the correlative LDS idea that God was once a man and has progressed to Godhood. I affirm the weaker sense of theosis but not the stronger.

V

Earlier in the chapter, in our quest for an ontology of the Holy Spirit, we arrived at four conclusions. First, the Holy Spirit is divine, is part of the Godhead, and possesses the standard divine attributes. Second, the Holy

---

13. Alston, "The Indwelling of the Holy Spirit," p. 140.

Spirit is a person, in the full-blooded sense of that term discussed above. Third, the Holy Spirit is a spirit (i.e., is not embodied). Thus the Holy Spirit does not have location in space, does not move at a certain velocity, is invisible, and so forth. Finally, the Holy Spirit acts in the world, both in nature and in the realm of human persons. God's actions in the world are actions of the Holy Spirit.

But now, having briefly discussed human nature, we are in a position to reach a deeper understanding of the nature of the Holy Spirit. First, it is part of the Spirit's nature to be intensely and intimately and lovingly related to humans. Some human persons do not seem to have such relations with other persons. But the Holy Spirit is capable of, and strongly desires, to be so related to all humans. Second, if humans are verbivores, it is part of the nature of the Holy Spirit to be a verbalizer. The Holy Spirit is the agent of divine revelation. Third, it is part of the Spirit's nature to dwell in (certain) human beings. Finally, it is part of the Spirit's nature to welcome and enable human beings to be "participants in the divine nature"—in other words, to be as much as possible like God.

3

Conscience and the Voice of God

FAITHFUL DISCERNMENT

Paul W. Gooch

Whatever creed be taught, or land be trod,
Man's conscience is the oracle of God.
GEORGE GORDON BYRON, *The Island* Canto 1:vi, 1823

Certainly it is correct to say: conscience is the voice of God.
WITTGENSTEIN, *Notebooks* for 1916

IS THE VOICE of conscience also the voice of God? There seems to be more than enough evidence in the history of conscientious human wrongdoing to dispute that simple identification, regardless of Wittgenstein's certainty or Lord Byron's optimism. The challenge set in this chapter, then, is to determine whether, and if so how, it is possible for the faithful to discern the voice of God in the deliverances of conscience. The task is not straightforward. We will see in the first part of the chapter that the language we use to describe conscience and its voice makes a clear and consistent definition close to impossible. In part two we find that the biblical tradition about the witness of the Spirit and the biblical references to "conscience" don't support the claim that conscience is the voice of God. However, in the third section we explore some clues about faithfully discerning the voice of God the Spirit in the deliverances of conscience—and suggest, more daringly, that that voice might on occasion speak against the voice of conscience.

I. Speaking of Conscience

Let us begin with some reflection on the experience of conscience as an aspect of our moral psychology. While competent English speakers may know when and how to use the term, it is not easy to provide a simple, clear definition. Etymology points us in the right direction for the word's root, *scientia*, the territory where knowledge, awareness, and consciousness are found. But the prefix *con*, meaning "with," brings perplexity: "knowing with" what or whom? Is it the self, a self-awareness? Or is it an inner entity, faculty or voice, even the *vox Dei*, the voice of God?[1] Only an examination of the actual uses of the term will throw light on that problem.[2]

Fortunately, the evidence is readily found in all manner of everyday speech and in various genres of literature. To mention but one source, the *Oxford English Dictionary* (OED) has about 350 citations for 12 senses and nine phrases, ranging in time from the 14th century to 2009. Less fortunate for those who seek precise definitions is the remarkable variety in this discourse. It seems difficult to listen to the discourse of conscience without encountering a range—perhaps even a jumble—of images and metaphors.[3] That the vocabulary of conscience is so varied and even inconsistent must have some significance for the ways in which we construct and understand our moral experience.

The OED's citations in sense I.2b under "Conscience" give us about 20 adjectives applied to conscience. Some are evaluative terms appropriate to

---

1. James A. Knight (who was Harkness Chair in Psychiatry and Religion at Union Theological Seminary) puts forward this view without qualification: "Conscience is the voice of moral man speaking to himself as a moral being and making moral judgments. This voice was placed by God in man at his creation, and man cannot rid himself of it. God has established this monitor in man, to urge him to do what man knows to be right and to restrain him from doing what he regards as wrong. God created man to be a moral being. Thus, he endowed him with the faculty to be moral." "Conscience," *Union Seminary Quarterly Review* 19(2) (1964): 133.

2. A helpful essay on the subject is the chapter "Conscience and Conscious" in C. S. Lewis, *Studies in Words*, 2nd ed. (Cambridge: Cambridge University Press, 1967). Lewis distinguishes the "weakened branch," where the meaning is pretty well just "consciousness" or "knowledge," from the "together branch," in which knowledge is shared with another— including oneself. He coins the term "consciring" to signify the experience of self-knowledge of a (usually) guilty secret; in this sense "conscience" has not yet become a judge or legislator of right and wrong. When it takes on this new additional meaning, it is a "remarkable development" and a "great semantic shift" (pp. 191, 192).

3. The OED adds a note to its first definition of the word: "Opinions as to the nature, function, and authority of conscience are widely divergent, including that it is: (i) practical reasoning about moral matters, which, though fallible, must be obeyed (Aquinas); (ii) the understanding which distinguishes between right and wrong and between virtue and vice; (iii) an infallible, God-given guide of conduct; (iv) a sense of personal or individual morality as opposed to customary or social morality (Hegel); (v) a sense of guilt and unworthiness which arises when aggressive impulses are denied external expression (Nietzsche); (vi) an aspect of the superego, the internal perception of the rejection of a particular wish (Freud)."

moral agents, such as "good," "bad," "evil," "ill," "guilty," "scrupulous," or "erroneous." Others refer to qualities of persons or personalities such as "sensitive," "perverted," "quiet," "glad," "strict," "troubled," and "kind." Still others apply metaphors of sensitivity to touch such as "tender" or "seared," or visual metaphors with ethical connotations like "clear," "pure," "clean," or "dark."

Among the actions that conscience undertakes are to prick or goad, to bother or trouble. These are directed to an inattentive, lazy, reluctant or recalcitrant body—which has to be other than the conscience itself. The discourse about conscience is not always consistent, as is demonstrated in its association with legal terms, for conscience may be made to play very different roles in and out of the courtroom. In one of its parts, conscience gives counsel about what is or is not to be done. In another, it is accuser, charging its owner with wrongdoing. It also plays the part of witness, supporting or disagreeing with an accusation. In determining guilt or innocence, conscience acts as judge. These are incompatible roles in legal systems, but this inconsistency has no effect upon our willingness to speak in these metaphors about conscience.

The main conclusion to draw from the ways in which the language of conscience is actually used is this: Conscience is assumed to be an entity, independent of but related to an agent, which is appropriately spoken of in the vocabulary of the *personal*. Not exclusively, of course, because of the metaphors related to tactility. Those metaphors might suggest that conscience is a bit like an internal organ that can be the locus of feelings like pangs, twinges, or pricks. Or perhaps, as a very large number of writers assume, it is a special faculty within a person.

If conscience is a faculty, however, it is rather different from those other functions traditionally known as faculties—the five senses of sight, hearing, smell, taste, and touch. They are perceptual functions related to the workings of the brain and nervous system. But conscience? Recent popular reports claim that scientists have "discovered the conscience" in the lateral frontal pole.[4] The rhetoric is exaggerated, but suppose that science does in fact locate brain activity when we experience the workings of conscience. It doesn't follow that conscience is perceptual in the way these other senses are. And the main reason is the one already presented: Conscience has an

---

4. John Walsh, in *The Independent* on January 24, 2014, writes rather grandly: "Without recognizing it, Oxford scientists appear to have discovered the conscience." http://www.independent.co.uk/voices/comment/you-say-lateral-frontal-pole-i-say-that-little-devilangel-that-whispers-in-my-ear-9094043.html (accessed July 25, 2014).

independent person-like role, unlike other senses. The faculty of sight isn't an entity that points out pictures on a mental screen. And even if we consider cognitive activity to belong to a faculty of reason, we don't think there is an internal thinker coming up with reasons and communicating them to us. We just reason, as we just see or hear. But conscience does engage in assessments, making use of moral "perceptions" such as justice or benevolence. Constructed as an internalized person-like entity performing its own functions, conscience is then different from other entities we call faculties—except, of course, when we treat it as though it were an organ.

The ways in which we speak of conscience, then, are confused and confusing whenever we attempt to articulate a comprehensive and consistent account of its operations, functions, and character. It is small wonder that C. S. Lewis refers to a "simmering pot" of meanings.[5] Yet we believe that the vocabulary of conscience attempts to reflect important facets of moral experience. This is especially so when this personalized entity is given a voice. We have so far ignored the pervasive language of voice in referring to conscience. That omission must now be remedied: The metaphor of the voice of conscience has direct significance for this study of its relationship to the voice of God the Spirit.

The Voice of Conscience

Much of the language associated with conscience considered above refers to nonverbal activities, but the legal metaphors require that conscience itself employ language. We need not here investigate where conscience first was supplied with *voice* as a means of communication. The locution "voice of conscience" is so pervasive in English (the first citation in the OED, under "Voice" sense 4.f, is from 1600) as to require no special evidence.[6] The question here is not about the history of use, but rather about what is gained or lost by attributing voice to conscience.

The precepts, commands, exhortations, and the like associated with conscience are formulated in language; but language can be written as well as oral. Both written and spoken commands are addressed to a

---

5. "A maze—or, better, a simmering pot—of meanings." *Studies in Words*, p. 196. Lewis adds later, "any ingredient may be flavoured by others" (p. 202).

6. If an example is needed, one could point out that on p. 2 of Paul Strohm's *Conscience: A Very Short Introduction* (New York: Oxford University Press, 2011), "voice" un-self-consciously appears three times.

subject capable of response and arise, elementally, from a source that is *independent of the subject,* and also *personal.* That follows from the nature of language as shared communication, written or oral, among persons.[7] So speaking of conscience in such terms is yet more evidence for the assumption that conscience has a certain person-like independence from the subject attending to it. But conscience does not write; it speaks. And communication in voice has two features distinguishing it from written communication.

Primarily, there is an *immediacy* to voice that writing need not share. As Plato most notably argued in the *Phaedrus,* the written word freezes thought and can only say the same thing over and over again (275d-e); it cannot address the particularities of a new or different context. In recent times, technology has managed to capture sound—to freeze in sound-wave tokens the thoughts expressed by voices, like letter tokens; recorded voice becomes, then, like written words and subject to Plato's comment. Direct address, though, remains attentive to its reception and creates a relationship that is alive, not frozen. And even if the voice of conscience repeats the same message, it is not a recording; it is immediate address to its subject.

But secondly, and contrariwise, writing has a permanent character that is accessible over time, at least in principle. Since it does freeze thought, it permits inspection by others who are not present at the time of writing. The immediacy of voice is also its evanescence. Speaker and hearer are left only with memory, which is internal, even private and privileged if there is no possible independent inspection of its claims.[8]

One more comment, about ambiguity and incompleteness of meaning. Writing can be indistinct if half-erased or poorly produced. Changes, too, may be difficult-to-hear murmurs or whispers whose meanings must be guessed rather than discerned. But there's also a pre-linguistic feature to voice that written language does not share. Voices can warn, alarm, disapprove, or affirm, through grunts, cries, shouts, or sighs. Where voices are inarticulate and cognitively deficient in themselves, it may nevertheless be important to heed them (as Socrates so thought about his divine sign, *Apology* 40a-b).

---

7. I ignore here the act of speaking to oneself, and the extended notion of "communication" as occurring among animals and insects. We use such expressions and vocabulary only because we have language as shared among persons.

8. One is reminded of Wittgenstein's dictum that relying on memory for confirmation is like buying several copies of the same newspaper to verify a published report (*Philosophical Investigations*, sec. 256).

Conscience, of course, is not vocalized in any physical way by an external entity; it's experienced internally, like memory. How this voice does or does not play out in the work and deliverances of conscience will require more work, in our third section, especially as we consider how the voice of God may be discerned in the voice of conscience. But so far, we've seen that the construction of conscience as a voice suggests that its utterances issue from a source that is independent of the hearer, personal, immediate, and private; and we are prepared to recognize that, as a voice, its utterances need not always be articulate or enjoy full cognitive content.[9]

If our speaking of conscience reveals the assumption that conscience is person-like in its functions, it should not surprise us that it's difficult to provide a neat, consistent definition of the term. The same person can play, at different times, very different and even incompatible roles. The prosecutor becomes a judge; the witness, articulate about one event, may stutter about another. It's no accident that conscience is portrayed as a separate, interior individual with its own voice—the angel on the shoulder, Jiminy Cricket.[10] But though personalized and distinguishable from its owner, conscience does not share all the characteristics of persons as responsible agents. For instance, it is rarely blamed by its owner.[11]

We will, in our next section, consider what we can discover in the biblical tradition about conscience and the witness of God as Spirit.

---

9. Thomas E. Hill has a description, rather than a definition, of conscience. The "core idea" is "roughly, the idea of a capacity, commonly attributed to most human beings, to sense or immediately discern that what he or she has done, is doing, or is about to do (or not do) is wrong, bad, and worthy of disapproval." See "Four Conceptions of Conscience" in Ian Shapiro and Robert Adams (eds.), *Integrity and Conscience*, Nomos XL (New York and London: New York University Press, 1998), p. 14. Such an account may downplay the positive functions of conscience (as in "defending the right of conscience"), its niggling ambiguities, and the vocal and aural metaphors in its vocabulary.

10. The little devil on the other shoulder, of course, is not a negative-conscience figure, but a tempter. Perhaps the earliest instance of two competing voices comes in mandate 6 of *The Shepherd of Hermes* (second century CE), with an angel of righteousness and an angel of wickedness, both in the heart if not on the shoulder (though the shoulder position is better for listening). Though Walt Disney's Jiminy Cricket is modeled on Carlo Collodi's Il Grillo Parlante, the "talking cricket" in *The Adventures of Pinocchio*, the Disney figure is given a substantial role, explicitly identified with conscience. For further comment, see Nomi Maya Stolzenberg, "Jiminy Cricket: A Commentary on Professor Hill's Four Conceptions of Conscience," in Shapiro and Adams, *Integrity and Conscience*, especially pp. 64–66.

11. Rarely, but not never. There has been much discussion of Huckleberry Finn's conscience and his rejection of its claims (in Chapter 33 he exclaims, "a person's conscience ain't got

As a transition to that topic, we can bring our reflection on the written and the oral to the Exodus 20 story about the giving of the Ten Commandments. As the narrative has it, these commandments were first uttered orally by God to Moses, then written out by the fingers of God on stone tablets.[12] The advantage of the written word, as we've remarked, is that it fixes and stabilizes content. While only Moses heard the voice of God, the tablets were at least in theory accessible to others and an authoritative source capable of correcting any deviations in reports of what was said. It's different where there is no deposit, where the law is (as Paul claims in Rom. 2) written on the heart. A move to the metaphor of heart internalizes law, opening the possibility of inaccessibility to others, with a potential lack of stability or fixity of content. This internality also begins to suggest something akin to a private voice, since what's written on the heart has to be present to consciousness in ways other than visual. We are approaching the language of conscience, though we have not yet arrived there.

II. Conscience and the Witness of the Spirit: The Biblical Tradition

Is there warrant in the biblical tradition for associating the workings of conscience with the voice of God, or the witness of the Holy Spirit? Some comment on the ways in which biblical writers apprehend the operations of the Spirit will assist us in exploring this question. Let me suggest that there are two distinctly different modes of relationship between human beings and the Spirit of the Lord (or the Spirit of God). We can call the first an *instrumental* relationship, and the second a *personal* one.

We can characterize the instrumental mode as particular, episodic, and mainly involuntary or even unpredictable. These are cases where human

---

no sense, and just goes for him *anyway*"). The discussion was sparked largely by Jonathan Bennett's article "The Conscience of Huckleberry Finn," *Philosophy* 49 (1974): 123–34, though the subsequent literature has not dealt with conscience per se; see, for a recent example, James Montmarquet, "Huck Finn, Aristotle, and Anti-Intellectualism in Moral Psychology," *Philosophy* 87(1) (2012): 51–63. An exception is Bernard G. Prusak, "When Words Fail Us: Reexamining the Conscience of Huckleberry Finn," *The Journal of Aesthetic Education* 45(4) (2011): 1–22.

12. Exodus 24:12, 31:18, 32:15–16 (where the tablets are called "two tables of testimony"). After Moses broke the tablets, they were rewritten, not by God but by Moses at God's instruction (34:27–28).

beings are used to accomplish divine purposes.[13] Possession by the Spirit overcomes human limitations, both physical and epistemological.[14] Often the experience involved is ecstatic in the primary sense of taking one outside one's self.[15] Prophetic utterance, which conveys a message from God otherwise inaccessible to human beings, is also the work of the Spirit of the Lord.[16] Examples of instrumentality are common in the Hebrew scriptures, and this mode of the Spirit's activity is also reflected in several New Testament passages.[17] In the Baptist's proclamation that the one coming after him will baptize in the Holy Spirit and fire (Luke 3:16), the association of the Spirit with divine judgment continues the instrumental mode; and the Pentecostal phenomenon of speaking in other languages (Acts 2:4) is another manifestation of ecstasy and prophetic utterance.

Although the prophet may be regarded as a social "conscience," an external voice of moral or spiritual assessment and rebuke, the particularity and episodic nature of the Spirit's activity in the instrumental mode is unhelpful when we attempt to understand conscience as the voice of God. Conscience, after all, is not the privileged possession of a few, nor does it function only on select occasions (at least if it is in good working order). If we are looking for the witness of the Spirit in the voice of conscience, the personal mode may be more promising.

We begin to glimpse this mode in Psalm 51, a confession and expression of repentance notable for its awareness of interiority. The psalmist exposes heart and spirit, asking for cleansing, renewal, and joy. Desiring to continue in the presence of God, he begs God: "do not take your holy spirit from me" (51:11). Although the petition might suggest the episodic character of the instrumental mode, it is possible to read it in a more personal

---

13. For the particularity of the interaction, see (in the book of Judges alone) the singling out of individuals such as Othniel (3:10), Gideon (6:34), Jephthah (11:29), and Samson (13:25).

14. For example, the Spirit "rushes on" Samson, giving him superhuman strength (Judg. 14:6, 15:14) and rousing him to anger (Judg. 14:19; the same holds for Saul in 1 Sam. 11:6). That the Spirit is the source of superhuman power is not surprising: The Hebrew scriptures open with the creative activity of God as Spirit, bringing order out of chaos (Gen. 1:2). It's the Spirit who sustains all life (Job 33:4, Ps. 104:30).

15. The Spirit may be thought to transport someone physically (2 Kings 2:16; cf. Ezekiel's experiences of relocation: "the spirit lifted me up" (3:12, 11:1, 37:1, 43:5)).

16. Numbers 11:25; Joel 2:28.

17. For examples: the driving of Jesus into the wilderness after his baptism (Mark 1:12), the episodic guidance of Philip by the Spirit (Acts 8:29), and the prophecy of Agabus (Acts 21:11; cf. 1 Cor. 12:10, 2 Pet. 1:21).

way, as constitutive of a lasting relationship. That kind of relationship underlies the rhetorical question of Psalm 139:7, "where can I go from your spirit?," though in the answer of the spatial ubiquity of God's spirit ("there is nowhere I can go where God is not") there isn't the interiority of Psalm 51 ("God is always present within").

Although the centrality of the heart is found earlier (Deut. 6:6, 30:1–6), this inwardness is proclaimed prophetically by Jeremiah as God's new covenant: "I will put my law within them, and I will write it on their hearts; and I will be their God and they will be my people" (31:33). It is Ezekiel who links the inward law written on the heart with the presence within of God's spirit, in 36:26–27: "A new heart I will give you, and a new spirit I will put within you; and I will remove from your body the heart of stone and give you a heart of flesh. I will put my spirit within you, and make you follow my statutes and be careful to observe my ordinances." Further, the episodic nature of prophetic utterance moves from particularity to the universal outpouring of God's spirit on sons and daughters, old and young, male and female slaves (Joel 2:28–29).

The New Testament writers take up these themes in order to develop the personal as the dominant mode of interaction between God as Spirit and human beings. While the narrative of the Spirit does begin in particularity with the baptism of Jesus, it is he who will extend baptism in the Holy Spirit to all his followers, and the story of those first followers unfolds with demonstrations of the presence of the Spirit on all those who believe in him. For an understanding of the early Christian material in the personal mode, two writers are especially important. In his Gospel, John provides an account of Jesus's own speaking of the Spirit, and Paul works out his understanding of inwardness and the Spirit especially in Romans and 2 Corinthians. While the scholarly literature on these two authors is vast, making simple claims difficult if not suspect, we will try to distill their views on what we're calling here the personal mode of relationship.

For John, the Spirit descends on Jesus at his baptism and (non-episodically) *remains* (1:32). The same will be true for those who believe in him: They will be baptized with the Holy Spirit (1:33), born from above of water and the Spirit (3:5–8). The Spirit will be given to them as an interior source, an inner lifespring (7:37–39: "out of his belly [*koilia*] shall flow rivers of living water"). After his resurrection, in an enactment reminiscent of God's breath to Adam, Jesus breathes out the Holy Spirit on the disciples (20:22). He had explained in his farewell discourse the meaning of the Spirit's activity, using the term *paraclêtos* (14:16, 26; 15:26; 16:7): helper or assistant (literally, someone called alongside). The term is used in a legal context of an advocate, a counsel for the defense. The range of translations in New Testament versions is wide—helper, advocate, counselor, friend, companion, comforter. Perhaps the simplest clue to meaning is in the phrase in 14:16: *another* helper (*allon paraclêton*), performing therefore the roles that Jesus himself has fulfilled (the disciples will not be left orphans, 14:18).

What sort of presence and assistance to be offered is spelled out a little more. The Spirit has a double role, one didactic and the other judicial. Jesus refers three times to the Spirit *of truth* (14:17, 15:26, 16:13), who will disclose to the disciples what he hears from the Father and from Jesus, guiding them into all truth (16:13–14), teaching them all things (14:26). He will also assist them to remember the words of Jesus (14:26). Translating *paraclêtos* as advocate in this context isn't very helpful; perhaps the notion of an authoritative mentor works better. While there is no explicit reference to interiority, the mentoring will have to be personally and inwardly appropriated to be successful.

The judicial role is found in 16:8–11: The Spirit will convict the world of sin, righteousness, and judgment. These verses have occasioned discussion about the precise meaning of the explanatory clauses, but it seems that this role is outwardly directed toward a world that does not recognize Jesus. The Spirit functions here, in Raymond Brown's term, like a "prosecuting attorney" in a courtroom.[18] In this judicial function there need be no subjective recognition or acknowledgment of wrong on the part of those convicted; those found guilty not untypically proclaim their innocence. However, there is ambiguity in the notion of conviction, which may also refer to the subjective state of being convinced.[19] The common understanding of the phrase "conviction of sin" does hold this subjective sense, and if the Spirit's work is to bring about this inner realization of

---

18. "Jesus is going to die on a cross—in the eyes of the world judged guilty and convicted. Yet after his death, the Paraclete will come and reverse the sentence by convicting the world and proving Jesus's innocence (16:8–11). He will show that Jesus did not sin; rather, the world sinned by not believing in him. He is the one who is just or righteous, as shown by the fact that he is not in the grave but with the Father. The judgment by his enemies putting him to death did not defeat him; ironically, it defeated his great adversary, the Satanic Prince of this world." Raymond E. Brown, "The Holy Spirit as Paraclete," *St. Anthony Messenger* 105(12) (May 1998): 12. http://myaccess.library.utoronto.ca/login?url=http://search.proquest.com.myaccess.library.utoronto.ca/docview/222637688?accountid=1477, 1 (accessed July 14, 2014).

19. The Greek is *elenchô*, which can mean to refute or convict, but also to convince—where there is in fact recognition of wrong thinking or action. D. A. Carson's reading of the passage

wrongdoing, then perhaps the operations of conscience may be involved. Before considering that possibility, however, we should consider the Pauline contribution to an understanding of the personal mode of interaction between the Spirit and believers.

Without using the Johannine term *paraclêtos* or invoking the promise of not being left orphans, Paul expresses a similar idea by referring to adoption (*huiothesia*) in Romans 8:14–17. It is the Spirit who bears witness with (*summartureô*) our spirit that we are children of God (verse 16) when we cry out, "Abba, Father." In perhaps the most striking passage with respect to interiority and intimacy in relationship, Paul goes on to write:

> Likewise the Spirit helps us in our weakness; for we do not know how to pray as we ought, but that very Spirit intercedes with sighs too deep for words. And God, who searches the heart, knows what is the mind of the Spirit, because the Spirit intercedes for the saints according to the will of God. (8:26–27, NRSV)

The Spirit not only provokes us into acknowledging our relationship as adopted children of God, providing assurance of that status, but the Spirit is also present in our inarticulate groanings. Whereas the instrumental work of the Spirit overcomes human epistemological limitations in prophetic utterance, the relational work of the Spirit accepts our limitations, identifies deeply with them, and presents them to a caring God. Paul sees these groanings as labor pains, mixing a birth metaphor with the language of adoption (8:22–23), the former a process and the latter a status not yet fully realized. When realized, the experience will be one of freedom, "the freedom of the glory of the children of God" (8:21).

The themes of glory and freedom recur in 2 Corinthians 3, where Paul presents a particular interpretation of the story in Exodus 34 of Moses's wearing of the veil after having spoken with God and having received the tablets of stone. His face shone with glory; but for Paul, the greater and unfading glory is not manifested in commandments on stone but in the freedom of the Spirit (3:17). The Spirit of the living God writes in tablets of human hearts (3:3). With Paul's contrast between law and spirit, this passage provides material for an antinomian assertion that the Spirit's

---

trades on this. See his "The Function of the Paraclete in John 16:7–11," *Journal of Biblical Literature* 98 (1979): 547–66. For more on this passage, see René Girard, "History and the Paraclete," *The Ecumenical Review* 35 (1983): 3–16.

freedom overrides the laws and commandments that a Jeremiah or Ezekiel saw written on the heart. This would be interiority and inwardness made not just personal but private, and it raises the question of private conscience as the voice of the Spirit.

Paul does not refer to conscience in the passages we've considered. He does do so, however, in many other places; in fact, two thirds of the New Testament occurrences of *suneidêsis*, translated as "conscience," occur in Pauline letters.[20] Unfortunately for the issue under consideration here, none of his references relate *suneidêsis* to the work of the Spirit. However, in Romans Paul speaks of the law written on the heart, allowing us to reflect on interiority again. In arguing for universal guilt, Paul writes:

> When Gentiles, who do not possess the law, do instinctively what the law requires, these, though not having the law, are a law to themselves. They show that what the law requires is written on their hearts, to which their own conscience bears witness; and their conflicting thoughts will accuse or perhaps excuse them on the day when, according to my gospel, God, through Jesus Christ, will judge the secret thoughts of all. (2:14–16, NRSV)

There's no antinomian sentiment here: What's written on the heart is the law given through Moses (as the prophets would agree, but for God's people rather than for the Gentiles). The witness bearer is not the Spirit (they are not, or not yet, the adopted children of God through faith in Christ), but *their own conscience (summarturousê autôn tê suneidêseô)*. Might it be possible, nonetheless, to see in this passage the work of the Spirit as the voice of conscience, even though the Gentiles might not appreciate the identity of that voice?

That possibility, unfortunately, places too much strain on the text, for two reasons. First, if conscience is an internal personal repository of moral precepts, that idea cannot be found here. *Suneidêsis* does not provide any content on which the Gentiles should or should not act; that is given in the law written on the heart. Divine activity lies, then, in the writing rather than the bearing witness. And second: *Suneidêsis* does not act as

---

20. The Greek *suneidêsis* occurs in the New Testament 30 times; 14 times in letters generally accepted to be by Paul and another eight in Pauline-related letters. Here I draw on material presented elsewhere. See Paul W. Gooch, "Conscience," *The New Interpreter's Dictionary of the Bible*, Volume 1 (Nashville, TN: Abingdon Press, 2006), pp. 719–26.

judge of actions. The ultimate judge is Christ, in light of whose judgment the Gentiles will experience "conflicting thoughts," an apt psychological description of self-accusation or self-exoneration when faced with ultimate judgment.

Underlying these points, however, is a deeper issue. It's this: All the instances in which Paul uses the concept of *suneidêsis* can be read without reference to our contemporary understanding of conscience in its manifold operations. Indeed, this is true of all occurrences of *suneidêsis* in the New Testament, most of which can be translated by referring to feelings of self-assessment, usually negative and guilty, rather than to a source of moral knowledge, counsel, or judgment.[21]

I have to conclude, then, that this search in the biblical texts for conscience as the voice of God or witness of the Holy Spirit has come up empty-handed. Indeed (in the alternative, as the lawyers say), were *suneidêsis* to be that voice or witness, it would carry only negative content; the witness would be the whisperings of bad feelings.

Nevertheless, we have some residue from this study that might prove useful in constructing a more positive account of conscience and the voice of God. The personal mode of the Spirit's relationship, for John, has didactic and judicial functions, instructing, convicting, or convincing. For Paul, the Spirit "bears witness," as does *suneidêsis*: Indeed, in Romans 9:1 Paul claims that his *suneidêsis* bears witness (*summartureô*, again) with him in the Holy Spirit. Are these instances of witness-bearing mere verbal parallels, or might they contain clues for developing an understanding of how the witness of the Spirit may—or may not—be involved in the operations of conscience?

III. *Faithful Discernment and the Deliverances of Conscience*

In this final section, we consider the formation of conscience and the variety of its deliverances in order to assess the claim that conscience is

---

21. 1 Tim. 4:2 ("seared" consciences) and Titus 1:15 ("corrupted" consciences) may be exceptions, as I note in "Conscience," 725. The general conclusion of my analysis of the biblical texts is that *suneidêsis* means simply self-awareness or a negative sense of wrongdoing. C. S. Lewis reads some of Paul's uses of *suneidêsis* as including moral judgments, "conscience" in the "shifted" sense. However, he is careful to say that it's not clear whether the shift has occurred in the New Testament use, or "whether a new meaning, arising from different causes, led to a misreading of these passages and was then, by that very misreading, greatly strengthened" (*Studies in Words*, p. 193). I have argued in favor of the latter.

the *vox Dei*, the voice of God. We need to press the question of whether this voice may be heard in conscience, and how one would faithfully discern the witness of the Spirit, especially if that witness seems to speak in unexpected ways.

Forming Conscience, Diversity of Consciences

We should not leave to developmental psychology alone the question of how conscience is formed. That's because it is not always clear what the subject of investigation is. As the first part of this chapter demonstrated, the word is used in multiple ways, with the "simmering pot of meanings" that Lewis points to, including self-consciousness, shame and guilt, witness, legislator, judge. Whatever imprecision or confusion marks the employment of the word "conscience" will create challenges for mapping the development of its manifold operations. Though it is far too simple to posit that the historical development of the concept is recapitulated in the development of moral awareness in the young, it's not wrong to think of a significant "shift" from consciousness of bad feeling about the self's past conduct to conscience as an internal judge, arbiter, and guide.[22] And philosophers as well as psychologists can ask about the conditions necessary for this shift to take place.

I'm going to assume, without argument, that a conscience can't be formed or function effectively without a self-conscious apprehension of basic moral concepts such as justice and benevolence. Suppose, further, for the sake of argument, that these concepts or sentiments are universally present as necessary to the very structure of conscience in all those who have such an entity. It does not follow, however, that the deliverances of conscience will be the same for everyone. In other words, the conditions of the formation of conscience may be shared, but the informed conscience may be significantly different for different individuals, groups, and societies.[23] Much will depend on what's thought to be right, just, or obligatory in a particular context or culture; and every first-year student of the social sciences can give compelling examples of differences, inconsistencies, and contradictions in ethical beliefs and practices across human spaces and times.

---

22. See note 2 above.

23. For an account of 53 different examples of evidence of a seared conscience that is tellingly colored by context, see Charles Finney's lecture XXXI on 1 Tim. 4:2 on April 28, 1841. One

Faced with the incontrovertible fact that the consciences of different persons will shamelessly and authoritatively issue incompatible decrees, those who claim conscience to be the voice of God are faced with a large problem. As C. S. Lewis puts it, "The more boldly men claim that *conscience* is, directly or vicariously, a divine lawgiver and 'the spotless mirror of God's majesty,' the more troublesomely aware they must become that this lawgiver gives different laws to different men; this mirror reflects different faces."[24] Lord Byron was too optimistic in claiming conscience as the voice of God in all creeds and lands. Nevertheless, since the *vox Dei* claim continues to be made, the claimants may have one of two different senses in mind.

The first is that "God" just *is* the voice of conscience: That's what is meant by "God." Why would someone make that claim? As we have seen, to experience the operations of conscience is to encounter an interior person-like independent assessor and judge who is privy to one's secrets. This voice is omnipresent in the sense that it always is where one is. It can be ignored, but it will keep saying the same thing from the place of rightness that it maintains, as it seems, infallibly. Since these attributes of conscience are predicated of God in the major monotheistic faiths, some may argue that what they mean by "God" is the experience and work of conscience, pure and simple. That there are different "Gods" where there are different consciences is, for them, an interesting feature of human experience, but it creates no metaphysical mischief or trouble. It is correct, for them by definition, to say with Wittgensteinian certainty that conscience is the voice of God.

For others, however, the differences in the deliverances of conscience require a different explanation. The God of Abraham, Isaac, and Jacob, Father of Jesus Christ, will not issue commands that contradict justice or love, nor will his voice forbid under all circumstances and also permit under some circumstances the same action—say, abortion of a fetus of

instance in the 46th example: "when you can buy tobacco, tea, coffee, and such like fashionable but pernicious articles without deep compunction and remorse, your conscience is seared with a hot iron." http://www.gospeltruth.net/18410E/410428_seared_consci_pt1.htm (accessed August 4, 2014). Elizabeth Kiss observes that understanding the psychological and sociological origins of conscience can lead to thoughtful moral reflection, in the third section of her "Conscience and Moral Psychology: Reflections on Thomas Hill's 'Four Conceptions of Conscience,'" in Shapiro and Adams, *Integrity and Conscience*, pp. 73–75.

24. *Studies in Words*, p. 199. In the mirror reference, Lewis refers to St. Bernard, citing it from Jeremy Taylor, *Works*, vol. XI (London: William Clowes, 1828), p. 369: "Conscience is the brightness and splendor of the eternal light, a spotless mirror of the Divine Majesty."

nine weeks. If conscience is indeed the voice of God, then problematic inconsistencies must arise for these believers from the hearing rather than the speaking. The Spirit, they will argue, can bear effective witness to the rightness or wrongness of a decision or action only where there is faithful listening. The notable differences in the dictates of conscience are the fault of human beings, not God.[25]

Nevertheless, we have seen throughout this chapter that the internalizing of voice makes it private and not amenable to easy adjudication, at least where there is no reason to doubt the intellectual and emotional honesty of the listener. Add to the problematic deliverances of conscience the conclusion of our previous section on biblical texts: that there is no evidence in Scripture that the voice of conscience is to be identified with the witness of the Holy Spirit. These considerations are sufficient, I think, to force the conclusion that conscience cannot be, *simpliciter*, the voice of God. It may well be God's intention and pleasure that human beings form and develop conscience, since it is crucial to moral growth, and to social and personal relationships. But particular consciences are informed by precepts and values inculcated through teaching and example, and neither the teaching nor the understanding is an infallible interpretation of the divine will. We're bound to get it wrong at least part of the time, with the consequence that the voice we hear as conscience may well be repeating the injunctions of some all-too-human figure.

It doesn't follow from this, however, that we can never discern the voice of God in the deliverances of conscience.

Faithful Discernment of the Voice of God and the Spirit's Witness

To bear witness is to provide evidence, confirming what might not be credible on its own testimony. As voice, witness has an independence from the subject that it addresses. When Paul, then, claims that the Spirit "bears witness with our spirit that we are children of God," the point is that we

---

25. "It is impossible that the voice of conscience in the heart of man should be his own voice alone.... But if, indeed, conscience is no other than the voice of God, it is yet necessary in order rightly to understand this voice, that men should have received a spiritual ear; and this is a gift of Divine grace, through the Holy Spirit." This from an unsigned article, "Conscience," in *The Sunday at Home: A Family Magazine for Sabbath reading* 882 (1871): 186–87. http://myaccess.library.utoronto.ca/login?url=http://search.proquest.com/docview/4002040/fulltext/1?accountid=14771 (accessed July 24, 2014).

may be in need of independent reassurance, beyond our merely telling ourselves over and over again that this is the case. Albeit in a different vocabulary, 1 John makes a similar point, recognizing that we may doubt our relationship to God: "And by this we will know that we are from the truth and will reassure our hearts before him whenever our hearts condemn us; for God is greater than our hearts, and he knows everything" (3:19–20). Although the word for conscience doesn't appear in the Johannine letters, "heart" can be so translated in this text.[26] The experience of self-condemnation that is the operation of conscience creates doubt about whether we are indeed loved by God, but we know "by the Spirit that he has given us" (3:24) that God does abide in us.

Note that the operations of the Spirit and the operations of conscience are distinct in such cases. When the voice of conscience whispers negative judgment because of our human failings and sinning, the voice of the Spirit affirms the permanence of our status as held within the love of God. This voice of reassurance has a completely different vocabulary from the voice of conviction, another Johannine operation of the Spirit, this time judicial and directed to the "world" rather than the faithful. We recognized in the previous section that conviction of sin may involve conscience, and if so, those of the "world" may be troubled by their Spirit-assisted recognition of wrongdoing. Nevertheless, even the faithful may find that their hearts condemn them for good reason: One can listen for the voice of the Spirit in a troubled conscience. If the Spirit's work is also didactic, leading into "all truth," then this will include uncovering the truth about one's own motives and actions or inactions.

This means, though, that sometimes the voice of conscience will be the vehicle of the Spirit, with the Spirit's reassurances consequent upon repentance; and sometimes—if its murmurings come from a false, unwarranted, or persistent guilt—conscience will need to be silenced by the more compelling witness of the Spirit. How does one begin to discern whether the voice heard should be the voice heeded? Is it the Spirit's? Or another voice mimicking the accents of the Spirit?

There may be no sure-fire answer to that. We may take some comfort from the apostle's description of the "fruit of the Spirit" as virtuous qualities of character,[27] and ask whether the advice, assessment, or judgment

---

26. See "Conscience" (cited in note 10), section C.3, p. 723.

27. ". . . love, joy, peace, patience, kindness, generosity, faithfulness, gentleness, and self-control" (Gal. 5:22–23).

we hear is consistent with these qualities. But even then we cannot don any iron-cladding against self-deception. Isaac was suspicious of the identity of the voice he heard, but duped by Jacob's false evidence of Esau's hands; and we may deceive ourselves by mistaking the work of our hands for the Spirit's work, wrongly confirming the voice of a misguided conscience as belonging to the Spirit.

Consciousness of our fallibility in discerning becomes even more acute when we are faced with the possibility that what we have taken to be the divine will may require rethinking and reform. In our discussion so far, we've asserted that the voice of God cannot be heard in consciences that contradict each other. But developments at the beginnings of the Christian community make this certainty problematic.

Issues of conscience around religious identity are particularly potent. When you disobey your conscience in a matter that defines your relationship with God, the disobedience is directed at God himself. Suppose your tradition makes it clear that it's God's will that you should not do X, or that Y is a divinely mandated mark of your belonging to God. A conscience so informed could not believe otherwise without experiencing spiritual and moral guilt. But suppose that X is not eating certain foods, and Y is circumcision for males. In these cases, the first Christian leaders struggled with the near-impossible idea that God's will had in fact changed, at least for a new class of believers.

The accounts (in Acts, especially chapters 10 and 15, and in Gal. 2) of how the Gentiles were accepted into the new community of Jewish believers in Jesus demonstrate the tensions and perplexities that must have been experienced by the early leaders, especially James, Peter, and Paul. To sort through the issues would be a long task for another and different project, but it may be sufficient for our purposes to note four common features of the accounts of what we can call an "experience of revision," First, there is a vision with a voice attributed to God, heard privately by one individual. The experience is surprising because it challenges entrenched beliefs. Second, the message is independently confirmed by another party. There is, third, evidence of the presence of the Holy Spirit, considered confirmatory of the revisionary message. Finally, the implications of the revision experience are discussed with others in a position to accept, modify, or reject the message.[28]

---

28. On the private vision not accessible to others, see (for Paul) the Damascus road experience at Acts 9:3–7, with the report of his vision of Ananias at 9:12, and (for Peter) his vision

Taken together, these features mean that the "experience" leading to a revised understanding of God's purposes is not simply an individual claim to have been the special recipient of a personal revelation, a privileged and secret hearer of the *vox Dei*. There are confirmatory public events, and a process for interpretative discourse about the import of the surprising revised understanding, related, perhaps, to fundamental principles in scripture. If what is being revised is an apprehension of the divine will, then it is important that there is witness from the Spirit in some form; this will provide assurance that God's mind itself is capable of being understood in new ways in new circumstances.

There are implications for conscience in any radically revised understanding of the divine will. Peter's experience is instructive: faithfully observant of Jewish dietary law, he is ordered in a vision to eat "unclean" food. He concludes that Gentiles are not profane; indeed, they receive the Holy Spirit though not circumcised. When criticized for eating with them, he explains his reformed understanding of God's will—and, as we would put it, he acts out of a revised conscience. But in Antioch, where he was in the habit of eating with Gentile believers, he succumbs to pressure from the "circumcision factor" and withdraws from table fellowship. Paul attributes this to fear (Gal. 2:12); that is, we might say, evidence of a conflicted conscience, unable to silence the whisperings of the old voice.

If even an apostle had difficulty with a reformed conscience, the rest of us faithful may have our own struggles with listening to the voice formed in us in the context of our own circumstances, and assessing its claims along with the witness of the Spirit. New circumstances and new understandings will challenge those who are open to the Spirit's uncovering of the mind of Christ.[29] The ability to distinguish the *voces famae* (the voices of tradition) from the *vox Dei* is especially difficult when the implication

---

at Acts 10:9–16. Independent confirmation is offered to Paul by Ananias (9:17) and to Peter by the three men sent from Cornelius (10:19–23). Ananias claims that Paul will be filled with the Holy Spirit, the evidence of which will be his sight restored (9:17–18); Peter takes the Gentiles's speaking in tongues as evidence of the Spirit and confirmation of the meaning of his vision (10:44–48). Barnabas vouches for Paul to the other apostles, who receive him (9:27); Peter's understanding that Gentile believers need not be subject to dietary laws is discussed and confirmed by James and the other apostles in Acts 15, and Paul's understanding is confirmed by the Jerusalem leadership (Gal. 2:2).

29. See section V.b, on philosophy as reflection on the mind of Christ, in my "Paul, the Mind of Christ, and Philosophy," in Paul Moser (ed.), *Jesus and Philosophy: New Essays* (Cambridge: Cambridge University Press, 2009), pp. 84–105. I noted there that two large issues are pressing for contemporary Christian thinkers: sexuality and religious pluralism. Paul's own

is that the divine purpose either has been long misunderstood or has changed. Nevertheless, Christian communities have managed to make such discernments, for instance over slavery, polygamy, and (with notable exceptions) the status of women. They have gained new understandings that contextualize past social norms considered divinely sanctioned, so that what then was approved by a devout conscience is now rejected by a reformed conscience.

Though successful discernment of the voice of the Spirit is never always assured beyond question, this effort is required of the faithful. There are spiritual practices that assist with discernment, such as examination of conscience.[30] Whatever those practices, they will involve prayer as a stilling of the heart and a listening beyond the self, to what one recognizes as the witness of the Spirit. That inward attentiveness may sometimes discover clarity of voice, but on other occasions only a groaning in need of further articulation, the prelinguistic workings of the Spirit. Sometimes it's simply a physical discomfiture that signals the need for self-examination: Marilynne Robinson's character John Ames, without explicit reference to conscience, makes this confession: "My custom has always been to ponder grief; that is, to follow it through ventricle and aorta to find out its lurking places. That old weight in the chest, telling me there is something I must dwell on, because I know more than I know and must learn it from myself—that same good weight worries me these days."[31]

If what one learns from within oneself—that is, from the voice of conscience or of the Spirit—turns out to challenge received opinion, apostolic example suggests that we should seek confirmation beyond the inward voice. That will include evidence of what is understood by the community as the presence of the Spirit in the lives and characters of those affected,

---

work in discerning the mind of Christ about circumcision and divorce, for instance, is not unrelated.

30. This practice is especially associated with Ignatian spirituality. Given the multiform uses of "conscience," the genitive "of" in the phrase could be objective or subjective. In the former sense, the object of the examination would be one's conscience, to uncover its condition (is it guilty? troubled? at peace?). In the latter, conscience would be doing the assessing of attitudes, motives, and behavior. That both are possible is only confirmation of the complexity of relationships of the self, consciousness, and conscience.

31. Ames is speaking of his heart, and muses on the double meaning of the word as he engages in self-examination: "My heart is greatly disquieted. It is a strange thing to feel illness and grief in the same organ. There is no telling one from the other." *Gilead* (Toronto: HarperCollins, 2004), p. 179.

and a willingness to offer to others one's interpretation of what's heard for the sake of discussion, revision, or correction. Even then, there can be no guarantee that the community's conscience will be receptive.[32] That risk, however, has been and always will be the core of faith: the commitment of one's own soul, acting in as much integrity as can be worn by frail human flesh, to God whose Spirit assures of everlasting care.[33]

---

32. The Canadian author Rudy Wiebe has a haunting fictional account of the privacy of hearing the voice of God and the attempt to seek confirmation, in "The Vietnam Call of Samuel U. Reimer," Chapter 12 of *The Blue Mountains of China* (Toronto: McClelland and Stewart, 1970). Samuel, like his namesake of ancient time, hears his name called; and the voice (of "the God of your fathers, the Lord your God") commands him to go to proclaim peace in Vietnam. Properly skeptical, and in fact not having read much about the war in Vietnam, Sam seeks evidence, so records the voice on the next occasion and takes the tape to his pastor—who cannot hear anything, though the needle on the tape recorder fluctuates as though someone is speaking. The desire to be faithful, the ambiguity of meaning, and the clash between "religious values to which many of us pay cautious lip-service and the actions (with all their attendant consequences) of our day-to-day lives" (W. J. Keith, in the Introduction) are painfully worked out in Samuel's descent into misunderstanding, illness, and death.

33. It is for this reason, among others, that we must respect the conscientiousness of those with whom we disagree. Difficulties arise, though, when those others do not reciprocate with the same respect, and attempt to impose the dictates of their conscience upon the rest of the world. That makes ecclesial reform impossible, and the development of social policy a matter of politicking rather than reasoned discussion.

4

The Testimony of the Spirit
and Moral Knowledge

C. Stephen Evans

ANY PLAUSIBLE ACCOUNT of the role that the Holy Spirit might play in ethics must presuppose some particular account of ethics. Since I have recently defended a divine command account of moral obligations, I will take such an account as my point of departure. Since the doctrine of the Trinity that includes a belief in the Holy Spirit is a distinctively Christian view, I shall also for the most part presuppose a Christian audience and context.

I believe that the Holy Spirit must play multiple roles in our lives as moral beings. In particular, it would seem vital that the gifts and fruits of the Spirit be present if a person is to make genuine moral progress, and this is probably the most important topic that connects the Spirit with the ethical life. However, in this chapter I shall focus mainly on another issue: the role the Spirit might play in giving us knowledge or true beliefs about what are moral duties are.

Divine Command Accounts of Moral Obligation

In my book *God and Moral Obligation*, I argued that moral obligations are best understood as divine commands or laws established by divine commands.[1] In this chapter I shall designate the claim that moral obligations

1. C. Stephen Evans, *God and Moral Obligation* (Oxford: Oxford University Press, 2013).

are divine commands as a DCT, short for divine command theory. A DCT
has both theological and philosophical strengths. From a theological view-
point it makes full use of the important role that divine law or Torah plays
in the scriptures, both in the Old and New Testaments. The view that
moral obligations are divine commands also gives a satisfying explanation
of why it is that all wrongdoing is sin against God, even though the harm
done by sin may often be directed at other humans or oneself.

A DCT has epistemic value that is both theological and philosophical.
It entails that anyone who is aware of a genuine moral obligation is aware
of God's call or claim to live in a certain way. Of course those who are
atheists may not experience those obligations *as* divine commands, and
thus may fail to realize that God is addressing them through conscience.
Still, if a divine command view is correct, then causal or explanatory arguments for God's existence may not be necessary for reasonable belief in
God, even if such arguments can be given. Rather, the epistemological
task might perhaps be to help those who are aware of moral obligations to
recognize God's address to them, to realize that they already have a *de re*
awareness of God.

The purely philosophical virtues of such a view are also multiple, particularly when compared with secular alternatives. It gives a satisfying
explanation of how statements about moral obligations can be objectively
true, and yet moral obligations be motivating. Moral realism is provided
by the fact of God's command, since that is a fact that is independent of
human beliefs and attitudes. The motivation is provided by the connection between the command and a relation to God, since such a relation
is essential to human flourishing. A DCT also explains why moral obligations provide reasons that trump other kinds of reasons for action, including non-moral obligations, since the relation to God for humans is more
important than relations to society, the state, and even the family. A DCT
also provides a satisfying response to the "evolutionary debunking argument" against moral knowledge. If naturalism is true, there is little reason
to suppose that moral intuitions shaped by evolutionary pressures to survive and reproduce would track moral truth. However, if evolution is the
method God employed to create moral beings, then there is every reason
to think that our intuitions are not inherently untrustworthy.

Some Christians may be inclined to think that other approaches to
ethics are more promising than a DCT, preferring to defend either some
form of natural law ethics or else some form of virtue ethics. However, as
I argue in my book, I do not believe these other two approaches are rivals

to a DCT.[2] Rather, all three types of approaches are necessary and complementary. A DCT presupposes some account of the good, since God's commands must be guided by his understanding of the good, and a natural
law account of the good seems well suited for this purpose. A virtue ethic,
on my view, provides the *telos* or end of divine commands. God gives us his
law for several reasons. One is to help us understand our sinfulness and
need for grace. However, another is to help us understand how the lives
we lead as forgiven sinners can prepare us for the kingdom of God. God's
commands are not given so that we can be rule keepers, but to help us
become, with God's help, certain kinds of persons with the character one
must have to be a friend of God.

A DCT of moral obligation of the type I defend must not be confused
with a general theological voluntarism that makes all moral truths dependent on God's will. A DCT is in fact incompatible with such a theological
voluntarism, since the divine authority that God's commands possess rests
on moral truths about God's character and goodness, and truths about our
relation to him, combined with normative truths about the implications of
those truths about God and our relation to God. It is because God is necessarily good and loving that his commands are good, and it is because it is
good to show gratitude to a benefactor that we owe God, who has given us
every good we have, our love and obedience.

It is also important to see that a DCT does not imply that moral obligations are in any way arbitrary. Thus the view is not defeated by the so-called
Euthyphro problem, as ethics textbooks often claim. God's commands are
not arbitrary because they are motivated and guided by his understanding
of the good. At least some of God's commands are fixed by that understanding. God could not possibly command us to make anything other
than himself the supreme object of our love and devotion, because it could
not be good to love anything other than God more than God. Some defenders of a DCT do hold that God has some discretion with respect to *some* of
his commands, because in some cases there might be equally good commands that God could give, but choosing between equally good options is
not an objectionable form of arbitrariness.

In any case the claim that God has such discretion is not an essential part of a DCT. It is fully compatible with a DCT to hold that *all* of
God's commands are determined by God's knowledge of the good. What

---

2. See *God and Moral Obligation*, pp. 53–87, for a fuller account of how a DCT relates to
natural law ethics and virtue ethics.

is essential to a DCT is the claim that God's commands add a new moral quality to an action. When God commands an act to be done or forbids an act to be done, a duty of a new type is thereby created. The act is now a moral *obligation*, even though the acts would be good or bad even without God's command. An act that is obligatory is not simply one that a person has good reason to perform; it is a special type of reason, one that can bring deliberation to closure. One can rightly be held accountable for failure to fulfill obligations. There are many acts that are good that are not obligatory.

How Are God's Commands Communicated?

There are various possible views one might hold about how God communicates his commands to humans. However, a DCT is committed to the claim that God's requirements must be communicated in some way. It is not simply God's *will* that creates an obligation but God's will as expressed to humans. That is in fact how I think of a divine command: not simply a speech act expressed in the imperative mood, but any expression of God's will that is communicated to humans effectively. In my book I defend the claim that God's commands are promulgated in a plurality of ways.[3] Those ways include for Christians the following:

(1) Special revelation, including the acts and words of prophets and apostles, as well as the divinely inspired written revelation of those acts and words that constitutes the Christian Bible.

(2) Special experiences and revelations given to individuals outside the biblical revelation. These could include dramatic experiences such as mystical visions, dreams, and voices, but could also include more mundane experiences, in which an individual simply becomes convinced that God is speaking to her and asking her to perform some particular action.

(3) Conscience: Although conscience is certainly shaped by culture and is mixed with some cultural "noise," there is good reason to think that humans have a natural ability to grasp some moral truths. This natural ability, like our natural ability to acquire mathematical knowledge, of course requires nurture for the ability to function properly, and can malfunction in various ways due to human sinfulness.

---

3. See *God and Moral Obligation*, pp. 37–45.

(4) Cultural transmission: Once some knowledge of God's commands (i.e., some knowledge of moral obligations) is present, then that knowledge can be transmitted culturally just as other kinds of knowledge are transmitted. (Obviously this introduces a possible source of error, but there is no reason to think that such errors would be total and pervasive.)

After this paragraph I shall not discuss cultural transmission. This is not because this is not a significant source of moral knowledge. It is highly likely that most of the moral knowledge that most people have is gained from what parents and other members of society teach, both through explicit instruction and through examples. However, it would seem that culture could only be a derivative source of moral knowledge. Someone must somewhere at some time acquire moral knowledge in some other way in order for that knowledge to be culturally transmitted. So I shall focus on the first three types of communication, asking with respect to each what role the Holy Spirit might play.

Conscience and the Holy Spirit

On the view that I want to defend, conscience is one of the ways God communicates his commands to humans. Laws must be promulgated to have binding authority; I cannot be expected to obey a human law that is made in secret; indeed, such a law would not be a proper law. The same is surely true for God's laws. If we limit God's communication of his moral requirements to special revelation that is only historically accessible and thus unavailable to some humans who lack access to the historical record, it would appear that many people would have no ability to know what is morally required of them. That would in turn imply that they could not justly be held responsible for failure to obey those laws. In addition to that philosophical point it is important to recognize that the Bible itself plainly teaches that there is a natural moral knowledge available to those who do not have access to divine special revelation.[4] So it is important for a DCT to accept the idea that God communicates his commands through some natural process, and I concur with the traditional view that this natural process is what we call conscience.

I understand by "conscience" a faculty or ability normal humans have to make moral judgments both of a particular nature ("It was cruel of him

---

4. See, for example, Rom. 2:14–15.

to kick that dog") and of a general nature ("Cruelty to animals is morally wrong"). I have argued elsewhere, but shall here simply assume,
that a good case can be made that conscience, even though fallible and
enmeshed in cultural accompaniments, is sometimes a source of genuine
moral knowledge.[5]

One might think that since conscience is a "natural" human cognitive faculty it does not involve any direct communication from God to
humans. However, I think this conclusion would be too hasty. I agree that
conscience is a natural human faculty; there is in fact good scientific evidence that at least the foundations of moral judgments are hardwired into
small children.[6] On my view communication involves the transmission of
information from one party to another in a form that the second party can
understand. Normally at least this requires some kind of causal process by
which the information is transmitted.

Some might think that because the information from conscience comes
from natural human capacities, it does not come from God. The person
who thinks this might hold that any communication from God would
have to be supernatural in some way, involving some kind of extraordinary
intervention by God in the natural order. However, this objection rests on
a deistic view of the relation between God and the natural world, and thus
a mistaken view of how God can act within the world. I do believe that God
can act in the natural world in extraordinary ways, and will discuss how
this might bear on God speaking to us later in this chapter. But we should
not think that God's actions in the world are limited to such extraordinary
actions. God is the creator of the whole of the universe. This does not
mean merely that he is responsible for the beginning of the universe but
also that he is responsible for its continued existence at every moment.
God is the ultimate cause of every substance in nature, and thus there is
no reason that the causal chain by which he transmits information to us
cannot involve natural processes. Whether a natural event is a communication from God depends on whether God intends that event to function
as communication and on whether it is possible for the human recipient
to understand what is thereby communicated.

Someone might object to this that the causal process required for
communication must be direct, and therefore that a causal process that

---

5. See *God and Moral Obligation*, pp. 169–181.

6. For a good summary of the scientific evidence, see Paul Bloom, *Just Babies: The Origins of Good and Evil* (New York: Broadway Books, 2013).

involves natural faculties cannot qualify as communication from God. However, the requirement that the causal process must be direct seems wrong to me. When my wife calls me on her cell phone, the causal process by which I hear her is surely highly indirect, involving radio waves and cell towers, with sound waves being digitized, transmitted, and then converted again to sound waves. Nevertheless, despite the indirect nature of the causal process, I hear my wife speaking to me.[7]

On my view it is literally true that God sometimes speaks to humans through conscience, even though the causal process is normally indirect. Since this speech occurs through a natural faculty, it is properly thought of as a form of general or natural revelation. Does this mean that we should think of conscience as a manifestation of the Spirit? I am not completely sure, but I think a case can be made for an affirmative answer.

To answer this question requires some view as to how one attributes particular actions to the various Persons of the Trinity. As I see things, we are often ignorant about such matters. In any case, given the unity of the Persons, it seems plausible that every action of one of the Persons of the Trinity also in some ways involves both of the other Persons. Nevertheless we do rightly speak of certain actions as especially attributable to one of the Persons, because of the special role that Person plays in it. For example, though no doubt the Incarnation was willed by all three Persons, we speak of it as a special action of the Son, and we also speak of the Son as the one who "gave his life as a ransom for many."

Some Christians may believe that the Holy Spirit is only manifested to believers, members of the body of Christ, and that it is therefore improper to speak of a natural revelation that is a manifestation of the Spirit. On this view the Holy Spirit is only active in the lives of believers. However, I doubt that this is correct. Perhaps it is God as a whole who speaks through conscience, rather than just the Spirit. If so, it may be that this activity of God is an activity of the Trinity as a whole, rather than just one of the Persons. Nevertheless, if the three Persons of the Trinity are speaking to humans through conscience, then this must at least also involve the activity of the Spirit.

If we look at the role of the Holy Spirit in the New Testament, one of the characteristic actions that are linked to the Spirit involves the giving of insight or knowledge. For example, in John 17:13 Jesus tell his disciples

---

7. George Mavrodes makes this point for religious experiences in general in *Belief in God* (New York: Random House, 1970), pp. 49–89.

that "When he, the Spirit of Truth, comes, he will guide you into all truth."
It is of course clear that Jesus is referring to the activity of the Spirit after
the Spirit is poured on the Church, and not about any general revelation.
However, the example does show that one of the characteristic activities
linked to the Holy Spirit is enabling the grasp of important truths. If
conscience is a means whereby God gives to humans knowledge about
his requirements for them, then one might think that the Spirit would
be powerfully involved in this divine activity. If so, one might correctly
describe this activity of God as a manifestation of the Spirit, even though,
as is probably true for all the activities of the Persons of the Trinity, the
other Persons are involved as well.

Thinking of conscience as a manifestation of the Spirit does not preclude the claim that the Spirit is manifested in a special way in the life of
the Christian believer. The voice of God in conscience may communicate
to us how God expects us to live. However, the Christian who is indwelled
by the Spirit does not just receive information but is "filled with the Spirit"
and endowed with gifts and fruits that enable the Christian to live as God
desires. I agree that the indwelling of Christians by the Spirit is something
special and supernatural and should not be confused with any natural or
general revelation. However, the fact that the Spirit can work in this special
way does not preclude the possibility that the Spirit is also at work giving
us general revelation.

The Role of the Spirit in Giving Moral Knowledge Through Special Revelation

Christians have throughout the centuries maintained that one of the ways
God teaches humans how to live is through God's authoritative special
revelation. By "special revelation" I here mean God's actions in history,
and the Bible, the inspired written revelation that provides an account of
those actions. God acted in history by electing Israel as a special people
for himself, and in sending Israel prophets and judges. This divine mission culminated in God sending his own Son in the person of Jesus of
Nazareth, and in the ministry, death, and resurrection of Jesus, culminat-
ing in the founding of a new people of God through Jesus's chosen apostles. The Church has traditionally accepted the Old and New Testaments
as a divinely inspired record of this divine mission. Since for the most part
our only access to God's revelatory actions is through the scriptures, I shall
mainly focus on the Bible in this section.

There is no doubt that both the revelation in historical deeds as well as the written revelation includes a substantial account of God's law expressed in the form of commands. There is of course the Decalogue, but much of the Old Testament is "Torah," law. The prophets, such as Isaiah and Jeremiah, also continually remind the people of Israel of God's commands to treat the poor and the stranger with justice and compassion. It is sometimes said that the Old Testament is about law but the New Testament focuses instead on love; however, this is a superficial view of both Testaments. The Hebrew Bible has plenty to say about God's love and mercy, and the New Testament is full of God's commands, including a reiteration of the Old Testament commands to love God and the neighbor. Jesus even tells his disciples that it is only the person who obeys his commands who loves Jesus (John 14:15 and 14:21). For the Christian, divine law should retain a fundamental importance.

One might here object that the Christian no longer lives by the law but is now under grace. I take it that this means that the Christian does not believe that it is by keeping the law that one can be forgiven for one's sins and restored to fellowship with God, but rather this happens through God's grace. However, this by no means rules out important functions for the divine law. For one thing, without the law we would not understand our status as sinners, nor our need for divine grace. However, in addition to this accusatory, "schoolmaster" function, God's law also gives those who are forgiven an understanding of how to show proper gratitude for that grace. The person who owes everything to God will want to live a life that is pleasing to God, and God's commands provide insight as to what such a life will look like. The Christian knows, as did the ancient Hebrews, that God's law is not an arbitrary restriction of freedom, but a gracious gift, spelling out the framework within which human life can flourish.

So there is little doubt that, for the Christian, God's law should have a fundamental importance even though salvation is by grace and the believer is free from the penalty of failing to keep God's law. In comparison with the communication of God's law found in conscience, the revelation of the law in scripture is clearer, more precise, and comprehensive. Our understanding of God's law through conscience is more subject to error, primarily because of the way conscience is always accompanied by cultural noise.

This is not to say that our knowledge of God's law through scripture is error-free, however. Traditionally, Christians have believed the scriptures themselves are infallible, but that does not mean that we humans do not make mistakes when we put the scriptures to use. The Bible is infallible only when it is properly understood, and exegesis and interpretation of scripture is obviously not always easy or straightforward. To mention one obvious issue that is relevant to moral knowledge, the reader of the Bible is often required to decide whether a divine command is directed to a particular people in a particular historical/cultural context or whether the principle applies more generally. If the former is the case, as it often is, then questions may arise as to whether the specific command in a particular cultural context is an expression of some deeper principle that may be of more general import. So even though the moral teachings that come through scripture carry some priority over those that come through conscience, it may sometimes be the case that a relatively clear dictate of conscience carries more weight than a principle that is claimed to be grounded in scripture, but that is interpretively dubious.

It is now time to raise the main question: What is the role of the Holy Spirit in the moral knowledge gained through special revelation? The first thing to note is that the activity of the Spirit plays a key role in providing the revelation in the first place. Christians have traditionally held that all scripture is inspired, "God-breathed," in the words of Paul in 2 Timothy 3:16, and the reference to "breathed" carries association with the Spirit, since the Hebrew word for Spirit is simply "breath." That the inspiration of the scriptures by God is primarily the work of the Spirit is also affirmed explicitly in 2 Peter 1:20–21: "Above all you must understand that no prophecy of Scripture came about by the prophet's own interpretation. For prophecy never had its origin in the will of man, but men spoke from God as they were carried along by the Holy Spirit."

The role of the Holy Spirit is also important in two other ways in relation to the scripture: first, in relation to how scripture is recognized as an authentic revelation, and second, in relation to the interpretation of scripture. In the next section I will discuss some of the obvious epistemic problems that arise when individuals claim to have received a direct word from the Spirit of God. My neighbor may claim that God has commanded him to stop cutting his grass, but I may wonder whether this is so and how I and my neighbor could know that it is so. However, it is important to see that analogous epistemic problems are raised by the claim that the scriptures provide a word that is from God. There are a number of books that are alleged to be divine revelations, including the Koran, The Book of Mormon, and a book in my office called

Salam: Divine Revelations from the Actual God, kindly sent to me by the human author. Why should I accept the Bible as a genuine revelation from God but not these others?

Christians have often responded to this question by attempting to give *evidence* that the Bible is divinely inspired. The evidence appealed to is of various kinds. Some have alleged that the sublimity of the Bible's moral teachings is evidence that it comes from God, but this argument is an awkward one to use for someone who wishes to hold that part of the value of the Bible lies in the superiority of its moral teachings to conscience. The awkwardness stems from the fact that it appears we would have to have prior and independent knowledge of moral truth in order to recognize the truthfulness of the Bible's moral teachings. A philosopher such as Kant, who holds that we have *a priori* knowledge of morality through reason, might indeed make such an argument, but it seems in this case that the authority of the Bible with respect to morality would thereby be subordinated to the authority of human reason. Of course people who have accepted the Bible as divinely authoritative, and who have been morally formed through their reading of scripture, may well find the biblical teachings on morality to be sublime and true, but that judgment seems more to be a consequence of their trust in the Bible than independent evidence for biblical authority.

A more promising line of evidence is an appeal to authenticating miracles, understood as events that could only be done by God, provided by God as signs to certify that some prophet or religious figure is actually speaking on behalf of God. A long line of theologians and philosophers have employed this kind of argument, and I have done so myself. Since the evidence is connected to the credentials of the messenger rather than being derived from the content of the message itself, this evidence is consistent with the traditional Christian claim that the teachings of the Bible not only are to be believed, but are to be believed *because they have been divinely revealed.*

However, rhetorically and dialectically, one may worry about how convincing such an argument will be in the contemporary world, where miracles themselves are objects of skeptical suspicion. A person will not be convinced by miracles that the scriptures are divinely inspired if that person is firmly convinced that miracles do not occur, or that, even if they do occur, we could never have enough evidence rationally to believe that they do. There are further difficulties. Much of the historical evidence for the miracles that are supposed to authenticate scripture comes from scripture itself, so those inclined to be skeptical about its historical veracity (as is common among contemporary historical/critical scholars) may be skeptical about the evidence for the miracle claims as well.

There is also the important consideration that what one is being asked to believe (the content of what the Bible teaches) is in many ways highly improbable. Kierkegaard of course makes this point by calling the incarnation, the central teaching of Christian faith, "the absolute paradox." Alvin Plantinga, sounding almost like Kierkegaard, makes a similar argument:

> What is being taught [in the scriptures], after all, is not something that chimes straightforwardly with our ordinary experience. It isn't like an account of an ancient war, or of the cruelty of the Athenians to the Melians, or of the overweening pride of some ancient despot. That sort of thing would be easy enough to believe. What we have instead is the claim that a certain human being—Jesus of Nazareth—is also, astonishingly, the unique divine Son of God who has existed from eternity.[8]

It is, I think, partly for such reasons that Plantinga appeals to "the testimony of the Holy Spirit" as playing a key role in his account of how Christians come to know the truth of the "great things of the Gospel." In *Warranted Christian Belief* Plantinga provides a "model" of how Christian faith can be known to be true if it is true. The model has three components: (1) scripture, which is divine testimony made possible by the work of the Holy Spirit inspiring human authors; (2) the internal testimony (or "instigation" to use the language of Aquinas, which Plantinga at this point prefers) of the Holy Spirit, which produces in Christians a disposition to believe that the teachings of the scriptures ("the great things of the Gospel") are both true and come from God; and (3) faith, which is, in the words of John Calvin, "a firm and certain knowledge of God's benevolence towards us, founded upon the truth of the freely given promise in Christ, both revealed to our minds and sealed upon our hearts through the Holy Spirit."[9]

I hold that the "great things of the Gospel" include God's teaching about how human life should be lived. Certainly, God's laws, expressed

---

8. Alvin Plantinga, *Warranted Christian Belief* (New York: Oxford University Press, 2000), p. 270.

9. Plantinga, p. 244, quoting Calvin's *Institutes* III, ii, 7.

in his commandments, form a significant part of scripture. Hence, on Plantinga's account the Holy Spirit played a key role not only in bringing scripture into existence, but also in making it possible for humans to grasp the truths of scripture, including the truths about the moral law. Plantinga rightly claims that this view that the Holy Spirit plays a key role in helping Christian believers know biblical truths is central to Reformed theology. However, its main elements can also be found in many other Christian theologians, and its roots are in the Bible itself. Space does not allow me to venture a full defense of such a view, though I have done so elsewhere.[10] I will just say that if something like Plantinga's model is correct, then the Holy Spirit not only provides moral knowledge through conscience, but is the source of the moral knowledge that comes through the scriptures.

I will not develop the point for reasons of space, but many theologians have also taught that the Holy Spirit plays a key role in coming to interpret the scriptures properly as well. I don't mean to say that the work of the Spirit in guiding interpretation occurs in isolation from other important hermeneutical strategies. Straightforward issues of grammar and meaning are of course important in interpreting any text, and in the case of scripture, there are important issues having to do with the reading of the message of the parts of scripture in the light of the meaning of the whole (again, a well-known, generally applicable, hermeneutical principle). Still, most Christians believe that in addition to these ordinary hermeneutical guides, the Spirit plays a role in guiding proper understanding. Given the importance of proper interpretation already noted, this is by no means an insignificant point.

Special Experiences and Revelations Given Outside the Biblical Revelation

The last source of moral knowledge I shall discuss are special experiences outside the biblical revelation. I wish to include in this category any kind of special experience whereby God might communicate his will to someone. This includes extraordinary experiences such as visions and voices, and special dreams. However, it also includes more mundane and ordinary experiences such as the following: I hear someone give a talk about a new

---

10. *The Historical Christ and the Jesus of Faith: The Incarnational Narrative as History* (Oxford: Oxford University Press, 1996).

Christian school in Sierra Leone, and during the talk I suddenly develop a conviction that I ought to donate a sizable gift of money to the school. I don't actually hear a voice in my head, but I nevertheless find it natural to describe the experience as one in which I have heard God say to me, "Steve, you should give some money to this school."

Many people will worry that such experiences will be objectionably "subjective" as a source of moral knowledge. After all, many people make bizarre and crazy claims about what God says to them, including obviously insane people who claim God has commanded them to do such things as kill their children. Given these facts, how can a person know an experience is truly one that embodies a communication from God?

That is certainly a good question, one that deserves careful thought. I take it to be obvious that the mere fact that someone claims and is even convinced that God has told that person to do something does not entail that the claim is correct. So we certainly must ask how a person might determine whether an alleged experience of a divine command is veridical. However, the fact that the question is one that we must ask does not imply that it cannot be answered.

We should also notice that the problem is not unique to special religious experiences. Conscience and scripture have also been the source of horrible actions. The Nazis regarded sympathy for Jews to be a moral temptation to be combated, and many seemed to have murdered Jews with a clear conscience. It is all too well known that scriptures have been used to justify slavery and even genocide. So the fact that a source of moral knowledge is fallible and that it can be used to justify horrible actions does not mean that it is completely unreliable, or else conscience and scripture would be unreliable sources of moral knowledge as well. Since I believe that conscience and scripture do provide such knowledge, I think the fallibility of special revelatory experiences is not a reason to exclude the category wholesale.

In dealing with this question, I want to distinguish the situation of a person who already has knowledge of God, perhaps including some knowledge of God's character, purposes, and characteristic ways of communicating with humans, from the situation of a person who lacks such knowledge. A comparison with human communication makes it clear how important this distinction is. Suppose I receive a message that purports to be from my wife. How can I tell whether or not the message is really from her? Clearly, having a prior knowledge of my wife is a great advantage. If the message is an email that appears to originate from Kazakhstan, that is pretty good evidence the message did not come from my wife, since she is not in Kazakhstan. Even if the message is an email that appears to come from her email account, if it asks me to do something that is inconsistent with my knowledge of her, I will suspect that her account has been hacked. I certainly would not send money to a terrorist organization on the basis of such an email. However, if I receive a message from her asking me to make a contribution to Christian education in Sierra Leone, I will be inclined to think it comes from her, because I know that is a cause she cares about. So it will be much easier to recognize a message from God if I already have some knowledge of God's character and purposes, and perhaps God's characteristic ways of communicating.

Let me first consider the case of a person who has no knowledge of God, but who receives an ethical message that purports to be from God. The epistemic difficulties here are substantial. If the person does not even know that God exists, then the message will have to have the ability to convince the recipient of God's reality, as well as to convince the recipient that this particular message comes from God. In this kind of case the likelihood of a mistake is going to be substantial. We can easily imagine genuine messages from God that fail to be recognized as such, as well as messages that are not from God that are mistakenly attributed to God. In fact, I think the epistemic burden is great enough that only God himself will be able to overcome the problems, either by performing an undeniable miracle as a way of authenticating the message, or simply by causally bringing it about that the person has an irresistible conviction that the message is from God. Even if God does this, and the person who receives the message thereby rightly believes God has communicated with him, this would of course not show that others should believe the person. In any case, others who are deciding whether to believe the person or not should surely take into account what they already know about God if they have such knowledge. Without such background knowledge, it is very difficult how one could actually know God has spoken.

If that is true, one might worry that a revelation from God is impossible. If we cannot recognize a message from God without already knowing a lot about God, how can God reveal himself to us in the first place? I think the answer to this question has already been given. God must either provide authenticating miracles or else, when he gives the message, act so as to produce an irresistible conviction in the recipient that the message is from God. This is perhaps how we might answer the question as to how such biblical characters as Abraham and the prophets recognized the word of God when they received it. God either performs a miracle, as was the case with Moses and the burning bush, or simply grants the person an undoubtable conviction that God is the source of the message. It is notable that in the case of Abraham, when God speaks to Abraham, Abraham is presented as someone who knows it is God who is speaking, even though no real account is given as to how Abraham knows this.

Let us turn now to the case of someone who already knows a good deal about God. Such a person will have a great advantage in recognizing a message from God. How does one acquire such prior knowledge? I am sure that some knowledge of God can be gained simply through conscience. The only God who could have a rightful claim on my obedience would be a God who is good. So, to the degree that I have some knowledge of good and evil through conscience, I have some knowledge of God. However, because of the ways conscience is shaped by human culture, this knowledge of God seems highly fallible.

Hence, as a Christian I affirm that it is primarily from the Christian revelation in the scriptures, as that revelation has been interpreted by the Church, that we gain knowledge of God. That revelation teaches me that God is a person who loves his human creatures, and wills their flourishing. He is "not willing that any should perish" and has suffered and died to save humans from the forces of evil in which they have enmeshed themselves. I am taught in that revelation that God has a special concern for the poor, that the follower of God should not return evil for evil, and that those who love God should love their neighbors. Furthermore, the category "neighbor" is not limited to friends and family but includes all human persons that one might have contact with, even including those who consider themselves enemies. Of course the scriptures, properly interpreted, provide a great deal more knowledge about God than this, but it would be foolish here to attempt anything like a complete summary.

Of course the fact that a purported message from God seems consistent with what I know about God does not show the message is authentic, but if a message contradicts what I know about God then this would provide strong evidence for its inauthenticity. If someone told me that he had a message from God that we should eliminate taxes on the rich because rich people are specially favored by God, I would quickly conclude that this person is mistaken in claiming that God has given him such a directive. The God of the Christian scriptures would give no such message. Similarly, if someone claims that God has told him or her to sacrifice a child, I would quickly call 911.

Why would I do this? How can I know with some confidence that my neighbor is deluded? One might think that my response here is similar to that of Immanuel Kant, who famously said that "Abraham should have replied to this supposedly divine voice: 'That I ought not to kill my good son is quite certain. But that you, this apparition, are God—of that I am not certain, and never can be, even if this voice rings down to me from heaven.' "[11] Kant makes this judgment because he is convinced that we can know what is morally right with certainty through *a priori* reason.

Even though I agree with Kant that we can know any such voice from heaven does not come from God, my reason for my belief is different. I am skeptical that we have any certain moral knowledge that comes from pure reason. Rather, my judgment that God would not ask my neighbor to kill a child is grounded in what I believe God has revealed about himself through his self-revelation. The Bible explicitly condemns child sacrifice as an abomination and makes it clear that God would never require any such thing. For example, Jeremiah 7:31 assures us that the idea of sacrificing a child "has never even entered God's mind."

One might here object that this cannot be so since God did in fact ask Abraham to sacrifice Isaac. However, on my view God never intended Abraham actually to sacrifice Isaac. Why did he make the request of Abraham? Perhaps for multiple reasons. The text says that God was thereby testing Abraham and perhaps thereby strengthening Abraham's faith through this test. I personally believe that one of God's purposes was precisely to teach Abraham and his descendants that, unlike some of the Canaanite tribes, child sacrifice was something God would not require of his people.

One might think that I have here abandoned a DCT of moral obligations, for one of the consequences of such a theory is the following proposition: "If God commands some person P to perform some action A, then P ought to perform A." Am I not saying that it would be wrong to sacrifice a child even if God commanded one to do it? No, I am not saying this. If God *actually* commanded a person to sacrifice a child, for some unfathomable reason, it would indeed be right for that person to attempt to obey God's command. Furthermore, it was right for Abraham to act as he did, assuming that God did command him to do this. (It is, I think, important epistemically that Abraham could not have known with certainty that

11. Immanuel Kant, *The Conflict of the Faculties*, in *Religion and Rational Theology*, trans. and ed. by Allen W. Wood and George di Giovanni (Cambridge: Cambridge University Press, 1998), p. 283n (Ak VII, 63).

God would never make such a request. After all, the surrounding tribes believed their gods did demand this, and Abraham certainly had not read Jeremiah.) So it is entirely consistent for me to maintain that I should perform any act that God commands, but also believe that God would never command certain acts. Of course I admit that my beliefs about what God could or could not command could be mistaken. However, if there is a case where God wills me to perform some action (again, for reasons I cannot fathom) that I do not believe God would ever will, then God would have to produce in me a belief about what I am to do in such a way that I would not be capable of doubting the belief.

There is one more worry that my epistemic concerns about special divine commands might raise. I have myself argued the importance for Christian theology of a principle I have already mentioned: that a revelation from God should not only be believed, but it should be believed *because* it has been revealed by God. In my book *Why Christian Faith Still Makes Sense* I call this the revelation authority principle.[12] This means we should not believe what God tells us simply because we can determine for ourselves that what God says is true, but that we should believe what God says because of our trust in God. This principle is especially important for a divine command theorist, since if I only believed that what God commanded was right because I independently knew it to be right, God's communicated commands would seem to be unnecessary. So it seems important that God can sometimes give us commands that *correct* our understanding of what is right and wrong, especially if that understanding is rooted in a natural human faculty such as conscience.

Paul Griffiths has recently argued, in a forthcoming essay that discusses Kierkegaard's treatment of his contemporary Adolph Adler, that Christians who are considering a purported contemporary special revelation should not respond by asking critical epistemological questions about that purported revelation.[13] Griffiths draws on two biblical stories of angelic communications to make his point. When Mary is visited by an angel speaking for God, she responds with a question as to how what the angel tells her can be true, but she does not doubt the truth of what she has

12. C. Stephen Evans, *Why Christian Faith Still Makes Sense: A Response to Contemporary Challenges* (Grand Rapids, MI: Baker Academic, 2015), pp. 84–91.

13. Paul J. Griffiths, "Kierkegaard and Apostolic Authority," in Paul Martens and C. Stephen Evans (eds.), *Kierkegaard and Christian Faith* (Waco, TX: Baylor University Press, 2016), pp. 55–74.

been told. The angel responds by telling her this will be done through the power of the Holy Spirit, and Mary then (in Griffith's words) "submissively ponders" what the angel has told her.

The case of Zechariah is different. Zechariah doubts whether what the angel has told him can be true, and thus seems to doubt the authenticity of the message itself. The angel is displeased and strikes Zechariah dumb "until the day that these things come to pass." The moral Griffiths draws from this is that epistemic worries about whether a message is really from God are misplaced, and that Christians who receive a purported special revelation directly from God ought to be like Mary and respond with "submissive pondering."[14] This does not mean that we should act on all such messages; some of them may be messages that are such that we must "leave what is said aside, as something we have, at the moment, no use for."[15] However, Griffiths thinks that even in these cases we do not have to judge that the revelation is not from God.

I do not believe Griffith is right about this, and I do not think that he has drawn the right moral from the biblical cases of Mary and Zechariah. In these two cases we have a message delivered by an evidently supernatural source, an angel. I take it that this means that both Mary and Zechariah had good reasons to believe the message was from God. It is true that in both cases a message is delivered that seems, humanly speaking, impossible. Despite this, Mary seems to think that seems the message should be believed since it evidently comes from God. She humbly asks for more information but expresses no doubt, and in the end expresses her obedient desire to be used by God in the way the angel announces. Zechariah, however, seems not to believe the angel. His attitude seems to be that of a person who will not believe something that he cannot make sense of even if the message comes from God, and he thereby does seem to exhibit a lack of trust in God. Certainly Mary's attitude seems the proper response of a person of faith.

However, I do not think this means that asking epistemological questions is always wrongheaded. In these two cases it is important that the message was delivered by what was recognized as an angel. The situation would be quite different if the purported message came in a way where it was not clear that it came from God. Suppose, for example, that a man receives a message that purports to be from God in a dream, in which he

---

14. Ibid., p. 69.

15. Ibid., p. 70.

is told to abandon his wife and children, and have an affair with another woman. In this case, "submissive pondering" does not seem like the right response. Rather, it seems that the person should recognize that people often have bizarre and unusual dreams, and though it is surely possible for God to communicate through a dream, one ought to ask how it can be known that a dream message is really from God. There is nothing untoward about such epistemological concern, and it does not indicate any lack of trust in God. For it is surely right that I should believe whatever God tells me, and obey any command God gives me, but also right that I should want to know that some message that purports to be from the Holy Spirit really is from the Spirit. After all, I John 4:1 enjoins us to "test the spirits to see whether they are from God." I conclude then that it is right and proper to seek to determine that a special experience that purports to be from God really is from God. One way of doing this would be to look for some kind of sign, such as a miracle, to authenticate the message. Another way would be to seek to determine if the message is the kind of message one would expect the Spirit of God to deliver, given what one already knows about God. For the Christian this means that any contemporary experiences or dreams must be tested for consistency with biblical teachings.

This means that in comparison with those biblical teachings, contemporary special experiences must play a subordinate, secondary role. This does not, however, entail that such experiences could not be significant in helping people understand what God wants them to do. The biblical teachings are usually general in nature and need to be made concrete by being applied to specific situations. I know from scripture that I have special obligations to care for the poor and those who cannot take care of themselves. However, which of the many needy people in the world should I seek to help, and how should I help them? To what extent should I be willing to sacrifice my own needs and the needs of my own family to serve others? It seems very possible that God could give a person specific answers to such questions. It seems highly likely that the answers God might give to different individuals will be somewhat different as well, and special revelatory experiences would be a good means of communicating such individual answers.

The answers will likely be different partly because the histories, abilities, and life situations of individuals are different. But the differences may also reflect God's knowledge of what individuals need to become more godly. When the rich young ruler asked Jesus what he should do to inherit eternal life, Jesus told him to sell all he had, give it to the poor, and come and follow him. Interestingly, Jesus does not seem to make this a universal requirement for everyone. Perhaps it reflects Jesus's understanding that the wealth of this young man was an idol that hindered his relation to God.

On my view the ultimate *telos* of moral obligations lies in the transformation of character. God gives us commands to help us become the kinds of people we must become in order to be friends of God. His commands help us understand how far from God we are and how much we need God's grace. However, they also help us in the process of sanctification as we seek to embody the character God wishes to implant in us.

I conclude that despite the secondary role that special experiences should play in our moral lives, God can through his Spirit communicate important truths about how we should live. The Spirit who gives moral knowledge to all through conscience, and offers moral knowledge to the Church through scripture, also offers moral guidance to individuals and communities through special experiences.

5

Diversity and Spiritual Testimony

Roger Trigg

Testimony and Truth

All religions have to appeal to the ideas of divine inspiration and divine revelation. The purpose of genuine religion is not simply to make practitioners feel good, or luxuriate in powerful emotional experiences. Religion can never be a totally subjective matter, of concern only to an individual. All religions typically claim truth about the nature of the world we live in and the place of humans in it. Furthermore, it is a kind of truth that bodies of knowledge, such as empirical science, cannot aspire to. When we talk of spiritual testimony, of a general or particular kind, it must always be regarded as testimony to something. It has to point beyond itself. It is a witness to a truth that has to concern others besides those receiving the testimony. Yet there is always a philosophical gap between human ideas of the divine and what the nature of the divine is itself. The idea of such testimony provides an answer as to how that gap can be crossed.

To appreciate the role of spiritual testimony in the way the infinite, which by definition transcends our understanding, has to reach down to the finite, we have to take seriously the logical gap between reality as it is in itself and human conceptions of it. That is the difference between ontology and epistemology. The issue is how humans can come to know anything of a realm of existence that seems by definition to be "wholly other," in the sense that it may be utterly different from our own physical existence.[1] We are all limited by our place in a particular time and space.

---

1. Roger Trigg, *Rationality and Religion* (Oxford: Blackwell, 1999), Chapter 10, esp. p. 207.

How can we comprehend anything of a wholly different level of reality, assuming that it is even possible meaningfully to speak of such a thing?

Plato faced a problem with a similar logical structure. Whatever we may think of his metaphysics, he had to bridge a logical gap. This appeared between the asserted reality of his eternal and necessary Forms (as unchanging universal standards), and our knowledge of them in a world of change and decay, where nothing has to be as it is. All is contingent. How can we know what pure goodness is, or have any glimmering of understanding about other objective standards, such as the nature of a pure circle or absolute equality in geometry? His own answer was that we were all born with innate knowledge of the world of Forms, and, in a prenatal existence, we had been in contact with them. For humans, therefore, it was a matter of recollecting this knowledge, and Plato devised a system of education in *The Republic* to do that. A metaphysical world, and our own familiar world that we experience every day, will be drawn together, so that the former can illuminate the latter.

This image of light casting out darkness, and of knowledge being a matter of illumination, has proved long-lasting. *Dominus mea illuminatio* ("the Lord is my light") is the motto of the University of Oxford. The idea of the light of reason in "Enlightenment" runs through the 17th and 18th centuries. It took a more atheistic turn in France in the 18th century, but in the 17th, at the dawn of modern science, reason could still be coupled with an idea of divine inspiration. "Reason is the candle of the Lord" was a favorite slogan of the Cambridge Platonists, the group of philosophers and theologians who were an influence on the development of science in England and the founding of the Royal Society.[2] They also influenced political philosophy through their contact with John Locke, who himself uses the same phrase several times.[3]

In all this, from Plato to his later followers in the 17th century, the idea of our knowledge and our reason being grounded in a reality beyond that of the ordinary empirical world gave universal grounding to human knowledge. Whether ultimate reality was conceived of as consisting of impersonal objective standards or, as the Cambridge Platonists thought,

---

2. Charles Taliaferro and Alison J. Teply (eds.), *Cambridge Platonist Spirituality* (New York: Paulist Press, 2004).

3. See John Locke, *Political Essays*, edited by Mark Goldie (Cambridge: Cambridge University Press, 1997), and John Locke, *An Essay Concerning Human Understanding*, edited by A. S. Pringle-Pattison (Oxford: Oxford University Press, 1924), p. 280.

the Christian God, one thing was quite evident: We all live within the same framework. The same reality sets the same standards of truth for everybody, even if we can only dimly recognize them. The image of the candle is particularly relevant here. We do not have the aid of a great searchlight illuminating what there is with great clarity. Instead, we are given the image of a pale, flickering light, which perhaps makes us as aware of the shadows cast as the objects it picks out. We are not given the luxury of clear sight, but have to struggle to pick out what might be there. This leaves open the possibility of doubt, diversity of belief, and even downright error.

The message of a Platonist view of things, however controversial it can be, is not just that there are two worlds with a problem connecting the two. It is that there are objective standards of truth. Human reasoning and human understanding may be fallible and unreliable. They are, though, constrained by a notion of truth independent of all such reasoning. Humans cannot construct truth, or reality. Their aim should be to understand its nature, and be guided by it. Where there is disagreement, not everyone can be right. Indeed, human limitations may dictate that we are all mistaken, and humility and mutual toleration is in order. Yet the great risk for any metaphysical structure that makes a logical distinction between humans and the reality they are attempting to grasp is skepticism. How can we be sure that we, or anyone else, can cross the logical gap to reality from our understanding of it? We may be in the position of the man who looked down a well, thinking he could see someone looking up at him. He was merely seeing the reflection of his own face.

The idea of any reality logically independent of human understanding and our own conceptual distinctions is central to any "realist" idea of the relation of humans and the world in which they are placed. It provides a spur to scientific research, and underpins the idea of scientific progress. Without a truth to be discovered, and a realm of reality to be explored, whether physical or not, we may as well rest content with whatever our present views may be. There would be no point in trying to increase our knowledge, as there would by definition be nothing independent of our present conceptual apparatus to be discovered. If any "existence" is only the shadow cast by whatever conceptual scheme we inhabit, we need not agonize about possible ignorance. When there is nothing to know, we can never be wrong or mistaken.

Despite the best efforts of philosophers over the centuries, ontology must be kept separate from, and underpin, epistemology.[4] Empiricist

---

4. Roger Trigg, *Reality at Risk: A Defence of Realism in Philosophy and the Sciences*, 2nd ed. (Hemel Hempstead: Simon and Schuster, 1989).

philosophers tried, for example, to relate stories of what there is to actual and possible human experience. Yet that is to build an edifice merely out of what is accessible to humans. It makes all that exists depend on human access to it. Reality then becomes anthropocentric. Yet how can we talk about what is by definition beyond our reach? What is the source of a reason that outstrips all possible contact with whatever reality we are positing, even the other universes that are talked about by some physicists?

Human reason has the power to outstrip our experience and still make sense of the reality beyond. What is the source of that capability? We are, according to Judeo-Christian thought, made in the image of God. If that is so, it is not perhaps fanciful to see the power of reason as itself grounded in the rationality of God, as "the candle of the Lord." It may perhaps be particularly fitted to understand what has been created by that rationality. The "logos" or reason within us could then comprehend the basic rationality or "logos" built into the very scheme of things.

General Revelation through Human Nature

In theological terms, all this can be put into the category of what is termed general revelation. A common testimony has been grounded in our common humanity. We are able to make sense of a physical world that, according to the theist, has a rational structure reflecting the mind of the Creator. As humans, we have been furnished with minds attuned to that structure, because we share in some small way in the very rationality that grounds all things. Our powers of reason are themselves God-given, and grounded in the reality that is God. Further, this rational understanding is not confined to the physical world. Recent research in the so-called cognitive science of religion has provided suggestive findings about the ways in which tendencies to religious understandings about disembodied agents, life after death, a built-in purpose in things, and other components of religious faith are part of the normal cognitive architecture of all human beings.[5]

Even an idea of an omniscient God can come easily to children, who start off by thinking that their parents know everything.[6] By the age of

5. Roger Trigg and Justin L. Barrett, *The Roots of Religion: Exploring the Cognitive Science of Religion* (Farnham: Ashgate, 2014).

6. Justin L. Barrett, *Born Believers: The Science of Children's Religious Belief* (New York: Free Press, 2012).

four, experiments indicate, they grow out of that optimistic belief. They come to understand that, for instance, a mother's point of view is limited. The child may have seen things happen that the mother has not, and can come to understand he knows something the mother does not. Each has a distinctive perspective. The point, though, is that it is easy for the child to go on believing that there is someone who still knows everything and shares in the child's knowledge, namely God. As with other branches of such research, this does not prove that the child is right; it just shows how easy it is to grasp some concepts, such as that of an all-knowing God, because they grow out of our earliest understanding as children. This could show that such ideas are merely "infantile," but they are certainly deeply ingrained in what it is to be human.

It is not outlandish to say that religion is natural for human beings. Religion is built up from various strands of human thought, but they are all deeply woven into characteristically human ways of thinking. Children naturally think in terms of purpose.[7] Even sophisticated scientists, under pressure of time, will easily lapse into describing things in terms of purpose.[8] It seems natural to want to see things in terms of their happening for a reason rather than just being a succession of cause and effect. It has been suggested that religion provides a more natural way of thinking than science.[9] We naturally respond to the world in a religious way, even though a scientific theory can be remarkably counterintuitive. Apparently solid objects are, for instance, revealed by physics to be masses of particles, which themselves ultimately seem to dissolve into something like pure energy. However we theorize about the quantum world, it requires years of training and expertise to be able to do so. On the other hand, natural religious impulses prompt everyone very easily to view the world in particular ways.

Religion is built into the very idea of what it is to be human, as the cognitive science of religion is demonstrating with considerable success.[10] That does not mean all will be religious. Just as we employ rationality to theorize in science, we can also use it to persuade ourselves that basic

---

7. Ibid., p. 44ff.

8. Ibid., p. 54.

9. Robert N. McCauley, *Why Religion Is Natural and Science Is Not* (New York: Oxford University Press, 2011); see also Roger Trigg, *Beyond Matter: Why Science Needs Metaphysics* (West Conshohocken, PA: Templeton Press, 2015).

10. Trigg and Barrett, *The Roots of Religion.*

human inclinations toward religious belief are misleading byproducts of cognitive mechanisms that have evolved for other reasons. That is not the issue, which is simply that religion is likely, given what we have learned, to have been a constant component in all human societies. That suggestion seems to be borne out by social anthropology and by archaeology. It is a suggestion that would indicate that the secularist thesis beloved by sociologists in the mid-20th century is deeply flawed. Religion is unlikely to be rooted out permanently by the march of scientific progress, or by any other social trend. It is too deeply entwined with other human characteristics.

The idea of reason as having a divine source, and of human beings as naturally inclined to a religious interpretation of events, goes against much philosophical thinking. The later Enlightenment, particularly in France, saw human reason as autonomous and religion as irrational. Similarly, empiricist philosophers have shown little patience with any idea either that reason has innate biases, or that it is capable of reaching out to any reality beyond human experience. For them, modern science encapsulates all that is within reach of human knowledge. It is therefore rather ironic that cognitive science, itself an example of the application of scientific method and empirical explanation, should conclude that the urge to religious forms of thought may be born in us. This reinstates the idea of a common human nature, stretching across human societies and cultures, and making them answerable to it. Yet it does not produce a common religious outlook. Robert McAuley,[11] writing about the cognitive science of religion, muses about the difference between religion and what he terms "the radically counterintuitive representations that the theories of science employ." He continues: "Their superficial diversity notwithstanding, religions share the same cognitive origins and vary within the same limited framework of natural cognitive constraints." He claims that religion follows those constraints and "replays minor variations on the same ideas time and time again." The idea is that, as the outcome of our common human nature, religions, in all their variety, are repeating the same themes. Their diversity is thus superficial.

Looked at as a natural phenomenon, it may be tempting to lump all religion under the same description. Yet once we look at the content of different religious beliefs, instead of just explaining why humans might have come to hold them in the first place, there is wide variation. We have seen

---

11. McAuley, p. 152.

that one of the most characteristic features of any religion is its claims to truth. Beliefs may be expressed in ritual or in other ways, but they mean nothing unless they take place in the context of a definite belief about the nature of the reality confronting humans.

Once we take seriously *what* religious believers hold, the sheer fact of religious diversity becomes a major challenge. It may be possible to see human beings in general as religiously inclined, and the fact of human reason as reflecting the rationality of the Creator. Human beings have, it may be said, an inbuilt testimony about a truth beyond themselves, and beyond the phenomenal world. Bridges have been built naturally between two worlds. Divine reality is, then, not in principle inaccessible, and we should expect sufficient common ground among all humans to enable them to converse with each other and understand the nature of their disagreements. Such commonality is worth remembering when we confront the diversity of religious views that is all too apparent in the present day. Such diversity is of course not new and was particularly prominent in the world of the New Testament.

Yet even if we all start with what has been termed by John Calvin, and in the present day by Alvin Plantinga, a *sensus divinitatis*,[12] that sense of some divine presence must fall short of a real *sensus Dei*, a knowledge of the presence of the one God, as described in Christian doctrine. The gap between an understanding of some vague reality beyond us, and a definite idea of the one God, let alone of the Father, Son, and Holy Spirit, remains large. The one may prepare the ground for the other, but we still need something more specific. That is the justification of special revelation.

We may stress the ability of human beings to understand the glory of God through the way we react to the physical world. Yet the interpretations and explanations that are embroidered around a primeval sense of divinity are many and various. How are we to choose between them? In a famous passage at the beginning of his letter to the Romans (1:19–20), St. Paul upholds the idea of a general revelation of God through the world around us. Natural theology has sometimes been regarded with suspicion by theologians such as Karl Barth, because it can seem to reduce the importance of special revelation. In the Christian context, it can appear to make superfluous the revelation of God in human form, according to the doctrine of the Incarnation. If we can already know God, why should there be any

---

12. See Alvin Plantinga, *Knowledge and Christian Belief* (Grand Rapids, MI: Eerdmans, 2015), p. 33.

further need of revealed knowledge? Putting it another way, if the Spirit can offer testimony through a human nature shared by all, what further testimony do we need?

St. Paul is sure that all that can be known of God lies plain for all humans. His everlasting power and deity have been visible in the things that have been made. Why, then, do we not all agree and fall down to worship the one God? St. Paul traces this back to human impiety and wrongdoing, in other words, to human sin. Humans exchanged "the glory of the immortal God for an image shaped like mortal man, even for images like birds, beasts and reptiles" (Romans 1:23).

What might be seen as the general revelation of one God has become transmuted into tremendous religious diversity. Just because of its roots in human nature, religion, as such, is not going to be quickly eradicated. Atheism and agnosticism are sophisticated philosophical positions, but, according to the cognitive science of religion, they go against the grain of basic human impulses.[13] The human mind is prepared for religious belief, even if so-called general revelation is very unspecific about the nature of the divinity being revealed. The notion of a *sensus divinitatis*, coupled with our basic cognitive impulses, still leaves open the possibility of many gods. It is in no way specific about the nature of one God. The venerable problem of evil may not permit an easy reading of the goodness of God from the alleged goodness of the world. Things are too ambiguous. Many would feel that they need to know more to enable them to trust the goodness of a Creator. The basic religious impulses, built into us, allow humans to go off into many directions. They explain animist beliefs, as well as the complicated theological structures of world religions. Arguably, they may explain the former better.

The Diversity of Special Revelation

General revelation can provide a basis for religious belief and preparedness to accept more particular intimations of divinity. It can help to bridge the logical gap between divine reality and human existence. Yet it underdetermines which religion should be held, and fails to fill out any details of what should be believed. We need a more specific revelation, and more detailed guidance. Many religions try to fill this gap, but we must remember that it is a gap between understanding and ultimate reality. Our beliefs

---

13. See Trigg and Barrett, *The Roots of Religion*.

must be constrained by that reality, which, by definition, must be the same for everyone.

Different religions have arisen with different understandings of what divinity consists in. Is it one or many, personal or impersonal? Does it have a moral character so as to be the source of goodness and justice? However dubious from a philosophical point of view, Plato's Theory of Forms was put forward as an attempt to establish an objective realm against which everything should be measured. Any religion that claims universal significance must also aspire to that kind of objectivity.

When we return to the question of how knowledge of such reality can be obtained, phrases like "the testimony of the Spirit" become more relevant. One can argue that general revelation provides general testimony, linked to our God-given reason. We need more, particularly if we have to contend with human wickedness, and a reluctance even to face truth. There is a general issue about how far-reaching the effects of human sin and general fallibility can be. Some accounts of sin would make it appear impossible to have any knowledge of God at all. We must not go that far, but we still have to recognize that all judgments can be fallible. How do we know which to rely on?

This problem arises even in the presence of so-called special revelation. Given that a general understanding of "divinity" is not enough and that we need more definite knowledge, how can we be sure that apparent knowledge is genuine? This problem arises at every level of revelation. If even general revelation can be ignored, the same doubts arise when things become more particular. Why are there so many different religions relying on so many alleged revelations? They cannot all be right. Why trust one rather than another? It is often alleged that the fact of conflicting religions providing different testimonies may only show that none of them can be reliable.

One ploy is to hold that different religions are not claiming different truths, and can be reinterpreted so that they are not seen to be in conflict. John Hick put forward a philosophy of religion that saw each of the world's main religions as centered on what he termed "the Real." Yet he says that "the Real in itself is not and cannot be humanly experienced."[14] Like Kantian *noumena*, things in themselves, it cannot be humanly experienced. We each can only experience it as a particular tradition teaches us. "The Real" is merely a presupposition of what makes the whole range of religious

14. John Hick, *An Interpretation of Religion* (London: Macmillan, 1989), p. 249.

experience possible. It is in itself neither personal nor impersonal, good nor bad. There is one reality, Hick believes, but it cannot correspond with any one tradition. It floats free of all particular understandings, so that its connection with real, lived religion is left unexplained. It is unclear whether it is directly concerned with us at all, as opposed to being a mere intellectual goal. Our religious concepts are formed by cultural conditioning.

Hick comments that "even in the profoundest unitive mysticism, the mind operates with culturally specific concepts."[15] All religious experience is culturally conditioned. We experience a manifestation of "the Real" only as it appears within a particular tradition. Yet this raises the question whether the beliefs of a particular tradition are in contact with anything at all. Since the latter is inaccessible, and at best could only have a causal, not a conceptual, connection with one religion or another, it is unclear what reason we could have for thinking that we have been granted any understanding of what lies beyond understanding.[16]

Hick's Kantian view of religion faces the same challenge that Kant's philosophy has historically faced. If we talk of an inaccessible reality, behind all appearances and manifestations, how can we know anything about it? By definition we cannot, and it is easy for the notion to drop out altogether. We cannot appeal to it to decide which of the different religious accounts is right. An object such as "the Real," beyond every specific religious tradition and beyond all possible experience, will be of no help in deciding which experience is related to the way things are. Forms of pluralism, such as that of Hick, take religious diversity at face value and can degenerate into an acceptance of diversity as an end in itself. We are left with relativism. John Hick was an avowed realist, not a relativist, but his conception of reality becomes so attenuated that it is not surprising that Joseph Ratzinger (then soon to be Pope Benedict) called him "a prominent representative of religious relativism."[17] The idea, though, that reality must recede beyond our grasp renders it so ineffective in human affairs that all we are left with is the mere fact of human diversity.

John Hick and others in the 1970s had tried to make Christianity more open to other religions and less exclusive in its claims by reinterpreting

---

15. Ibid., p. 295.

16. Roger Trigg, *Rationality and Religion* (Oxford: Blackwell, 1999), pp. 59ff.

17. Joseph Ratzinger, *Truth and Tolerance* (San Francisco: Ignatius Press, 2004), p. 121.

the doctrine of the Incarnation. In a book provocatively called *The Myth of God Incarnate*,[18] the contributors describe Jesus as "a man approved by God" for a special role. In other words, he was not God. Indeed, they say that "the later conception of him as God incarnate, the second person of the Holy Trinity living a human life, is 'a mythological or poetic way of expressing his significance for us'." They go on to assert that this has major implications "for a relationship to the peoples of the other great world religions."

According to this approach, acceptance of religious diversity is made to inform all our other judgments. If we hold beliefs that clash with those of others, we must, it seems, be prepared to modify them, just as we must recognize the dependence of religious experience on our tradition. The alternative to a revision of beliefs in the interests of harmony between world religions seems to be the relativism that Ratzinger was afraid of. Yet if religion should be oriented toward what is true for all, acceptance of relativism must be self-destructive. A belief that purports to put us in touch with what is ultimately real, and hence real for everyone, will destroy itself if it meekly celebrates diversity, thinking that each set of beliefs is merely true for its holders.

Hick saw everything from the side of humans, but if we believe that there is a personal God, who wishes us to be in relation to Him, the chasm between reality and purported knowledge has to be crossed. There must be an alternative to a portrayal of a God who is totally detached from the universe that has been created. Any such deistic idea is likely to be discarded as irrelevant to human life. The Christian doctrine of the Trinity may be hard to understand, but the denial of the relevance of any of the three Persons is not only fatal to Christian belief; it poses questions for any other religion, too. It may be easy to see a connection with the idea of God as Creator. What, though, of the Son and the Holy Spirit? The position of Jesus is bitterly contested by other religions, not least Islam. Yet Jesus forms a bridge between God and the reality of this world. Without Jesus, some other form of special revelation is necessary. Above all, however, the notion of the Holy Spirit points to the immanence of God in the world, as an antidote to the notion of absolute transcendence, which Hick seems to advocate in a way that has to empty religion in general, and Christianity in particular, of any significance.

---

18. John Hick, ed., *The Myth of God Incarnate* (London: SCM Press, 1977), p. xi.

The Holy Spirit

We thus come to the necessity of the Spirit's testimony within Christianity, as a special source of our knowledge of the transcendent God. We still have to face the question of how it can be properly ascertained. The problem, too, of any particular revelation is why this person, rather than that, should be spoken to. Why then and not another time? Why there and not somewhere else? Spiritual revelation can appear to be exclusive. It can seem to have its favorites. Yet claims about the guidance of the Holy Spirit are a central part of Christian belief. Even so, conflicting claims about that guidance have been rife through Christian history, and we have to decide which is right.

While diversity has always been a feature of the world in which Christianity took root and was propagated, it has never stopped at the gates of the Church. Religious diversity, in the shape of cultural differences and styles of worship, can reflect the diversity of humanity itself, although we should never lose our grip on the notion of a common humanity. It has been a sad fact about the Christian Church that it has splintered into myriad factions. Some of them may be the legacy of political and other disputes that have little to do with appeals to revelation. Many, however, claim the authority of the Spirit in maintaining their own distinctiveness. There is a constant tension between the idea of the Holy Spirit inspiring the whole Church and guiding it to a common mind with that of individual inspiration. Should we be concerned if we are out of step with our fellow Christians? Should we pray for guidance so that we are all brought to the same position? Should we, on the other hand, be so certain that we have received direct spiritual testimony that we can be confident of our own position regardless of the views of others?

There is not only diversity between religions and diversity between the nonreligious and the religious. Beyond that, different groups of Christians claim insights that other Christians do not share, and individuals claim to have a Spirit-given knowledge not given to other individuals. Christian denominations not only point to a diversity of guidance from the same Holy Spirit, but cannot agree at times whether the body of the Church or the conscience of the individual should be seen as the final authority. Protestant denominations have traditionally given much more emphasis to the idea of an "inner light" given to individuals. Roman Catholics instinctively look to collective guidance within the structures of the Church, and there are many combinations of these positions.

Whether the Holy Spirit works only through Church or individual can be contentious, but exclusive stress on either leads to philosophical dangers. The more that the rules of an institution are stressed, the more it can appear that truth is relativized to the institution. On the other hand, if everything is brought down to the level of the individual, the danger is then not relativism but extreme subjectivism. The reply will come that neither relativism nor subjectivism is a danger because what is being conveyed in each case should be truth. This brings us back to the issue of truth and its universal applicability. A Church can claim that it is the repository of the whole truth and the only means to salvation. A particular individual can claim that personal illumination has conveyed a truth of universal import. Church or individual will each claim to have special access to knowledge, and could feel an urge to compel others to recognize the truth it has received. The stress on truth then leads to intolerance.

Yet the alternative celebration of diversity, and of disagreement, as ends in themselves implies that we do not really believe that truth matters. The claim to truth may seem more important if direct testimony by the Holy Spirit appears to have been given. The acquisition of such knowledge may appear to be of such enormous significance that one has a positive duty to impart it to others for their own good, whatever means are used. Such spiritual testimony might be thought to carry with it absolute certainty about its correctness. It will be said that the Holy Spirit can hardly be thought to be speaking with an uncertain voice and must surely be infallible.

This brings us back to the perennial question as to how we can be sure that we are being guided by the Holy Spirit. It was Thomas Hobbes who, in the 17th century in his *Leviathan*, notoriously pointed out that there seems to be little difference between God speaking to me in a dream and my dreaming that God spoke to us. Similarly, John Locke warned that we must be on our guard against what he termed "enthusiasm."[19] Conviction and commitment are not enough, but, as he says, while we "await the inspiration of the Holy Spirit, we honour and worship our own dreams." In his eyes, reason and scripture must also constrain us so that we are not led astray. Personal experience and individual commitment must go in tandem with our other sources of guidance.

We must be sure that it really is the Holy Spirit guiding us or speaking through the Church. I may be unconsciously seeking to rationalize my

---

19. John Locke, *Political Essays*, edited by Mark Goldie (Cambridge: Cambridge University Press, 1997), p. 209.

own desires. The Church may in reality merely wish to expand its own authority and power. It always faces the danger, too, that it may imagine it is being led by the Holy Spirit when in fact it is in thrall to the "spirit of the age." Those who claim that the Holy Spirit is speaking to us through contemporary society may merely want the Church to go with the crowd, rather than run the risk of unpopularity and isolation. People within the Church can as easily as those outside be seduced by the fashions and preoccupations of the time.

Freedom and Unity

Putting aside the perennial question of how the purported guidance of the Spirit can be tested, we must return to the problem of the apparent certainty and infallibility implied by appeal to the Spirit's testimony. It may appear that having access to such testimony means that one has been directly inspired by God, and that may suggest one should tolerate no opposition. We have here an inexorable progress from spiritual guidance to certainty about what is true, and from there to an apparent right, or even a calling, to convey it to others. If the recipient of spiritual testimony is superior in knowledge, from there it might seem a short step to coercion of those who do not share that knowledge, or indeed actively repudiate it.

The idea of theocracy is much feared in many societies. The notion that everyone should be governed in the name of God can sound frightening to those brought up to believe in the ideals of democratic pluralism. The idea of objective truth, with which we started, can itself be made to seem oppressive. Are not my choices restricted if I have to accept that I can be mistaken? Is not personal autonomy attacked if I am told there is a truth that I ought to acknowledge?

The idea of personal freedom is at stake. People who think they know what is true, it is often said, do not respect others if they tell them what they ought to believe. The Enlightenment ideal of autonomy is put at risk. With spiritual inspiration goes, it appears, the right to claim an authority over others, who may see things differently. Yet the idea of objective truth, it may be said, is not being honored if we allow falsehood to exist as the apparent equal of truth. One only has to look at the history of the Inquisition in Europe and in Latin America to see how apparent truth was upheld at a terrible and cruel cost. It was hardly surprising that the various forms of the European Enlightenment explicitly reacted to the ways in which the Roman Catholic Church was ready to impose its claim to spiritual insight on those who wished to challenge its authority. Claims to be custodians of spiritual guidance can become mere exercises of power over others.

Part of the solution to this juggling of truth and freedom from a Christian point of view is to see that the exercise of freedom is inseparable from any proper recognition of truth. The latter is impossible without the former. For a Christian believer, God wants an unforced acceptance of the truth. As John Locke often stresses, Christianity does not accept the value of coerced conformity. He says that the way to salvation is not "any forced exterior performance, but the voluntary and secret choices of the mind."[20] He concludes that God would not approve of means that were at odds with that.

The balance to be struck is between the acceptance of the importance of objective truth, and a recognition that there can be genuine disagreement about what that truth may consist in. If human freedom is God-given, we have to respect it, as part of the truth we want to live by. An apparent certainty about the nature of what is true on our part does not give us the right to ignore such freedom on the part of other people.

There is a temptation at the present day to deride as intolerant "fundamentalists" those who claim to know what is true and want to impart that truth to others. Yet that comes very near to dismissing not just the right to claim knowledge but also to suggest that there cannot be a truth that all should recognize. The fear of coercion and intolerance seems to follow from the recognition of what Locke refers to as "enthusiasm." One might reflect that present-day Christians could often do better to be enthusiastic in the presentation of their faith, but this is to make a play on words. What those in the 17th and 18th centuries saw as "enthusiasm" was not just wholehearted commitment; the word itself comes from a Greek one with a specifically religious connotation, itself meaning "being inspired by a god."

One can see from the gradual slippage in the meaning of the word that any divine inspiration came to be seen as a dangerous fanaticism, which may get out of control. It was not subject to the constraints of reason. If such inspiration was indeed divine in origin, it could be respected. Once, however, it was seen that there were many alternative forms of inspiration and enthusiasm, the recipe for dangerous conflict became obvious. Writers such as Locke were writing in the aftermath of an English civil

---

20. Ibid., p. 138.

war that, at least in part, had been fueled by such enthusiasts, with many attempts to force others to conform to whatever was being promoted. "Cool reason" seemed a much safer option, and it is perhaps not surprising that Locke himself, as a committed Christian, wanted to stress the "Reasonableness of Christianity" (the title of one of his books). Reliance on apparent spiritual testimony alone could produce civil conflict and even civil war.

Christianity preaches the importance of the Holy Spirit as a central part of its doctrine. The Spirit ensures that God is not absent from the world but is working within it. The Creator is not hidden, beyond our grasp and comprehension, but is immanent. Humans are free to worship God or turn away, as some people did when they met Jesus. Spiritual testimony cannot be coercive. Freedom entails the fact that people can and will accept different beliefs. What is certain to one person may not be to another. Just because human freedom has to be taken seriously, it is inconceivable that the Holy Spirit would force anyone into belief. It is clear from the reports of those who have undergone great spiritual experiences, from St. Paul to John Wesley, that the ground has been prepared. Revelation was not forced on someone unready and unwilling, but was the culmination of much seeking.

Just because truth is at stake, though, we should never assume that personal religious experience can be the only route to truth, any more than apparent collective guidance would be. Fervent belief, whether on the part of an individual or a group, does not make something true. Holding fast to the concept of objective truth should make us all the more aware of the potential gap between beliefs and reality. Inspiration, or spiritual testimony, may seem to provide a way out of this dilemma, but the diversity in claims to such truth imposes a warning. Such testimony or apparent testimony still has to be tested.

Christians believe that spiritual testimony, particularly through the workings of the Holy Spirit in the world, can help to bridge the logical gap we are faced with between the objective reality of a transcendent God and human understanding. The diversity of understandings, both within and beyond the Christian Church, can appear a major obstacle to this. It can cast doubt not just on the possibility of knowledge of God but on the very idea of God, who is so hidden as to drop out of sight. Yet against the background of a general revelation, human minds are primed to expect and to receive a more detailed understanding of the nature of God. The doctrine of the Holy Spirit helps to bridge the logical gap between reality known and the subject of potential knowledge. God is then seen not as a passive regulative ideal in some Kantian sense, but as an active personal Creator trying to enter our hearts and minds.

The Holy Spirit can well say different things to different people at different times and circumstances, but spiritual testimony, if genuine, can never be contradictory. If we take to heart the idea of one common reality, and one God, such guidance could never undermine itself. We dare not take all claims to have received divine teaching at face value. Truth may be applied differently in different circumstances, but in itself it can never vary. The nature of objective reality, and our collective or individual understanding of it, should not be confused. Different testimonies about the character of a single reality cannot all be right.

Although some religious experience can be so overwhelming that it would seem impossible to doubt its veracity, it must cohere, according to Christian understanding, with everything else we know about the nature of God and God's will. Other people's experience, our own reason, and the tradition of the Church as a whole, based on scripture, must all enter into our judgment. We can take the brave course of saying that we are right and the rest wrong, when faced with divergences. Yet things are not true just because I want them to be. The objectivity of God puts any total reliance on subjective assurance into question. We should never be tempted by outright skepticism, but still have to acknowledge the need for a certain humility because of knowledge of our own fallibility, let alone sinfulness.

From its earliest days, the Christian Church has depended on spiritual insight thought to be derived from the Holy Spirit. Yet it has also often been put into peril by the arrogance of those who embraced a certainty to which they may not have been entitled. A willingness to coerce others does not take their God-given freedom seriously. It is a sad fact that, throughout the history of the Christian Church, the more alive churches seemed, the greater their propensity for quarrelling, disputes, and ultimately division. The more people care about what is right, and the more they feel they have received genuine divine guidance, the more intolerant they can become. On the other hand, the celebration of diversity can easily lead to an indifference to truth, and finally to the view that it does not matter at all what is true. Nihilism can then beckon.

The hardest part of truth is to couple genuine commitment to what is seen to be true with an acceptance that there are other views that must also be respected. The problem is that if the Spirit is apparently on one side, how can we sit lightly relative to what one has been inspired to believe? If one believes one's views are true, must one believe that those contradicting them are spiritual enemies and treat them as such? There is always the danger of this, and we can see such religious extremism at work in our contemporary world in other religions besides Christianity. The danger is as real outside religion as inside. Marxist-Leninists, for example, felt that they had a deep insight into what was true about human societies, and for that reason allowed no opposition in societies they could control.

In the 18th century, enthusiasm, as seen for example in the early Methodists, was often regarded as a very "horrid" and dangerous thing. Yet it was in part through Methodism that the Church of England of the time was raised from its indolence and torpor. A similar Evangelical Revival had a lasting influence in the newly formed United States. Without the continued testimony of the Spirit, Christianity is in peril. It is part of the teaching of Christianity that such testimony is always available. Yet at the same time it is right that Christians do not take all apparent testimony at face value. A divided Church at odds with itself seems to proclaim a fractured God who is not the same for everyone. Such a God could hardly be a means of reconciliation. The idea of one Reality should always constrain us. To be consistent, the Church should try to reflect the oneness of that Reality.

Claims to diverse spiritual testimony can strike at the root of what the Church as a whole should stand for. A diversity of apparent spiritual guidance puts a question mark against the idea of there being one Christian Church. The disunity of the contemporary Church in the 21st century does little to point to any universal truth. We started with the idea of the divine as it is in itself. The notion of spiritual testimony stops that idea being absorbed into some Kantian notion of inaccessible reality. Yet the very diversity of claims to spiritual revelation of various kinds can lead us away from such a vision.

Diversity should never be celebrated as an end in itself. That does not give the right to one group to impose its views on others, and we must all be willing to put our dearest convictions to the test. That, among other things, involves taking the judgment of others seriously. If we each persistently want to be true to whatever spiritual testimony we think we have received, regardless of all other considerations, we shall each find ourselves in a church of one person. If we genuinely believe we are encountering what is true, we must believe that the same truth can constrain others as well as ourselves. The purpose of the guidance of the Holy Spirit, according to Christian doctrine, is to guide *everyone* to a knowledge of truth, a truth that is not just tailored for one person but is the same for all.[21]

21. For more on the philosophical significance of religious diversity when faced with the issue of truth, see Roger Trigg, *Religious Diversity: Philosophical and Political Dimensions* (New York: Cambridge University Press, 2014).

6

The Testimony of the Spirit

INSIGHTS FROM PSYCHOLOGY AND NEUROSCIENCE

Malcolm Jeeves

Introduction

The *Concise Oxford Dictionary* gives the basic meaning of "testimony" as "evidence" or "demonstration." Traditionally, some of the most widely available "evidences" of the work of the Spirit are seen in the "spirituality" of individuals and groups. It would be wrong, however, to assume that there is a universally agreed definition of "spirituality." In an extensive and detailed review of the varied ways in which spirituality is used today, Victor Copan has summarized the contemporary situation:

> For more than two decades now, there has been an increasing fascination about all things spiritual in the western world—and it is everywhere. The term spirituality is a buzz-word in popular culture. . . . But what do we mean when we use the word "spirituality"? . . . What is a biblical understanding of spirituality and spiritual formation? . . . It is one of the astonishing developments of the last decades that spirituality has made a strong comeback after years of being out of vogue. Do a Google search on the term spirituality, and you'll get over 141,000,000 hits.[1]

---

1. Victor Copan, *Changing Your Mind: The Bible, the Brain, and Spiritual Formation* (Eugene, OR: Cascade Books, 2016), p. 1.

In similar vein, Sarah Coakley, a Cambridge theology professor, warns that spirituality has become a "buzzword" whose meaning often does not go beyond mere hand waving.[2] She notes that spirituality is, in some circles, a "controlled religious high" devoid of content normally necessary to faithfully represent the spirituality of Christian churchgoers: namely, something with the content of clear doctrinal beliefs. Such spirituality, as a "religious high," excludes many people for whom spirituality, first and foremost, is living out a Christian worldview in a world that they believe is upheld moment by moment by the Creator God whom they worship.

For Professor N. T. Wright, the central aspects of Christian spirituality are anything but vague or mere hand waving. For him, they include formative spiritual experiences such as new birth and baptism, prayer, reading of scripture, participation in the Lord's Supper, and the capacity to give and respond to love. The concreteness in action of manifestations of true spirituality has been further underlined by Miroslav Volf: "Some people like to keep their spirituality and theology neatly separated, the way someone may want to have the main dish and the salad served separately during a meal. I don't. Spirituality that's not theological will grope in the darkness, and theology that is not spiritual will be emptied of its most important content."[3] But, as we shall see in detail later, spirituality is not "something" to be located "in an immaterial immortal soul," hidden somewhere in our heads; nor is it "something" securely protected from the effects of the chances and changes of this fleeting world, which include the effects of illnesses of old age, increasingly prevalent in today's world.

Reference to "an immortal soul" will alert the reader to an ongoing debate among biblical scholars and theologians. For example, more than a decade ago N. T. Wright wrote, "Despite what many people think, the Bible does not envisage human beings as split-level creatures (with, say, a distinct body and soul) but as complex, integrated wholes."[4] As a mere scientist, it would be impertinent of me to claim any competence to enter into this ongoing biblical/theological debate. However, since what one believes

---

2. Sarah Coakley, in the introduction to Sarah Coakley (ed.), *Spiritual Healing: Science, Meaning, and Discernment* (Grand Rapids, MI: Eerdmans, forthcoming).

3. Miroslav Volf, *Free of Charge: Giving and Forgiving in a Culture Stripped of Grace* (Grand Rapids, MI: Zondervan, 2005), p. 236.

4. N. T. Wright, from his cover endorsement of Malcolm Jeeves (ed.), *From Cells to Souls— and Beyond: Changing Portraits of Human Nature* (Grand Rapids, MI: Eerdmans, 2004).

about the soul is intimately related to what follows in discussing embodied spirituality, I offer my current understanding of what theologians and biblical scholars are saying. It is true that for centuries, traditional Christian thought saw the body as frail and finite, but the soul as immortal. Today, biblical scholars recognize it as a gross oversimplification to repeat the longstanding and pervasive view that there was a dichotomy between Hebrew thought (which affirms some form of psychosomatic unity—what I call elsewhere in this chapter *psychobiological unity*) and Greek thought (which affirms some form of dualism—a separate soul and body). Greek thought was in fact much more varied on the nature of the soul than Plato's views would suggest. As one scholar has put it, "There was no singular conception of the soul among the Greeks, and the body–soul relationship was variously assessed among philosophers and physicians in the Hellenistic period."[5]

In what follows, I shall outline the way spirituality, as the testimony of the work of the Spirit, manifests itself, as does all of religion, through the experience, belief, and action of the whole person, not in some "bit" of the soul. I shall summarize for the non-specialist cumulative evidence demonstrating how spirituality is both embodied in our physical make-up and embedded in our social and cultural groups. In doing this, we shall note in particular that it has been, first and foremost, the rapid advances in psychology and neuroscience that have underlined repeatedly the psychobiological unity of the human person. Our approach, therefore, is to discern the new insights that God has given us through research into God's creation, of which we are a part, and to ask how this new evidence may give fresh insights into the basis of true spirituality (while mindful of its frailty, vulnerability, susceptibility to internal and external challenges, and vulnerability to false and counterfeit manifestations).

In saying "to discern," I have in mind a danger that has been highlighted recently of being so dazzled by the discoveries in neuroscience that if an explanation can be given that refers to neuroscience, then that explanation is accorded more weight and validity than other explanations.[6] For example, a recent article in the *Journal of Cognitive Neuroscience* reports the work of Diego

---

5. Joel B. Green, *Body, Soul, and Human Life: The Nature of Humanity in the Bible* (Grand Rapids, MI: Baker, 2008), p. 53.

6. See *Research Digest*, "Psychology students are seduced by superfluous neuroscience," *Research Digest*, a blog on the British Psychological Society website (April 17, 2015). http://digest.bps.org.uk/2015/04/psychology-students-are-seduced-by.html.

Fernandez-Duque and his colleagues,[7] who were following up what seems to have been "a near consensus among commentators that there is something distinctly persuasive about neuroscience."[8] However, the *Research Digest* blog comments that, "In fact, besides anecdotal argument, there's little solid evidence to suggest that this is true (and some that it is not)." In four studies, Fernandez-Duque and his colleagues asked U.S. psychology students to rate the quality of short true and false explanations for psychological phenomena such as "face recognition" and "emotional states."

The researchers discovered that "The main takeaway is that when superfluous neuroscience information (i.e., information that offered no further insight) was added to the end of these explanations, the students rated explanations more highly.... All this suggests there is something uniquely convincing about neuroscience in the context of psychological phenomena."[9] They believe the most plausible reason is that psychology students endorse a "brain-as-engine-of-the-mind" hypothesis—that is, they "assign to neuroscience a privileged role in explaining psychological phenomena not just because neuroscience is a 'real' science but because it is the most pertinent science for explaining the mind." The fact that "the students who endorsed dualist beliefs (seeing the mind as separate from the brain) were just as wooed by superfluous neuroscience information somewhat undermines this interpretation."[10] What follows, I believe, avoids this temptation of giving undue weight to neuroscientific explanations of psychological phenomena since it is based on first-hand experience of working in psychology and neuroscience over many decades.

This chapter's focus will be:

- to examine new insights into understanding the work of the Spirit in the lives of individuals and groups through discoveries in neuroscience and psychology,
- to explore the vulnerability of individuals in coping with the inevitable changes in our awareness of the work of the Spirit through, for

7. D. Fernandez-Duque, J. Evans, C. Christian, and S. D. Hodges, "Superfluous Neuroscience Information Makes Explanations of Psychological Phenomena More Appealing," *Journal of Cognitive Neuroscience* 27(5) (2015): 926–944.

8. *Research Digest*, 2015.

9. Ibid.

10. Ibid.

example, the normal processes of aging and the abnormal processes of disease and degeneration,

· to highlight the pervasive challenge of reductionism, which claims to "explain away" the result of the work of the Spirit as "nothing but" the abnormal firing of neurons in the brain. This, in turn, leads to questions about how we should constructively relate the knowledge that God gives us through scripture with the knowledge that God gives us through the scientific enterprise leading to the enrichment and deeper understanding of life in the Spirit.

Mind and Brain

The landscape to be viewed is so vast that the challenge is to highlight the salient features of the current scene for the non-specialist without distorting the scientific picture. There are two basic approaches in attempts to investigate the possible links between brain mechanisms and mental events: the *bottom-up* and the *top-down* approaches.

Historically, the bottom-up approach focused on the effects of brain damage on mental processes and behavior, and contributed much of the early knowledge of brain–mind links. This was because the techniques then available made it the most scientifically possible. Only with the remarkable increases in the diversity and sophistication of techniques for imaging and monitoring brain activity online have the top-down approaches begun to bear so much fruit.

Early proponents of different theories of mind–body links held a variety of views about where to locate the mind or the soul. Some argued for the heart, some for the brain, and others for the ventricles—the prominent spaces within the brain. Each assumed that there is a separate immaterial part of us, a soul or mind, that lives within our body somewhere. With the advent of more scientific approaches to the study of mind–body relations, there was a largely shared assumption that the mind was not "something" located somewhere but, rather, it referred to a functional property of the brain.

Debates continued well into the early years of the 20th century between opposing schools of thought. One group sought to relate mental processes to circumscribed areas within the brain regarded as an aggregate of separate organs. Another group assumed that mental activity is a single, indivisible phenomenon, the function of the whole brain working as a single entity. Underlying these varying attempts, occurring at different times and using different techniques, was a consistent outcome, *the accumulating evidence of tightening links between mind and brain.*

One result of this intense research activity was that in less than a hundred years the assumption that brain events and mind events were not linked changed to a recognition of clear links between brain, language, and intellectual functions generally. There were also hints of links between brain and personality, including social and ethical behavior.

The Current Scene: The Inexorable Tightening of Mind–Brain–Behavior Links

Research has consistently shown how specific mental processes tightly link to particular regions or systems in the brain. Within those regions, moreover, there often emerged a further specificity indicating that certain columns of cells are involved when a particular aspect of a task is being performed. This general statement applies to cognition and behavior. How we see the world, how we think about the world, how we feel about the world, and how we react and behave in the world, all depend on the intact functioning of very specific brain parts or systems. This is why the emphasis today is on the need to recognize the psychobiological unity of the human person. Here are a few examples to give the non-specialist a feel for the kind of evidence that makes possible this general statement.

More than half a century ago, neurophysiologists David Hubel and Thorsten Wiesel used single-cell recording techniques to study the neural underpinnings of vision in cats.[11] This prompted others to follow with similar studies in awake and alert monkeys. For example, attempts to pin down more accurately the ways in which the brain handles face perception have been the focus of detailed work by neuropsychologists using animals. Thirty years ago, following an observation by Charles Gross at Princeton, researchers such as David Perrett at St. Andrews, using single-cell recording techniques, discovered cells in monkeys' brains that responded selectively to the sight of human faces.[12] This was a surprising finding, since,

---

11. D. Hubel and T. Wiesel, "Receptive Fields, Binocular Interaction and Functional Architecture of the Cat's Visual Cortex," *Journal of Physiology* 160(1) (1962): 106–54.

12. D. I. Perrett, P. A. Smith, D. D. Potter, A. J. Mistlin, A. S. Head, A. D. Milner, and M. A. Jeeves, "Neurons Responsive to Faces in the Temporal Cortex: Studies of Functional Organisation, Sensitivity to Identity and Relation to Perception," *Human Neurobiology* 3(4) (1984): 197–208.

with further research, the specificity of the links between what the monkey was seeing, such as the identification of the faces, seemed to become stronger with every experiment. Important determinants of face perception were the direction of gaze of the eyes and the direction the head was pointing. Cells that were responsively selective for faces were found in the superior temporal sulcus on the monkey brain. When the researchers changed the size of the faces, these cells were not affected. However, if the individual features of the faces were scrambled, the responses of the cells reduced. Others, such as Nancy Kanwisher, have replicated these findings.[13]

A similar story can be told about a cognitive process that we all rely on every moment every day—namely, remembering. Half a century ago, British neuropsychologist Brenda Milner and her colleague, working in Canada, fortuitously discovered that the ability to form new memories was lost due to surgical removal of the hippocampus in the brain.[14] This also led to a whole new scientific industry of studies studying the effects of hippocampal damage in animals.

Another intensively researched and widely publicized area has been the attempt to understand whether the hemispheres of the brain are specialized. This has led to a widely accepted view for the past 30 years that the functional organization of the human cerebral cortex can be best understood in terms of differences between the left and right cerebral hemispheres. The left hemisphere is seen as specialized for language, logical thinking, mathematical, and analytic processing, and the serial processing of sensory information. The right hemisphere is seen as specialized for emotional expression, intuitive thinking, recognizing faces and musical sequences, parallel processing, and visual-spatial encoding. In short, the left hemisphere is verbal, logical, and rule-bound; the right, intuitive and creative. These findings have been widely publicized and the results in general are well founded. However, to underline the tentative nature of this and all scientific research, it is important to remember how the foundations of this approach were shaken when three of today's leading cognitive neuroscientists, Gregoire Borst, William Thompson, and Stephen

13. N. Kanwisher and G. Yovil, "The Fusiform Face Area: A Cortical Region Specialised for the Perception of Faces," *Philosophical Transactions of the Royal Society of London B* 361 (2006): 2123.

14. W. B. Scoville and B. Milner, "Loss of Recent Memory After Bilateral Hippocampal Lesions," *Journal of Neurology, Neurosurgery, and Psychiatry* 20(1) (1957): 11–21.

Kosslyn, published a paper in which they argued that "a top bottom divide, rather than a left-right divide, is a more fruitful way to organize human cortical brain functions."[15] What was at issue was not that all of these cognitive and behavioral capacities are localized in the brain but rather a debate about where this happens. The psychobiological unity of each of us was further underlined.

But what about the relationship of the brain and the way that we behave? Here again, dramatic results have underlined the tightness of the links.

We all make moral choices every day. Sadly, some people seem habitually to make moral choices that adversely affect both themselves and those near to them. When this happens repeatedly, and in extreme form, it may be diagnosed as demonstrating psychopathic behavior. There was a time when applying psychoanalytic theory that aspects of psychopathic behavior were attributed to deep processes going on in the minds of these people attributable to their early experiences. Today, this kind of explanation seems increasingly unlikely. Brain scanning studies comparing the brains of psychopaths with those of normal people have shown clear differences between the brains of the two groups when they were confronted with making moral decisions. This, of course, raises issues such as this: If the evidence showing that the brains of psychopaths in some cases are different from the range of the rest of the population, then in what sense can we hold them responsible for their behavior and any moral decisions they make that seem correct to them but unacceptable to us? The possibility of close relationships between the intactness of a person's brain and his moral behavior may be dramatically exemplified by the well-documented account of the onset of extreme pornographic behavior by an otherwise highly respected schoolteacher.

In the year 2000, a male schoolteacher began collecting sex magazines and visiting pornographic websites that focused on images of children and adolescents. In his own words, "he could not stop himself doing this." When he started making subtle advances to his stepdaughter, his wife called the police. He was arrested for child molestation. He was convicted and underwent a 12-step rehabilitation program for sex addicts. The day before his sentencing, he voluntarily went to the hospital emergency room with a severe headache. He was distraught and contemplating suicide. The

15. G. Borst, W. L. Thompson, and S. M. Kosslyn, "Understanding the Dorsal and Ventral Systems of the Human Cerebral Cortex: Beyond Dichotomies," *American Psychologist* 66 (October 2011): 624.

medical staff who examined him said that "he was totally unable to control his impulses" and "he had propositioned the nurses." An MRI taken of his brain revealed an egg-sized tumor pressing on his right frontal lobe. The tumor was removed and his lewd behavior and pedophilia faded away.

But a year later, the tumor partially grew back and the man started once again to collect pornography. A further medical operation was undertaken to remove the regrowing tumor, and his urges again subsided.[16]

There was widespread comment on this case. A neurologist said he "saw people with brain tumors who would lie, damage property, and in extreme rare cases, commit murder." He further commented, "The individuals simply lose the ability to control impulses or anticipate the consequences of choices."[17] A psychiatrist who specialized in behavioral changes associated with brain disorders, and who had studied the way brain tumors can affect a person's behavior commented, "This tells us something about being human, doesn't it?" And he went on, "If one's actions are governed by how well the brain is working, does it mean we have less free will than we think?"[18]

All these specialists know that human behavior is governed by complex interactions in the brain. Many neuroscientists believe that so-called executive functions—that is, decisions with major consequences—are dependent upon the intact functioning of systems within and/or linked to the frontal lobes (regarded as the most highly evolved area of the brain). Tumors in this area can squeeze enough blood from the region to effectively put it to sleep, thus dulling someone's judgment in a way similar to drinking too much alcohol. However, only in very rare cases will the tumor turn the person to violence or deviant behavior.

The dramatic changes and then reversal in the behavior of the schoolteacher are a vivid illustration of how our moral behavior is embodied in our physical make-up. Similar dramatic effects have been on record for a long time. Every student of neurology and neuropsychology has heard about Phineas Gage, whose frontal lobe was damaged in an accident and whose behavior was permanently changed for the worse. From being a reliable industrious pillar of society, he became dissolute and

16. Jeffrey Burns and Russell Swerdlow, "Right Orbitofrontal Tumor with Pedophilia Symptom and Constructional Apraxia Sign," *Archives of Neurology* 60 (2003): 437–40.

17. Chris Kahn, "Doctors: Pedophile 'Cured' After Surgery," Associated Press (July 28, 2003). http://www.freerepublic.com/focus/f-news/953765/posts.

18. Ibid.

irresponsible. Frans de Waal, commenting on two similar patients recently studied by Antonio Damasio, has written, "It's as if the moral compass of these people has been demagnetized, causing it to spin out of control. . . . What this incident teaches us is that conscience is not some disembodied concept that can be understood only on the basis of culture and religion."[19] Morality, he claimed, is as firmly grounded in neurobiology as anything else we do or are.

Changes in Subjective Experiences

The workings of the billions of nerve cells and trillions of ever-changing connections between the cells are modulated by the release of tiny packets of chemical messengers called neurotransmitters. It is important to understand that not just our overt behavior but our subjective experiences are dependent upon neurobiological processes. Changes in what we feel and how we feel are fundamentally tied to alterations in brain activity. Although we do not fully understand the nature of the relationship between subjective mental phenomena and observable brain processes, advances in neuroscience have made it clear that there is an intimate link between the two. For example, one area of neuroscience where the relationship between mental state, neural activity, and healing has been studied extensively is that of bodily pain. It is beyond doubt now that one's mental attitude—what one expects to experience—has a robust and measurable effect on the degree of pain reported when the body is stimulated. The so-called *placebo analgesic effect* is a well-known example of this.

A typical experiment would be for someone to be trained with an infusion of the powerful painkiller morphine and subsequently given an infusion of an inert solution such as salt water (which the subject believed was morphine), with the result that this also dramatically reduced her reported pain. When brain imaging is also carried out on such subjects who show the robust placebo analgesia effect, it further confirms their subjective reports by showing reduced activity in brain areas normally activated by painful stimuli. In addition, other brain areas, including those activated by morphine, showed increased activity. A further discovery is that the analgesic effect of a placebo can be reversed by a molecule that blocks the brain's receptor for opioids.

---

19. Frans de Waal, *Good Natured: The Origins of Right and Wrong in Humans and Other Animals* (Cambridge: Harvard University Press, 1996), p. 218.

It is not surprising that placebo analgesia has become an important component in pain management, even though the basic mechanisms are still poorly understood. From what we do understand, it has been suggested that this placebo analgesia, in addition to involving endogenous opioid systems in the brain, also significantly involves higher-order cognitive networks. It has been shown that parts of the brain called the rostral anterior cingulate cortex and the brain stem are implicated in opioid analgesia, and it has been suggested that a similar role is played for these structures in placebo analgesia. A study using positron emission tomography to study the brain has confirmed that both opioid and placebo analgesia are associated with increased activity in the rostral anterior cingulate cortex. In a word, what we believe, what we think, modifies the activity of our brain.

There is one further aspect of all these discussions of the relationship between brain and behavior that we need to remember: namely, that first and foremost we are social animals.[20] It is not surprising, then, that in the past decade, the emphasis among some researchers has turned to what they call *social neuroscience*. In the final part of a significant volume entitled *Social Neuroscience*, the editors remind us that "Social and biological approaches to human behavior have traditionally been contrasted, as if the two are antagonistic or mutually exclusive. The readings in this book demonstrate the fallacy of this reasoning and suggest that the mechanisms underlying mind and behavior may not be fully explicable by biological or a social approach alone, rather, a multilevel integrative analysis may be required."[21]

Making Sense of It All

As emphasized at the beginning of this chapter, it is one thing to demonstrate intimate interrelationships between what is happening at the conscious mental level and what is happening at the level of the brain and the body. But it's another thing to answer the question: How can we most accurately characterize this intimate relationship without making claims or assumptions about what we know about the relationship between the

---

20. Christopher D. Frith and Daniel M. Wolpert, *The Neuroscience of Social Interaction: Decoding, Imitating, and Influencing the Actions of Others* (New York: Oxford University Press, 2003).

21. John T. Cacioppo and Gary G. Berntson (eds.), *Social Neuroscience* (New York: Psychology Press, 2005), p. 241.

two that have not yet been demonstrated? What is clear is that there is a remarkable interdependence between what is occurring at the cognitive level and what is occurring at the physical level. We could perhaps describe this as a relationship of *intrinsic interdependence*, using the word "intrinsic" to mean that, as far as we can see, it describes the way the world is in this regard (*Concise Oxford Dictionary*: intrinsic, belonging naturally, inherent). Could we perhaps go further than this and say that, based on our present knowledge, it is an *irreducible* intrinsic interdependence—meaning that we cannot reduce the mental to the physical any more than we can reduce the physical to the mental. In this sense, there is an important duality to be recognized, but it is a duality without dualism.

Brain Processes and Embodied Spirituality

From the few examples given above, the take-home message is clear: There are intimate links between what is happening in our physical make-up in our brains and bodies and how we perceive, think, feel, and behave. Given these very close links, we may ask the further question: Is there any evidence that would lead us to believe that some of the most cherished aspects of our human personhood, including our religious beliefs and behavior and spirituality, will be totally shielded from the effects of changes in our physical nature? As we seek to answer this question, we shall once again seek to put it in a proper historical perspective, and then go on to consider more recent and contemporary studies of the relationship of the activities in our brains to our spiritual awareness and our religious behavior.

Brain Processes and Religion: A Long History but a Short Past
Brain Chemistry

There are well-documented accounts of the ways some ancient religious rituals have used plants to facilitate ecstatic and mystical states. For example, the use of mushrooms by the Aztecs, peyote cactus in Mexico, and *ayahuasca* by the natives of northwestern South America come readily to mind. Today we know a little more about some of the chemicals that create hallucinogenic experiences. Normally, they fall into one of three categories: the *tryptamines*, the *phenylamines*, and the *ergolines*. The common subjective experiences elicited by these drug-related changes in brain systems include "altered perception of reality and self; intensification of mood; visual or auditory hallucinations, including vivid eidetic imagery and synesthesia; distorted sense of time and space; enhanced profundity and meaningfulness; and a ubiquitous sense of novelty."[22] Whether these experiences are interpreted as a psychedelic "trip" or as spiritual and transcendent, they are hypothesized to be due primarily to one's experience-based expectations, the setting in which the drugs are taken, and the cognitive/theological network out of which one provides a *post hoc* interpretation of the experience.

Neurologic Processes

There is a well-documented literature in clinical neurology suggesting that some individuals with temporal lobe epilepsy experience intense religious states as part of the aura before a seizure. In such cases, the intense experiences of religious ecstasy or of an ominous presence may be produced by the brain's abnormal electrical activity that brings on the seizures. Although such cases are rare, they are sufficiently well documented to suggest that something about the physical processes may be associated with normal religious experiences.

Since the days when epilepsy was regarded as a sacred disease, it has been referred to many times in the world literature. For example, Fyodor Dostoyevsky (who himself had a seizure disorder) gives a particularly graphic literary description of subjective feelings during some seizures, in his account of the experiences of Prince Myshkin in *The Idiot*. The following is a passage from this book in which Dostoyevsky describes (in the thoughts of Myshkin) the sort of religious experiences that are sometimes associated with temporal lobe seizures:

> his brain was on fire, and in an extraordinary surge all his vital forces would be intensified. The sense of life, the consciousness of self were multiplied tenfold in these moments.... His mind and heart were flooded with extraordinary light; all torment, all doubt, all anxieties were relieved at once, resolved in a kind of lofty calm,

22. David E. Nichols and Benjamin R. Chemel, "The Neuropharmacology of Religious Experience: Hallucinogens and the Experience of the Divine," in Patrick McNamara (ed.), *Where God and Science Meet*, vol. 3: *The Psychology of Religious Experience* (Westport, CT: Praeger, 2006), p. 3.

full of serene, harmonious joy and hope, full of understanding and the knowledge of the ultimate cause of things. . . . If in that second— that is, in the last lucid moment before the fit—he had time to say to himself clearly and consciously: "Yes, one might give one's whole life for this moment!" then that moment by itself would certainly be worth the whole of life.[23]

A recent literary reference to this phenomenon can be found in Mark Salzman's modern novel, *Lying Awake*. Salzman writes about a nun with religious visions associated with temporal lobe seizures.[24]

Whatever the most appropriate statement of the meaning of this phenomenon, it is clear that certain patterns of electrical activity involving the temporal lobes (sometimes occurring during a seizure) can cause intense, personally significant experiences that some persons describe as religious.

Neuro-theology

Today, localized brain stimulation studies have attracted media. A leader in this field has been Michael Persinger. Abnormal activity of the temporal lobes can be induced artificially in non-epileptic individuals using a noninvasive procedure called *transcranial magnetic stimulation*. Persinger reports experiments where electromagnetic stimulation of the right temporal lobe resulted in the person reporting a "sense of presence." This "sense of presence" is sometimes experienced by the person as the presence of God or angels or other supernatural persons. This has led Persinger to suggest that all persons who have religious experiences are having microseizures of the right temporal lobe. A similar explanation is given by Persinger for other paranormal experiences, such as reports of encounters with aliens.[25]

While the extrapolation of this form of brain stimulation to an account of normally occurring forms of religious experience seems unwarranted, this research does suggest that magnetically induced physical changes in

---

23. Fyodor Dostoyevsky, *The Idiot*, trans. Henry and Olga Carlisle (New York: Signet Classic, 1969), p. 243.

24. Mark Salzman, *Lying Awake* (New York: Alfred A. Knopf, 2000).

25. See Michael A. Persinger, *Neuropsychological Bases of God Beliefs* (New York: Greenwood Press, 1987), and Michael A. Persinger, "Religious and Mystical Experiences as Artifacts of Temporal Lobe Function: A General Hypothesis," *Perceptual and Motor Skills* 57 (1983): 1255–62.

the temporal regions of the brain can result in experiences that, in some cases, are interpreted as religious. Persinger's findings, however, should be treated with caution. A recent report of an attempted replication of his studies that used better-controlled experiments, including double-blind techniques, failed to replicate Persinger's results.

Currently, much research has focused on the use of modern brain-imaging techniques aimed at monitoring the ways different parts of the brain are selectively activated with different experiences, including religious experiences. Andrew Newberg and his collaborators have studied brain activity during various religious states. In these studies, they observed changes in regional cerebral blood flow using *single-photon emission computed tomography* (SPECT scans). They first studied religious meditation in both Buddhist monks and Catholic nuns. In both groups, the results showed increased bilateral frontal lobe activation and decreased right parietal lobe activity when the meditator reported reaching a state of total absorption and "oneness." Decreased activity of the right parietal lobe was interpreted as a neural correlate of the absence of a sense of self that is experienced in such meditative states.[26]

Newberg and colleagues have extended this research to include another religious state that is very different from meditation—the ecstatic religious state involving *glossolalia* (speaking in tongues). They compared this state to merely singing along with gospel music. Activity in the frontal lobes decreased significantly during glossolalia, consistent with the self-reported loss of intentional control of behavior in this state. This change in the frontal lobes is opposite to that seen during meditation. Decreased activity was also observed in the left temporal pole and left caudate nucleus during glossolalia. In contrast to the reduced right parietal activity seen during meditative states, glossolalia was associated with increased activity in the left superior parietal area.[27]

Thus, these studies suggest both that religious states are associated with identifiable changes in the distribution of brain activity, and that different religious states are associated with different patterns of brain activity—in some cases quite opposite changes in brain activity.

---

26. Andrew Newberg and Mark Robert Waldman, *How God Changes Your Brain: Breakthrough Findings from a Leading Neuroscientist* (New York: Ballantine Books, 2009), p. 101.

27. A. B. Newberg, N. A. Wintering, D. Morgan, and M. R. Waldman, "The Measurement of Regional Cerebral Blood Flow During Glossolalia: A Preliminary SPECT Study," *Psychiatry Research: Neuroimaging* 148 (2006): 67–71.

Perspectives on Brain Function
and Religious Experiences

Religious states and experiences may be drug-induced, seizure-related, or caused by magnetic stimulation; alternatively, brain changes may be associated with normal religious states. In any case, it is clear that the functioning of the brain is intimately involved in our religious states and experiences. The question is, what is to be made of such relationships?

V. S. Ramachandran argues that a "God module" exists within the temporal lobe in the form of a neural area dedicated to religious experiences. In essence, he believes that increased activity in this brain area would be necessary and sufficient for a person to have a religious experience. Thus, if this area becomes abnormally active during a seizure, the person will necessarily have a religious experience and not some other form of experience. This would be the case regardless of the person's prior life experiences, expectancies, habitual ways of interpreting life experiences, the context in which the seizure occurs, and so forth. Thus, religious experiences are, in the view of Ramachandran, a unique and intrinsic class of experiences served by a unique brain structure.[28]

A different interpretation of the same clinical data has been offered by J. L. Saver and J. Rabin.[29] They argue that certain temporal lobe seizures activate a brain system that marks mental processes with a quality of deep significance, harmoniousness, joy, and so forth. Whether or not the experience is described in religious terms is a product of the prior experiences and interpretive networks of the person having the seizure. This explains why some persons have temporal lobe seizures that have similar experiential qualities but are not described or experienced by the person as religious. The scientist and science writer Richard Dawkins, appearing in a BBC *Horizon* science documentary series, did not have a "sensed presence" experience but instead felt at times "slightly dizzy" and "quite strange" and had sensations in his limbs and changes in his breathing. He summarized his experience as follows: "It pretty much felt as though I was in total darkness, with a helmet on my head and pleasantly relaxed."[30]

---

28. V. S. Ramachandran, W. Hirstein, K. C. Armel, E. Tecoma, and V. Iragui, "The Neural Basis of Religious Experience," *Society for Neuroscience Conference Abstracts* (1997): 1316.

29. J. L. Saver and J. Rabin, "The Neural Substrates of Religious Experience," *Journal of Neuropsychiatry* 9(3) (1997): 1316.

30. "God on the Brain," BBC's *Horizon* series episode, transcript (London: British Broadcasting Corporation) (April 17, 2003). http://www.bbc.co.uk/science/horizon/2003/godonbraintrans.shtml.

Persinger explained Dawkins's limited results in terms of his low score on a psychological scale measuring temporal lobe sensitivity.[31]

In contrast, the experimental psychologist and former parapsychology researcher Susan Blackmore said, "When I went to Persinger's lab and underwent his procedures I had the most extraordinary experiences I've ever had. . . . I'll be surprised if it turns out to be a placebo effect!"[32] The reports of Dawkins and Blackmore suggest that prior beliefs and worldviews strongly influence how brain processes will be interpreted. Thus, religious meaning is not intrinsic to the experience but is applied by the interpretive network of the experiencer. Thus, it is possible that a general-process neural system (not a "God module") is activated by certain forms of temporal lobe seizure activity, and that when this area is subject to abnormal activation, it is fitted into wider brain cognitive systems that provide one or another sort of interpretation.

We shall hear much more of this, so it is therefore worth pausing and examining the logic leading to claims to have found "the God module" in this or that region of our brains. This is an important question because, on the one hand, there will be those who, believing that it has now been demonstrated that there is a "God spot" in our brains, will be tempted to use this as evidence for proof of the existence of God. On the other hand, there will be those who appeal to the same evidence to demonstrate that, as they have believed all along, religious experience and behavior is "nothing but" the unusual activity of a particular part of the brain; perhaps they will refer back to Sigmund Freud's famous book *The Future of an Illusion* and conclude that they have now discovered the seat of that illusion. We must examine these issues.

Spirituality and the Logic of the God Module Claims

At the beginning, we noted, as Victor Copan reminded us, the ubiquity today of references to "spirituality," some of which may have few or no links to any traditional Christian beliefs. For example, one widely practiced "spiritual exercise" is meditation. This takes various forms in

---

31. "God on the Brain," BBC's *Horizon* series episode, program summary (London: British Broadcasting Corporation, 2003). http://www.bbc.co.uk/science/horizon/2003/godonbrain.shtml.

32. Roxane Khamsi, "Electrical Brainstorms Busted as Source of Ghosts," *Nature* (December 9, 2004). http://www.nature.com/news/2004/041206/full/news041206-10.html.

different religions and also among groups who claim no religious affili-
ation at all. Meditation, it is widely claimed, calms one's thoughts, mod-
erates one's passions, and may lift one's spirits and induce a feeling of
contentedness. During such experiences, there is no doubt that, in principle, it would be possible to explore which parts of the brain are most
active and involved and which less so. Indeed, such studies have already
been carried out by Andrew Newberg and his colleagues. But the question remains, how are we to interpret the links between these forms of
spirituality and what is happening in the brain? Does it prove anything
about the object or focus of the induced spiritual experience? Does it
prove the existence of God?

Perhaps an analogy may help answer this question. My favorite sport
is fly fishing. There's a classic book on the subject entitled *The Complete
Angler*, written by Sir Henry Wotton. He describes fishing as "a rest to
his mind, the cheerer of his spirits, the diverter of sadness, the calmer
of unquiet thoughts, the moderator of passions, a procurer of contentedness."[33] Such a description might indeed suggest a brain state similar to
some forms of religious meditation. But, says Sir Henry, it comes when
he is enjoying fly fishing. I can testify that I know the feeling! Let's do a
thought experiment and imagine that we could study Sir Henry's brain
with modern fMRI techniques while he's fishing. Imagine we find certain
brain areas more active than others. Suppose we do the same experiment
on me and a half a dozen of my fly-fishing friends, and the result is that,
behold, the same areas are active in each of our brains! Have we discovered the brain areas for fishing? Does the observation that the same area
lights up in all of us prove the existence of fish? Either the fish are there
in the river or they are not. Casting a fly over them and observing that a
particular part of our brains lights up won't prove they exist. Brain imaging alone is not going to provide unequivocal evidence for or against the
existence of fish or the existence of God.

The logic is the same when we study the brains of people engaged in
spiritual activities or the brain correlates of atheism. Because certain brain
areas light up can never prove the existence of the God on whom the spiritual activities focus. Either God exists or God does not. As Christians, we
vary enormously in how we became Christians, how we practice our faith,
and the variety of reasons that underpin our belief in the existence of God.

---

33. Izaak Walton and Charles Cotton, *The Compleat Angler* (1676; reprint, Oxford: Oxford
University Press, 2009), p. 379.

The weight that each of us accords each of these different reasons will vary from person to person. Some Christians have seen what personal belief in Jesus Christ has done for a friend. Others have studied the scriptures with an open mind and become convinced of the claims of Jesus Christ and responded to his invitation to come to him, to put their trust in him. Others have come in other ways. You only have to read the lives of the first disciples and of Christians down the centuries to see the variety of ways in which people became Christians.

Ultimately, basing spirituality on subjective experiences alone as the grounds for belief is an unsure and shifting foundation. It was certainly never one used by the early Christians. If you read the accounts given in the New Testament, for example, you will find the constant grounds appealed to for taking the claims of Jesus Christ seriously were not subjective feelings or times of ecstasy, but the many and varied accounts of the life, teaching, and activities of Jesus and his disciples. Likewise, the key manifestations (evidences) of the work of the Spirit are as much external as internal. For example, the apostle Paul, writing to the Galatian Christians, describes the fruit of the Spirit as "love, joy, peace, patience, kindness, goodness, faithfulness, gentleness, and self-control." As John Stott has commented, "Love, joy, and peace characterize our relationship with God; patience, kindness, and goodness our relationship with others; and faithfulness, gentleness, and self-control our mastery of ourselves."[34] You could almost say that "spirituality" as manifest in the fruit of the Spirit is based fundamentally on relationships—the first three on our relationship with God, the second three on our relationship with others, and the third three on our relationship with ourselves. Perhaps here we find echoes of a theme pervasive in discussions today about what is meant by human beings made "in the image of God"; namely, that it is first and foremost focused on our capacity for relationships—proper relationships with our Creator, our fellow humans, and ourselves. There are no references to unusual experiences that seem nebulous, wishy-washy, or airy-fairy. Rather, the emphasis is fairly and squarely on behavior and on relationships.

Hermeneutics scholar Anthony C. Thistleton, in a wide-ranging survey entitled "The Image and the Likeness of God: A Theological Approach," notes that "to fulfil the vocation of representing God as his image and

---

34. John Stott, *Through the Bible Through the Year* (Grand Rapids, MI: Baker Books, 2006), p. 348.

likeness, humankind is called to reach beyond the self in love and communion with God and the other, which includes other human beings." He later comments, "relationality has always found a place among the more traditional attempts to explain 'image of God,'" and he quotes with approval the work of Daniel Migliore, who had commented, "being created in the image of God means that humans find their true identity in coexistence with each other and with all other creatures.... Human existence is not individualistic but communal."[35] In support of his argument emphasizing the relationality aspect of what it means to be made in the image of God, Thistleton draws upon the insights of theologians from a variety of different traditions.[36]

For example, the Greek Orthodox theologian John Zizioulas, in his book *Being As Communion*, declares, "God is a relational being ... 'God' has no ontological content, no true being, apart from communion ... nothing exists as an 'individual.'"[37] Thistleton accepts that some think that Zizioulas may go too far, but nevertheless he restores the balance after Enlightenment individualism. Thistleton also quotes Stanley Grenz, from another tradition, who has written about "the near consensus that person is a relational concept."[38] Each of them argues from the nature of the Trinitarian God to the image of God in humankind, rather than from humankind to God. And so Grenz concludes that "In the final analysis, then, the imago dei is not merely relational, it is ultimately communal: it involves 'the quest for completeness that draws humans out of isolation into bonded relationships'."[39] (In the book in which Thistleton's chapter appears, we find scientists, psychologists, philosophers, and others all reinforcing, in their different ways, the centrality, as one aspect of what it means to be made in the image of God, of our capacity to make, to accept, and to share relationships with others both as individuals and in groups.)

---

35. Daniel L. Migliore, *Faith Seeking Understanding: An Introduction to Christian Theology* (Grand Rapids, MI: Eerdmans, 1991), p. 12.

36. See Anthony C. Thistleton, "The Image and the Likeness of God: A Theological Approach," in Malcolm Jeeves (ed.), *The Emergence of Personhood: A Quantum Leap?* (Grand Rapids, MI: Eerdmans, 2005).

37. John Zizioulas, *Being as Communion: Studies in Personhood and the Church* (New York: St. Vladimir's Seminary Press, 1997), pp. 17, 18.

38. Stanley J. Grenz, *The Social God and the Relational Self: The Trinitarian Theology of the Imago Dei* (Louisville, KY: Westminster John Knox, 2001), p. 9.

39. Ibid., p. 303.

Embodied Spirituality in Pastoral Settings

Evidence suggesting links between aspects of the religious life, such as spirituality and what is happening in the brain, have important practical and pastoral implications. In recent years, these implications have been brought to the attention of the wider Christian public by the very helpful and open personal accounts of Christian leaders who have suffered from conditions such as depression, Alzheimer's disease, and Parkinson's disease.

We began this chapter by noting that, traditionally, some of the most widely available testimonies or evidences of the work of the Spirit are seen in their manifestations in the "spirituality" of individuals and groups. These testimonies to the work of the Spirit are experienced in individual lives and observed by fellow members of Christian groups. How does this work out in the everyday lives of Christians? Consider two brief scenarios. Jane, in her mid-30s, has been an active and lively member of a local Christian church. She is well known for her bright witness and dedicated Christian life in the church and the local community. For reasons she doesn't quite understand, she finds that for no apparent reason it is becoming increasingly difficult to make time for her daily private devotions. When she is attending church she no longer feels the deep spiritual encouragement and uplift that she has become so accustomed to. Given all that she has been taught about the Christian life, she has no doubt that for some reason she is failing in the closeness of her walk with God, and this is having effects in all of her life. But the more she struggles, the worse things get. Some of her closest Christian friends begin to hint that she doesn't seem to be as keen and dedicated as she once was. That troubles her even more. She feels she is letting down her Lord and Master as well as her local church. Eventually, on the advice of a very close friend, she decides to seek help from a local physician. He is most helpful, and, quite soon, it is apparent that she is suffering from a depressive illness. With suitable medication, her energy returns and her appreciation of the spiritual dimensions of her life return to where they once were.

The second scenario is of John, in his mid-60s, who, for five decades, has been a pillar of his local church. His participation in the church's activities, sharing in responsibilities, and, in particular, his leadership in his home Bible study group, has been the hallmark of a wonderful, fulfilled Christian life. For no reason that he can understand, he begins to find that his ability to lead his Bible study group is not what it once was. His ability to recall relevant passages of scripture when leading or answering questions in the study group begins to fail him. Soon, other members of the group begin to notice it. What, they wonder, is happening to him? Has he lost the deep spirituality that he once embodied? Again, on the advice of a close friend, he consults a neuropsychologist and, on that doctor's advice, his personal physician, who has known him for many decades. With the confirmation of well-tried psychological testing, it is apparent that he is in the advancing stages of Alzheimer's disease. His medical condition is affecting his brain and that, in turn, has consequences for his normal psychological functioning. His spirituality, it turns out, is not immune to the changes taking place in him as a fully embodied psychobiological person. It is possible to give him some temporary remedial assistance and much more personal support, and he is helped to see that he should not be judging himself because of his changed ability to contribute to the life of his Christian community; rather, he can be appreciating how they, as individuals and as a group, manifest the fruit of the Spirit by their support and encouragement of him.

Fortunately, in recent years, some high-profile Christian leaders have shared publicly the experiences they have been through as they have faced challenges such as those faced in our two scenarios of Jane and John. For example, Lewis Smedes, a former professor at Fuller Theological Seminary, wrote about his experiences of depression in his book *My God and I*. He noted his feelings of helplessness and alienation from God during that time. He also very helpfully described how eventually his depression was alleviated. In his own words, he wrote, "Then God came back. He broke through my terror and said: 'I will never let you fall. I will always hold you up'. . . . I felt as if I had been lifted from a black pit straight up into joy." Smedes added the following comment, "I have not been neurotically depressed since that day, though I must, to be honest, tell you that God also comes to me each morning and offers me a 20 mg capsule of Prozac. . . . I swallow every capsule with gratitude to God."[40] Lewis Smedes recognized that the biochemistry of his brain that had been changed by depression needed rebalancing, and part of the way to do this was by taking a drug. Biochemistry and spirituality are intimately interrelated.

---

40. Lewis B. Smedes, *My God and I: A Spiritual Memoir* (Grand Rapids, MI: Eerdmans, 2003), p. 133.

But what about John's experiences? Another leading Christian, this time a high-profile Presbyterian minister, Robert Davis, was diagnosed with Alzheimer's dementia when he was 53 and at the height of his ministerial career. With the help of his wife, he wrote a remarkable account of his spiritual experiences well into the middle stages of his disease. It documented how his progressive brain disease affected his spirituality. It was graphically illustrated in his own words. He wrote:

> My spiritual life was still most miserable. I could not read the Bible. I could not pray as I wanted because my emotions were dead and cut off. There was no feedback from God the Holy Spirit. My mind could not rest and grow calm but instead raced relentlessly, thinking dreadful thoughts of despair. My mind also raced about, grasping the comfort of the Savior whom I knew and loved and for the emotional peace that He would give me, but finding nothing. I concluded that the only reason for such darkness must be spiritual. Unnamed guilt filled me. Yet the only guilt I could put a name to was failure to read my Bible. But I could not read, would God condemn me for this? I could only lie there and cry "Oh God, why? Why?"[41]

Davis further writes, "I can no longer be spiritually fed by sermons. I can get the first point of the sermon and then I am lost. The rest of it sends my mind whirling in a jumble of twisted unconnected ideas. Coughing, headache, and great discomfort have attended my attempts to be fed in all the ways I am accustomed to meeting God through his Word."[42] These are heartrending words, but they underline graphically how the testimony or evidence of the work of the Spirit in our lives can become masked even to the point of seeming to have disappeared because of disease processes in our brains.

Lewis Smedes and Robert Davis have demonstrated clearly how, at times, the testimony of the Spirit—that is, the evidences of the work of the Spirit—may be masked or even eliminated in the lives of committed, earnest Christians. There is always a possibility that this may be due to wilful disobedience, something the apostle Paul warned the early believers of frequently. However, the theme of this chapter has been prompted by what

---

41. Robert Davis, *My Journey into Alzheimer's Disease* (Wheaton, IL: Tyndale, 1989), p. 53.
42. Ibid., p. 115.

God has revealed to us through the fruit of the scientific enterprise, including the work of dedicated Christian scientists, to alert us to new understandings of how someone's "spirituality" may be reduced, masked, or, at times, in the experience of extreme suffering, obliterated. But it has also shown how it may be partially or wholly restored by a proper application of that selfsame new knowledge we have today of our psychobiological unity. The opportunity for the manifestation of the evidences of the Spirit, then, lies first and foremost in ourselves and in the lives of fellow Christians as individuals and in groups.

7

Freedom, Community, and Language

OUTLINE OF A "NEUROANTHROPOLOGICAL" PNEUMATOLOGY

Oliver Davies

Introduction

There is no other term of Christian theology that is so fundamental and yet so historical in the sense of being bound up with the passage of time than the "Holy Spirit." There is one very simple reason for this. While there has of course been a rich and varied nuancing of christology and the figure of Christ over the centuries, the incarnate Word has remained definitionally human. Christ simply is material form: We just recognize his human body, in whatever age we live. The Holy Spirit, on the other hand, is not as such material form; rather, it is defined by its relation to matter. The Spirit "descends," is "breathed out," and "gives life." The Spirit "resurrects," "cleanses," and "sanctifies." The Spirit drives like "the East wind." It governs the efficiency of speech. We inherit a "spiritual body." In short, in biblical texts the Spirit is known in its evidencing of the power of God within material form. It unmistakably manifests and testifies to the sovereign power of the Creator in the midst of the creation.

If, in Christianity, the Holy Spirit has been understood to be bound up with a dynamic relation to the material, then, more than the Father who *creates* materiality, or the Son who *becomes* materiality, the intelligibility of the Holy Spirit has stood in—often unclear—proximity to the presuppositions that obtain in our understanding of the relation between the material world and immateriality as such (e.g., *nous* and the "noetic," *pneuma, mens,* the "angelic," "spirit" or *Geist*, or indeed "consciousness"). The translation of biblical terms and conceptualities into very different languages, in different historical contexts, means that Christian understanding concerning the Holy Spirit in its relation to the material, with its underlying presuppositions, has itself tended to coalesce with a variety of notions of immateriality or "immaterial substance" (to mention one classical configuration) in different times and cultures.

This state of affairs has one very significant consequence for this chapter. A properly critical exploration of the human reception of the Holy Spirit will require that we are aware of how this cultural recontextualization of the Holy Spirit has occurred in our own Western tradition, and indeed precisely at the point of the historical intersection between the medieval and modern periods. It is then that we can see a very deep change in understanding of mind and matter, which quite naturally touched on the foundations of our self-understanding—as mind and body—in ways that resisted, rather than favored, objectification. Between the early 16th and the later 18th century, the rise of the scientific method led to significantly new understanding of matters (and so also of mind). We can look back on this period now as one of *cosmological* change (and can compare it, in fact, with our own times of fundamental change in terms of quantum physics, astrophysics, genetics, and nanotechnology). Beyond the rise of technology, the gulf that separates us today from premodern times shows us that there obtains a very intimate relation between how we are in the world as body and mind and how we conceive of the relation between body and mind, in terms of both explicit and tacit knowledge. In short, what mind thinks matter is (or how mind "envisages" matter) can deeply shape our embodied living in the world. The transition from medieval to modern teaches us that culture can at times reconfigure the mind–body relation in the world, and so also our living experience of being human.

In consequence, then, a close philosophical-doctrinal reflection upon the testimony of the Spirit faces a particular problem in that the transition from what Charles Taylor has called the premodern "porous self" to the modern "buffered self" entailed the problem of re-envisaging the mind–body relation, with significant implications for conceptualizations of the human "spirit" and the divine "Spirit" alike.[1] "Porosity" is a feature of our sentient, embodied, and communal life, while "buffering" is a feature that

---

1. Charles Taylor, *A Secular Age* (Cambridge: Harvard University, Belknap Press, 2007).

is typical of an alert, self-possessing, and controlling consciousness. Both are equally characteristic of us, as sentient and intelligent human beings. Each received a different cultural weighting in the transition between the premodern and modern periods, however, with real effects that are deeply influential down to the present day.

Realigning Matter and Spirit

Highly informative traces of this "cosmological change" and its effects can be found in a body of texts from the early Reformation that concern the so-called Eucharistic controversy (in which leading reformers debated whether the new Protestantism should continue, emend, or reject Catholic teaching on Eucharistic Real Presence).[2] Here the point at issue was how the materiality of Christ's body in heaven should be understood. Was this "glorious" and so "transformed" flesh, as Scripture records, or was it "real" flesh as understood according to the incipiently materialist humanism of the day? If it was the latter, then there could be no real presence of Christ in the Eucharist as understood by the medievals. It was their belief in the particular ontology of the glorious and heavenly body of Christ that allowed Christ to be "locally" and "substantially" present in heaven while also being "substantially" present in the Eucharist on earth below.[3] In this debate, Zwingli reflected a transitional age, since he lived before the influence of Copernicus, and so held to a traditional, scriptural account of the geocentric universe, but equally he came after the emergence of materialism. Therefore he found himself depicting a physically "untransformed" (i.e., "unglorified") Christ seated at the right hand of the Father in heaven, reflecting a clash between medieval realism about the whereabouts of heaven and a new modern scientific realism about the nature of matter: "and so we can see that we should measure our understanding of the consuming of his flesh in part from the fact that he sits until the Last Day, and then eternally, in an *untransformed* state to the right hand of the divine majesty."[4] For Zwingli, it was the very

---

2. Brian Gerrish, *Grace and Gratitude: The Eucharistic Theology of John Calvin* (Edinburgh: T & T Clark, 1993).

3. *Summa Theologiae*, 3a, q.76 and 3a, q.57, art. 4 and 5.

4. "Antwort über Straussens Büchlein, das Nachtmahl Christi betreffend," *Huldrich Zwinglis Sämtliche Werke*, 14 volumes; Corpus Reformatorum 88–101 (Berlin/Zürich: Theologischer Verlag Zürich, 1905–1959), Vol. 92, p. 841: "so man offenlich sicht, das wir den verstand des

nature or truth of a real body that it should be "circumscribed, limited and particular."[5] Zwingli, for whom the question of the reality of the body of the living Christ was at stake (on the grounds of the authority of the new science), ingeniously defended his position to Luther, also protecting the principles of faith. But this was only possible at the price of a retreat from what Luther called the "order of salvation." According to tradition, the Holy Spirit does not act directly upon spirit, but rather acts first upon matter and embodiment.[6] It is the question of the *ordo salutis* that underlies Luther's celebrated insistence upon *hoc est corpus meum* in his debate with Zwingli at the Marburg Colloquy.[7]

What we glimpse in Zwingli, then, is the beginnings of a configuration around spirit and matter and their relation that will become hugely influential, and not just in modern theology. In this early materialism, matter becomes the site of efficient causation and resists the work of the Spirit, as scripture records this. Luther rightly critiqued Zwingli for replacing an *ethical* opposition between Spirit and matter with an *ontological* one.[8] One of the consequences of this substitution was that Holy Spirit and human spirit both came to be defined with respect to the resistance of matter and its efficient causation. As material causation/efficient causation (in which prior causes lead ineluctably to their effects), which is so central to the rise of modern science, comes to the fore, Holy Spirit and human spirit—now both in opposition to matter—begin to overlap. By the time of the foundation of the University of Berlin (1810), which was the birthplace of modern theology as well as an icon of the development of modern science and

essens sines fleischs zum teil dahar messend, dass er an den grechten götlicher maiestat *unverwandelt* sitzt biß an jungsten tag, und demnach ewklich" (my translation and italics).

5. Zwingli, "Über D. Martin Luthers Buch, Bekenntnis gennant", in *Huldrich Zwinglis Sämtliche Werke*, Corpus Reformatorum, Vol. 93, p. 167: "Die ist ein lyb, ein umbzyleter, umbfasseter, umpryßner lyb" (my translation).

6. "Ad Mattheum Alberum de coena dominica epistola," *Huldrich Zwinglis Sämtliche Werke*, Corpus Reformatorum, Vol. 90, p. 337. Zwingli's position is captured in Paul Althaus's apt phrase: "Spirit has an effect only on spirit" (Paul Althaus, *The Theology of Martin Luther* [Philadelphia: Fortress Press, 1966], p. 395). For a discussion of Luther's theology here, with references, see Regin Prenter, *Spiritus Creator: Luther's Concept of the Holy Spirit* (Philadelphia: Muhlenberg Press, 1953), pp. 252–55.

7. Gerhard May (ed.), *Marburger Religionsgespräch 1529* (Gütersloh: Gütersloher Verlagshaus Gerd Mohn, 1970), p. 54.

8. This accusation forms a substantial part of *That These Words of Christ, "This is my Body", etc., Still Stand Firm against the Fanatics* of 1527, *Luther's Works*, 37, *Word and Sacrament 3* (Philadelphia: Muhlenberg Press, 1961), pp. 13–155, and it returns in *Confession Concerning Christ's Supper* of 1528 (*Luther's Works*, 37, see for instance pp. 287–88).

technology, there is a far-reaching congruence between the human mind and the work of the divine Spirit, or what Fichte calls the divine "supra-sensible" or "Spirit world."[9] In an important theoretical justification for the new research university, Fichte writes:

> Knowledge however determines itself, and is not at all determined by anything outside itself, which it might be said to mirror. And it is this absoluteness which makes it the image of the inner being and essence of God. God alone truly transcends the senses and is the real object of every vision. Knowledge only exists as the image of God, and by virtue of being the image of God, and is only maintained by the appearance of God within it.[10]

The alliance of divine and human *Geist*, in a new age of Idealism and technology, is unsurprising, but it had the significant theological effect of effacing the wholly created and dependent nature of human "spirit." Properly in theological terms, the human mind is no less created than the human body, and mind and body both need to be understood to be entirely the object of the uncreated Spirit's work.[11]

Neuroanthropology and Philosophy

Questions about the volitional or motivational conditions for the work of the Spirit in us are inevitably bound up, then, with deep evolutions in the philosophical or cultural framework that surrounds the Spirit/spirit—matter relation. We have biblical and premodern resources that generally reflect the nondualism of the traditional cosmos, and we have the dualist emphases of modernity seeking to respond to reductionist science. And third, under pressure from the new scientific, "nondualist" paradigms of "non-reductive physicalism" (Murphey), or "reflexive monism" (Velmans), we are witnessing an incipient, though nevertheless unmistakable, return

9. See, for instance, his discussion in "Fünf Vorlesungen über die Bestimmung des Gelehrten," *Fichtes Werke*, 11 volumes, ed. I. H. Fichte (Berlin: Walter de Gruyter, 1971), Vol. 11, pp. 145–220, here 193–95.

10. Ibid., p. 151.

11. Oliver Davies, "Spirit, Text and Body," in Paul S. Fiddes and Günter Bader (eds.), *The Spirit and the Letter: A Tradition and a Reversal* (London: Bloomsbury T & T Clark, 2013), pp. 179–94.

to a nondualist perspective, with significant implications for philosophy.[12] Although we may assume that the testimony of the Spirit and its association with life, sanctification, love, freedom, and sureness of faith are Christian constants, the issue of what kind of philosophy, and what kind of philosophical presuppositions about the relation that obtains between spirit and matter (or consciousness and matter), will be central as a framework for the articulation of a pneumatology today. There is here a moment of choice, then, and the philosophical framework developed in this chapter will reflect the nondualism of contemporary science, in the belief that it is this that offers a future orientation.

We are helped here by the rise of the new term "neuroanthropology," which sets out specific constraints for understanding the human today that arise from the biological sciences, while also allowing the rich confluence of new philosophical and cultural thinking.[13] The results are not entirely surprising for readers familiar with a biblical account of the human, from the "Word made flesh" to the creedal affirmation of Christ's rising from the dead, our own bodily resurrection, and the final transformation of the world as New Creation. In the first place comes the principle that consciousness and brain (mind and matter) are "simultaneous" in us, or inseparably different (two sides of the same coin), with the consequence that mind and body together constitute an "integrated" system of embodied life or "intelligent embodiment." But precisely this unity of the self gives rise to a second principle that concerns our unity, namely, the question: How can we be free, as persons, if there is no separation between mind and body in us? From a neuroscientific perspective, then, the unity of the self and the freedom of the self can appear to be at odds. And so we are left with the question: What do we *mean* when we say that we are free?

The unity of our body and mind, and questions concerning our human freedom, are not without precedent, of course. In fact, in *De esse et essentia* Thomas Aquinas very precisely outlines such a comprehensively

---

12. For the terminology of "non-reductive physicalism," see the bibliography in Philip Clayton's "Toward a Christian Theology of Emergence," in Nancey Murphy and William R. Stoeger, SJ (eds.), *Evolution and Emergence: Systems, Organisms, Persons* (Oxford: Oxford University Press, 2007), p. 320, n. 11. See also Max Velmans, *Understanding Consciousness* (Hove, East Sussex, and New York: Routledge, 2009).

13. Daniel H. Lende and Greg Downey, "Neuroanthropology and the Encultured Brain," in Greg Downey and Daniel H. Lende (eds.), *The Encultured Brain: An Introduction to Neuroanthropology* (Cambridge: MIT Press, 2012), pp. 23–65.

integrated model of the self, *contra omnes*, as both body and mind, where he discusses the unicity of the soul, explicitly defending a thoroughgoing materialist conception of the knowing self.[14] A similar note is struck in Kant's late work *Anthropology from a Pragmatic Point of View* (1798), where the author of the three critiques focuses upon the unity of the human being in terms of our embodied habits and practice. Kant sets out his new project in "anthropology" as combining science and ethics:

> A doctrine of knowledge of the human being, systematically formulated (anthropology), can exist either in a physiological or pragmatic point of view. Physiological knowledge of the human being concerns the investigation of what *nature* makes of the human being; pragmatic the investigation of what *he* as a free-acting being makes of himself, or can and should make of himself.[15]

Kant continues with the assertion that the "pragmatic" approach is based on the observation and analysis of our human behavior and that it is "participative" and requires as broad a database as possible. He believes that the pragmatic approach "contains knowledge of the human being as *citizen of the world.*"[16] On the other hand, in the physiological perspective we are "mere observers" who "must let nature run its course, for we do not know the cranial nerves and fibers nor do we understand how to put them to use for our purposes." He concludes, therefore, that "all theoretical speculation about this is a pure waste of time."[17]

The question of our human freedom lies deep in Kant, of course, but attains a new prominence in the Romantics and Idealists. The question of freedom and the unity or *interdependence* of body and mind appears in a paradigm way in the work of Schelling, for instance, who argues in *Philosophical Investigations into the Essence of Human Freedom* (1809) that "spirit" and "ground" are co-positing and that Idealism and Realism

---

14. Denys Turner, *Thomas Aquinas: A Portrait* (New Haven, CT: Yale University Press, 2013), pp. 62–69.

15. Immanuel Kant, *Anthropology from a Pragmatic Perspective*, ed. Robert B. Louden (Cambridge: Cambridge University Press, 2006), p. 3. It is also worth considering Kant's proximity to Hamann and especially to Herder with respect to his understanding of language (though not in the three Critiques). On this, see the illuminating study by Michael N. Forster, 'Kant's Philosophy of Language,' *Tijdschrift voor Filosophie*, 74/2012, pp. 485–511.

16. Kant, *Anthropology*, p. 4.

17. Ibid. p. 3.

therefore need to be conceived of as interdependent: "Idealism is the soul of philosophy; realism is the body; only both together can constitute a living whole. The latter can never provide the principle but must be the ground and medium in which the former makes itself real and takes on flesh and blood."[18] In a parallel way, the Romantic poet and philosopher Friedrich Schiller develops an account of our unity as body and mind in terms specifically of freedom and beauty. In his piece on communication, *On the Necessary Limits of the Beautiful*, Schiller argues that the "thickly" embodied communication of ideas has a strongly aesthetic or attractive effect upon others. He identifies this with poetry and art, but the principle remains for Schiller that our ethical rationality comes to expression in our bodily form as freedom and in a way that triggers "taste" or the apprehension of beauty.[19]

Paul Ricoeur

An emphasis upon the unity of the self as both body and mind, and the accompanying question of our human freedom, appears in a particular way too in the philosophical hermeneutics of Paul Ricoeur. Ricoeur is potentially one of the closest interlocutors for the new "neuroanthropological perspective." His emphasis upon the "pre-thematic" as a dimension of our experience (or locatedness within the world) is an important prefiguring of the contemporary neuroscientific concern with extensive brain activation that underlies phenomenal consciousness. Neurological data locates consciousness as a feature of the mind–body relation, and processes of meaning are already co-terminous with our embodiment (in our "embodied cognition"), at a point prior to the distinctively self-aware processing of information that takes place within consciousness. It can be difficult to judge the boundary at which processing and feedback loops become self-aware or enter consciousness. Consciousness in this sense can be associated with the interconnectivity of the brain, which, according to Bernard Baars's "global workspace theory," suggests that a key function of self-aware consciousness is the managing of conflicting brain activation

---

18. F. W. J. Schelling, *Philosophical Investigations into the Essence of Human Freedom* (Albany: SUNY, 2006), p. 26.

19. There is an interesting contrast here with Kant, of course. David C. Schindler offers extensive discussions of both Schiller and Schelling, together with Hegel, in his engaging *The Perfection of Freedom* (Eugene, OR: Cascade Books, 2012).

at the pre-thematic level.[20] This supports Ricoeur's important intuition that consciousness is already placed *in medias res* and in ongoing processes of interpretation and "participatory sense-making" in the world.[21]

In *Phenomenology and Hermeneutics* (1975), Ricoeur develops his critique of Husserl's self-positing, preferring to emphasize the more fundamental and embodied nature of our "belonging to the world" (in Gadamer's phrase[22]) as being prior to the cogito. Ricoeur identifies this "belonging-to" most directly with our "live" intensity of our human face-to-face encounters. But at the same time, he measures the immediacy of the pre-thematic dimensions of this encounter against philosophy's requirement for a "distantiation" within experience that will support a structure that oscillates between "remoteness" and "proximity."[23] Our philosophical understanding cannot function in the face of pure immediacy or unadulterated difference: The very process of interpretation involves discovering ourselves within language, and yet also doing so at an objectifying distance. It is not the "polysemy of words in conversation," then, to which we should turn, for Ricoeur, but rather the "polysemy of texts." Here "the meaning of the text has become autonomous in relation to the intention of the author, the critical situation of discourse, and its first addressee," with the consequence that we can now find the "distantiation" that allows proper critical or, in fact, self-critical understanding.[24]

What he calls "the moment of suspicion" and "the critique of ideology," which form the basis of this critical self-understanding, are grounded, not in the original intentionality of the author of the text, but rather in the text's capacity to *refer*[25]: "By this I mean that what is finally to be understood in a text is not the author or his presumed intention, nor is it the immanent structure or structures of the text, but rather the sort of world intended beyond the text as its reference."[26] Ricoeur identifies what he calls this "world of the

---

20. Bernard J. Baars, *In the Theater of Consciousness* (New York: Oxford University Press, 1997).

21. Ezequiel Di Paulo and Hanne de Jaegher, "The Interactive Brain Hypothesis," *Frontiers in Human Neuroscience* 6 (2012): 163.

22. Paul Ricoeur, "Toward a Hermeneutic of the Idea of Revelation," *Harvard Theological Review* 70(1/2) (January–April 1977): 1–37, here 28.

23. Paul Ricoeur, "Phenomenology and Hermeneutics," *Noûs* 9(1) (1975): 85–102, here 88–92.

24. Ibid., p. 90.

25. Ibid., p. 98.

26. Ricoeur, "Toward a Hermeneutic of the Idea of Revelation," p. 23. In a memorable phrase, Ricoeur also says of the cogito here that it is "as abstract and empty as it is invincible."

text" with the communication of our "belonging-to," at a level that is deeper than the thematic or discursive levels of the text itself, just as it lies deeper, too, than the cogito (whether of the reader or the author). For Ricoeur it is precisely the task of the responsive reader to "display" or "unfold" this sense of "world" in a relation that Ricoeur describes as being "before" (or "in front of") the text.[27] Since it is the belonging-to that is disclosed in the text, as the form of its fundamental reference, Ricoeur identifies here the possibility of a real self-critique that lays bare the authenticity and inauthenticity of our "pre-comprehension" (or presuppositions) that we bring to the text and that the text, in its newness, has the power to dispel.[28] This is based in the discovery of a potential world that I could inhabit, or a potential mode of being in the world. And so it is in "the moment of suspicion" or "critique of ideologies" that we can discern new possibilities of existence.[29] "The question is no longer to define hermeneutics as an inquiry into the psychological intentions which are hidden in the text, but as the explication of the being-in-the-world shown by the text. What is to be interpreted in the text is the projection of a world which I could inhabit."[30]

From a neuroanthropological perspective, then, the key point in Ricoeur's hermeneutics will be precisely the principle that consciousness is not self-sufficient for meaning, but that "consciousness has its meaning beyond itself."[31] Ricoeur draws this out clearly in his embrace of the phenomenological inheritance in terms of its intentionality and *noemata*, which means to say the affirmation that there exist within consciousness, in traceable form, the same relational structures of reality that are presupposed in the natural attitude. This has the consequence that Ricoeur's turn to hermeneutics, and to language, does not mean that language replaces world. Rather, for Ricoeur's *phenomenological* hermeneutics, language is the "articulation" of the world's structures as "denomination, predication, syntactical liaison etc."[32] For Ricoeur, language always stands in relation

---

27. Ricoeur, "Phenomenology and Hermeneutics," p. 93.

28. Ibid. p. 92.

29. Ibid., p. 98. In his text "Toward a Hermeneutic of the Idea of Revelation," Ricoeur explores the possibility of developing this hermeneutical approach explicitly in terms of "revelation."

30. Ibid., p. 93.

31. Ibid., p. 94.

32. Ibid., pp. 98–99.

to world, which in some sense always exists beyond language. It is world, then, which is to say our meaningful relation with or in the world, that must be the starting point for a philosophy whose concern with meaning is finally grounded in our answerability to something that is beyond ourselves: "Even if it is true that every experience has a 'linguistic dimension', and that this *Sprachlichkeit* permeates every experience, it is not, however, with the *Sprachlichkeit* that a hermeneutical philosophy must begin. It is first necessary to say *what is brought to language*."[33]

New Hermeneutics

In great part, the modern Western philosophical tradition has itself been defined in terms of its extensive and productive internalization of new scientific knowledge, or alternatively in terms of its resistance to science and to "scientific" philosophies, whether of an empiricist or Idealist kind. Looking back to Descartes, Hume, and Kant, it seems reasonable that we should at least pose the question: What is changed *philosophically* by the new knowledge about ourselves that comes to us from contemporary neuroscience as this interacts with culture? Arguably, neuroanthropology stands in a tradition that goes back to Kant's *Anthropology from a Pragmatic Point of View*, in which Kant laments that we do not understand "the cranial nerves and fibers" of our physiology.[34] Since today we do have a far greater understanding of these, the implication might be that we can therefore potentially grasp the human more fully than before, precisely in philosophical or "anthropological" terms.

To address the key issues of our unity as both body and mind (our "nondualism"), together with the problematic of our "freedom," and their relation philosophically, from a neuroanthropological perspective, we need to look more closely at brain activation at the point of our "belonging-to" the world, as envisaged by Paul Ricoeur. We can begin by noting that social cognition (cognition of the other) is effectively the "default position" of the human brain, and so may be judged to offer quite fundamental access to the human.[35] But since high levels of social

---

33. Ibid., p. 98 (my italics in final line).

34. See p. 157 above.

35. Rogier B. Mars, Franz-Xaver Neubert, Mary Ann P. Noonan, Jerome Sallet, Ivan Toni, and Matthew F. S. Rushworth, "On the Relationship Between the 'Default Mode Network' and the 'Social Brain,'" *Frontiers in Human Neuroscience*, doi.10.3389/fnhum.2012.001.

cooperation have been typical of hominins for more than two million years, this may not be so surprising. Strong, communicative sociality is also the common inheritance of higher primates and other advanced animals. If cooperative sociality has been our evolutionary specialization, from very early times, then it is small wonder that the brain should turn out to be above all a social organ.

Contemporary neuroscience gives us access to the deep and ancient sociality of the human brain.[36] Its structure has been identified as cognitive, affective, and empathetic, even though it is prior to consciousness, which is to say that it is pre-thematic or prelinguistic (evidence for advanced human language being relatively recent in the archaeological record). In the interactive face-to-face, a set of physical reflexes are in play whereby rich information is exchanged within spontaneous, interactive, inter-body reflexes that often occur at intervals of milliseconds, and so are too fast for conscious perception.[37] The pre-thematic reflex processes of "social cognition" can be defined in the following way: "The point of departure is a fundamental understanding of cognitive processes: a cognitive system is a system which in its reaction to environmental stimuli shows some degree of flexibility, a factor that is made possible by internal information processing."[38]

This means that the interrelational communication that takes place between bodies in "online" social cognition (i.e., in the actuality of the face-to-face) is itself "organic" in that our interactive responses are guided by the information about each other that is constantly being exchanged. We are familiar with this at the thematic or linguistic level of speech by which we exchange information consciously, but it is thought-provoking to realize that a comparable exchange is taking place in the primitive "motor system" of our purely physical responses. This has been summarized in the following terms: "When we interact with another person, our brains and bodies are no longer isolated, but immersed in an environment with the other person, in which we become a coupled unit through

---

36. I am grateful to Prof. Kai Vogeley and Prof. Gary Bente of the University of Cologne, and to Prof. Rüdiger Seitz of the Heinrich-Heine University, Düsseldorf, for their generous advice on this topic and fully acknowledge any shortcomings as my own.

37. Ezequiel Di Paulo and Hanne de Jaegher, "The Interactive Brain Hypothesis," *Frontiers in Human Neuroscience*, doi:10.3389/fnhum.2012.00163.

38. K. Vogeley, L. Schilbach, and A. Newen, "Soziale Kognition," in G. Hartung and M. Herrgen M (eds.), *Interdisziplinäre Anthropologie* (Heidelberg: Springer VS, 2014), pp. 13–39.

a continuous moment-to-moment mutual adaptation of our own actions and the actions of the other."[39] What is being described here is a series of very rapid interactions that are "complex, multi-layered, self-organizing," involving a whole set of mutual responses ranging from eye movement, facial expression, and gesture to the synchrony of brain waves: a subtle and pervasive "alignment of behaviour" that includes "synergies, co-ordination and phase attraction."[40] One person engages with another through neural coupling or imitation and through phase symmetry as the rhythms of breathing and heartbeat align. In other words, not just posture, gesture, and speech become shaped to one another, but also the internal rhythms of brain and anatomy synchronize.

We are used to thinking of the pre-thematic dimensions of our bodily self as being somehow blank, lacking the sophisticated capacities of our conscious, linguistic self. This is our creaturely "instinctive" self. We have operated with a sharp distinction between our linguistic, rational self and the "subliminal" self of our biology and unconscious life. But the data from the neuroscience of social cognition show a quite different state of affairs. In addition to the affectivity, empathy, and interrelationality of our socially cognitive motor system, very high levels of *valuation* (associated with the medial prefrontal cortex) are also in play.[41] The evolutionary advantage lies in *accurate* reading of the other, through "participative sense-making," which also unlocks rapid and robust forms of bonding.[42] The motor system state of "rapport," as it has been called, includes within itself evaluative systems that assess the relative success of the "dance" or formation of the social matrix that functions between human beings. That this is genuine reasoning, albeit "implicit" reasoning, is borne out by the considerable challenges it poses to the human brain, in the live encounter with the human other. Integrating incommensurable sources of first- and second-hand knowledge about the other in the face-to-face can prove too demanding and is associated with cognitive impairment in social

---

39. Ivana Konvalinka and Andreas Roepstorff, "The Two-Brain Approach: How Can Mutually Interacting Brains Teach Us Something About Social Interaction?" *Frontiers in Human Neuroscience*, doi.10.3389/fnhum.2012.00215.

40. Ibid.

41. Rüdiger J. Seitz, Matthias Franz, and Nina P. Azari, "Value Judgments and Self-Control of Action: The Role of the Medial Frontal Cortex," *Brain Research Reviews* 60(2) 2009: 368–78. doi:10.1016/j.brainresrev.2009.02.003.

42. See note 36.

cognition.[43] The "participatory" nature of this particular form of interhuman "sense-making" reaffirms just how deeply within reality, with all its organic complexity, these rich processes of evaluation are taking place. We are, of course, largely unaware of them as such (although they communicate to us as a "feeling" we have about the other), but contemporary brain imaging shows that they are nevertheless in themselves real enough and that they constitute the deep structure of our sociality at the intense level of our prelinguistic, preconscious life.

Our conscious, social responses are, of course, dominated by our language use, entailing the choosing of *parole* from *langue* (as de Saussure has it), which brings with it the kind of reflexive and responsible judgment we associate with culture and freedom.[44] But it would be wrong, nevertheless, to think that these are wholly different spheres. In effect, each stands in continuity with the other, within the unity of the self as both body and mind. It is this structure of the overall dynamic unity of the self that allows us to read the relation between our conscious, linguistic socioethical reasoning and our preconscious, prelinguistic evaluative-social reasoning in terms of a possible convergence of the former with the latter. Where we are guided by a socioethical concern for the human other, our conscious self-embarks on a journey of decentering self-dispossession, as we feel our way into, or receive, the affective promptings, empathetic, compassionate perceptions, and sense of interdependence and vulnerability—even mortality perhaps—within contingency, of our pre-thematic embodied self. Here the conscious, linguistic self begins to lose its fine-grained control, and reasoning becomes an open, participative process within the complex real, ultimately moving beyond all possibility of a calculative resolution.[45]

Paul Ricoeur and Neuroanthropology

We need now to ask what kind of philosophy might be generated by this new scientific knowledge of the self we have today, in the context of the

---

43. Bojana Kuzmanovich, Leonhard Schilbach, Fritz-Georg Lehnhardt, Gary Bente, and Kai Vogeley, "A Matter of Words: Impact of Verbal and Non-verbal Information on Impression Formation in High-Functioning Autism," *Research in Autism Spectrum Disorders* 5 (2011): 604–13. doi:10.1016/j.rasd.2010.07.005

44. Ferdinand De Saussure, *Course in General Linguistics*, 3rd ed., transl. R. Harris (Chicago: Open Court Publishing Company, 1986), pp. 9–10, 15.

45. Paul D. Janz, *The Command of Grace: A New Theological Apologetics* (London and New York: T & T Clark, 2009).

hermeneutical turn of Paul Ricoeur, as the basis for a pneumatology in an neuroanthropological perspective. For Ricoeur, what he calls our "belonging-to" the world is the site of an irreducible immediacy, which is not accessible to philosophical analysis at all, since it lies deeper than the subject–object divide. Ricoeur's critique of the Husserlian cogito is precisely that it is self-positing at the level of objectifying consciousness or the subject–object divide, whereas it is in fact preceded by a "relationship of inclusion," prior to the subject–object divide. This is what Ricoeur captures in the term "belonging-to" as "the ontological condition [. . .] thanks to which the inquirer shares in the thing he questions."[46] Ricoeur speaks here of the need for a methodological "regression from the idea of scientificity to the ontological condition of belonging-to."[47] Of course, for Ricoeur, that ontological condition becomes critically accessible to us, or "objectifiable," only through the study of texts where, as readers, we allow the primary power of reference of the text to come into view. This is the way in which a text can convey to us the sense of a "world" (the "world of the text") as a "world" in which we might belong. It is this testing and renewing of our capacity for belonging to the world, through texts, that underlies Ricoeur's commitment to a far-reaching "critique of ideologies."

For our present discussion, we need first critically to interrogate Ricoeur's key term of "scientificity," by which he means the objectifying, determining, and ultimately controlling power of the Husserlian cogito. The findings of contemporary neuroanthropology suggest that science now affords a visibility that goes beyond the Husserlian "scientificity" and extends directly into the pre-thematic "belonging-to." Here the multiple, self-organizing reflexes that are "outside our full control" exhibit a highly ambivalent ontology.[48] They constitute a structure that is both "myself" or "ourself" and "world" at the same time. The observed synchrony, symmetry, and resonance *between* human beings is said "to enact a world," pointing to the ambiguity of this social "in-between," which is foundational to who we are, but also self-regulating material processes, which are equally

---

46. Ricoeur, "Phenomenology and Hermeneutics," pp. 88–89.

47. Ibid., p. 89. Ricoeur rejects the Husserlian designation of ontology as "finitude," since it poses the "limit" to subjectivity, on the grounds that it "designates in negative terms an entirely positive condition." Perhaps we can hear a subtle appeal here to a Levinasian framework of "infinity" that Ricoeur associates with our search for meaning as such in the world to which we belong (Ricoeur, "Phenomenology and Hermeneutics," p. 88).

48. See note 36.

to be defined as "world," or as "world in us."[49] Another team has referred to it as "dark matter," using metaphor to emphasize its "strangeness."[50] We should think of our modern, advanced linguistic consciousness as arising from the ancient interactivity of the face-to-face that itself is world that is in us and between us.

This returns us to the question of how "world" is understood in Ricoeur and how it can be refigured philosophically on the basis of the contemporary neurology of social cognition. The key point of difference between a Ricoeurian and post-Ricoeurian, neuroanthropological perspective lies, therefore, in how we answer the question of what appears in language. For Ricoeur, the hermeneutical philosophy he is advocating cannot begin with linguisticality (*Sprachlichkeit*), but first it is necessary "to say *what is brought to language*."[51] World is defined as that which is inscribed in language, to which we belong most fundamentally in our pre-thematic belonging-to. But from a neuroanthropological perspective, our belonging to the world is already defined differently: as a structure that is both "myself" or "ourself" and "world" *at the same time*. As a structure, this accords with Ricoeur's need for a certain "distantiation" or oscillation between "remoteness" and "proximity" that is the primary basis for philosophy. But what kind of philosophy will the structure of the "in-between" support? Not an extension into texts, certainly (at least not primarily so). Rather, it finds its necessary objectivity within the face-to-face itself, and in the structure that neuroscience observes of a certain symmetry between the pre-thematic processes of evaluation within "rapport," and our own higher-level, socioethical reasoning for or with another. In other words, it is not our potential relation to world that is prior here, according to this observed structure, but something more immediate and more fundamental. *It is the relation of the mind itself to its own embodiment, precisely as this is mediated according to the freedom that is a given of language.* In other words, the unifying process we have defined as "convergence" is itself the precondition for our being in the world, at the critical depth to which Ricoeur rightly aspires. But this is not now a relation of reference and the critique of ideologies; it is rather a critical relation that is internal to the human

---

49. See note 36.

50. Leonhard Schilbach, Bert Timmermans, Vasudevi Reddy, Alan Costell, Gary Bente, Tobias Schlicht, and Kai Vogeley, "Towards a Second Person Neuroscience," *Behavioural and Brain Sciences* 36(4) (2013): 393–414. doi:10.1017/S0140525X12000660.

51. Ricoeur, "Phenomenology and Hermeneutics," p. 98 (my italics in final line).

being concerned, though one that is mediated by the exchange with the other and by the full, linguistically performed recognition of the other, as one who is equal to ourselves.

In both a Ricoeurian and post-Ricoeurian hermeneutics, *Sprachlichkeit* is key, then, but its freighting—or what is *"brought to language"*—differs. For Ricoeur, it is world that is brought to language. For neuroanthropology, on the other hand, it is the human body itself that comes into presence in our decentered and other-oriented language, as integral to our authentic being in the world. In short, then, between our linguistic consciousness (the cogito who speaks and thinks) and the world to which we belong in pre-thematic ways, a post-Ricoeurian hermeneutics inserts the human body itself, *in its interrelation with another human body*. On the basis of what we know at second hand, or scientifically, it is reasonable to affirm, too, that this conscious, linguistic, social relation is itself a self-reflexive recapitulation of the social matrix of our pre-thematic "in-between." From a neuroanthropological perspective, this would then mean that that matrix can be said to come to expression in language, as the fertile and vital power of our ancient embodied life.

Pneumatology in Neuroanthropological Perspective

A scripturally and dogmatically grounded pneumatology in neuroanthropological perspective for today will ground the work of the Spirit in the movement of the creation itself toward God and the Incarnation. This movement can be identified with the emergence of the "enacted world" of the human "in-between" as the possibility of culture, personhood, and relation. Here again our unity as body and mind on the one hand, and our freedom on the other, as established within the neuroanthropological perspective, will be uppermost, captured now in the distinctively theological idiom of glorification.

Any pneumatology has to begin with the moment of the descent of the Holy Spirit at Pentecost, and so the establishment of a new field of social and personal possibilities we can identify with Church. According to Acts 2:33, the source of the Holy Spirit is the exalted body of Jesus and it is Jesus in heaven, who "received from the Father the promise of the Holy Spirit" and "has poured out" the Spirit upon the people (in a way that impacts upon their senses: "this that you both see and hear"). Exaltation is a state of glory that affirms the unity of Christ as the embodied fullness of divine-human hypostasis, but also his freedom as sovereign Creator in the midst of creation. It affirms his unparalleled freedom from sin and death and from the limits of the natural material order.[52] Indeed, the life of Jesus in the scriptural narrative is the realization of the unity of the created order in him, and its liberation "into the freedom of the glory of the children of God" (cf. Rom. 8:21).

To highlight the structure of our own negotiations of this freedom and calling to freedom, in the reception of the Holy Spirit, we can consider two texts: from Ezekiel 36 and from 2 Corinthians. In the Old Testament text, following God's command, Ezekiel prophesies that the land of Israel is to be liberated from foreign dominion and is to become once again their home and a time and place of flourishing for God's people: "I will take you from the nations, and gather you from all the countries, and bring you into your own land" (Ezek. 36:24). At Ezekiel 37:1–14, the prophet continues to prophesy to the "dry bones," and the Spirit gives life to the bones, through the utterance of the prophet at God's command: "Thus says the Lord God to these bones: I will cause breath to enter you, and you shall live" (Ezek. 37:5). The motif of freeing the land, which has fallen into "the possession of the rest of the nations" (Ezek. 36:3), is matched by the motif of freeing the people of Israel from their state of death and restoring to them the freedom of physical movement that is the ground of embodied human life in its personal, responsible, and receptive capacities.

We can already see here that a link between speech and Spirit is in play. It is the force of prophecy that gives life to the dry bones, through the Spirit. Moreover, Ezekiel's life-giving prophecy is specifically performed at God's command, and so the prophet's own human freedom is fulfilled through his self-offering in the power of speaking for God's sake. This sacrificial motif is further affirmed in the passage: "I will sprinkle clean water upon you, and you shall be clean from all your uncleannesses, and from all your idols I will cleanse you. A new heart I will give you, and a new spirit I will put within you; and I will remove from your body the heart of stone and give you a heart of flesh" (Ezek. 36:25–26). From the perspective of a neuroanthropological pneumatology, therefore, we can say that the prophet is being set free in his own "deep sociality" (interactive, self-organizing, social matrix), which is his own point of contact with, or

---

52. René Virgoulay captures this very well in his two-part article "Phénoménologie du corps et théologie de la résurrection," *Revue des sciences religieuses* 54 (1980): 323–336, and *Revue des sciences religieuses* 55 (1981): 52–75.

rootedness in, the world (the prophet's own "creatureliness" or embodied proximity to life). This transformational liberation occurs through divine grace and is the Spirit's work. Indeed, we can say that this same fount of life comes into presence, with healing and sanctifying effects, through the Spirit's work *as he speaks* (since speaking is also the expression of that interior embodiment or belonging to the world). This presence can be associated with the realization of the prophet's own personhood in the here and now of his speaking, but it is nevertheless greater than himself. It is also the coming to expression culturally of world as created and as formed by the Holy Spirit. It is the place in which the prophet is both unified in himself and also set free since, in his inspired speaking, he is one with the world, which exists in him, as it is now flooded with the life of the Spirit and taken up into God.

The structure that comes into view here is one of Spirit-indwelling and Spirit-inspired freedom, in which it is the hidden life of the ancient inheritance within us—the interactive, self-organizing, social matrix as world—that comes to living expression in the prophet's live and active speech to Israel. We can see this same combination of freedom, Spirit, and self-decentering speech in 2 Corinthians 3, where St. Paul is concerned to distinguish the authority of the true apostle from the false. The false apostles are in possession of a letter or letters that have a purely secular authority.[53] Here we find an allusion to the same Ezekiel passage in St. Paul's reference to the community at Corinth as being "a letter of Christ, prepared by us, written not with ink but with the Spirit of the living God, not on tablets of stone but on tablets of human hearts" (2 Cor. 3:3). St. Paul contrasts the two covenants, noting that even with the letters written on "stone tablets" rather than the living human body, the glory of Moses's face (who had received the tablets of the covenant in the face-to-face with God) was too great for the people of Israel to look upon him and so Moses "put a veil over his face" (2 Cor. 3:7–8, 13). But the evangelist of the second covenant has far more boldness to proclaim the Good News openly, since "Now the Lord is the Spirit and where the Spirit of the Lord is, there is freedom" (2 Cor. 3:17). The true Christian can preach for "we do not proclaim ourselves; we proclaim Jesus Christ as Lord and ourselves as your slaves for Jesus's sake" (2 Cor. 4:5).

---

53. Oliver Davies, "Spirit, Body and Letter," in Paul Fiddes and Günter Bader (eds.), *The Spirit and the Letter: A Christian Tradition and its Late Modern Reversal* (London: T & T Clark/Continuum, 2013), pp. 179–94.

Once again, then, we can say that the social matrix of our deep belonging in the world comes into presence in how we speak (here as proclaiming Christ), effecting change in others, and constituting the new shared
life of a Spirit-filled ecclesial community. In the proclamation of Jesus, the
social matrix, as this is shaped and enlivened by the Holy Spirit, comes
into view as the place of Christ's indwelling and, as such, is a Trinitarian
space of material social enactment (cf. Matt. 18:20: "where two or three are
gathered in my name, I am there among them").

But what might that mean for our own inner orientation, as this is
brought about through the presence of the Holy Spirit within us? If speaking "in the Spirit" brings our own linguistic consciousness into convergence with the far more ancient inheritance of social cognition that we
bear within us, then what might the testimony of the Spirit in us be, at this
embodied, pre-thematic level? How might we recognize as self-possessing
human spirit the Spirit's work? The answer to this question lies in the
nature of freedom as such and of our capacity to be free. Our own human
freedom sits most deeply in the pulse and breath that give us life. This
freedom of movement is utterly our own, but it is nevertheless a dependent freedom: We do not freely control the movements of our own pulse
and breath. It is a freedom that is gifted to us: Whatever our beliefs, this is
our *createdness*. Being *free* is how we are made.

But what are the human conditions of our being free, dependently?
What is the signal that we are working with our createdness? Or to put
this in Pauline terms: Where does the "hope" come from that is "poured
into our hearts through the Holy Spirit" and that "does not disappoint
us" (Rom. 5:5)? We are looking here for an orientation within the human
that begins before proclamation and that is even more fundamental than
"hope." And perhaps the answer lies elsewhere in Romans, in St. Paul's
"spirit of adoption": "For you did not receive a spirit of slavery to fall back
into fear, but you have received a spirit of adoption. When we cry 'Abba!
Father!' it is that very Spirit bearing witness with our spirit that we are
children of God, and if children, then heirs" (Rom. 8:15–17). "Adoption"
or "sonship" evokes the powerful, pre-thematic language of human bonding. Here linguistic consciousness is contracted to its most essential core
("Father!"), and we are brought before our most essential human "belonging together," which is predicated on present, interpersonal relation in the
face-to-face rather than past causality, or social hierarchy.

If the Spirit is already active at a pre-thematic level prior to linguistic
consciousness, then the signature of the work of the Spirit at this most

fundamental level may be as simple, though essential, as our willingness to look the other in the eye: to turn our face toward them. Such a reception of the other, through the exchange that is face-to-face relation, is arguably the most basic freedom we have, as linguistic consciousness. It is always in our power as adults to refuse the invitation of the other's face. Here, then, is the ground of our freedom to choose rather than to resist relation. And we are already instinctively drawn to the other's face, to the face of our neighbor, through our social biology. The Spirit, at work in the creation, has shaped us in that way. And so, perhaps, it is the reception of the neighbor, which is the first work of our spirit as the Spirit's creature, that is also our first acceptance of the work of the Spirit in us and between us; and so too is the ground of our hope.

8

Art, Beauty, and the Testimony
of the Spirit

Steven R. Guthrie

THE PHRASE "TESTIMONY of the Spirit" is often associated with Calvin's discussion of the *testimonium spiritus sancti internum*, a discussion that asserts the authoritative status of scripture. Even as he insists upon the authority of scripture, however, Calvin points beyond scripture alone. He writes:

> If we regard the Spirit of God as the sole fountain of truth, we shall neither reject the truth itself, nor despise it wherever it shall appear, unless we wish to dishonor the Spirit of God.... We ought not to forget those most excellent benefits of the divine Spirit, which he distributes to whomever he wills, for the common good of mankind. The understanding and knowledge of Bezalel and Oholiab needed to construct the Tabernacle had to be instilled in them by the Spirit of God. It is no wonder, then, that the knowledge of all that is most excellent in human life is said to be communicated to us through the Spirit of God.... He fills, moves, and quickens all things by the power of the same Spirit, according to the character that he bestowed upon each kind by the law of creation.[1]

---

1. John Calvin, *Institutes of the Christian Religion*, trans. Ford Lewis Battles (Philadelphia: Westminster, 1960), pp. 273–74, 275.

It is worth observing that in insisting upon the Spirit's widespread and ongoing testimony, Calvin—not usually noted as a champion of the arts—specifically mentions Bezalel and Oholiab. These are the artists who in the Old Testament were "filled with the divine spirit . . . to devise artistic designs" (Exod. 31:3, 4, NRSV). And of course, Calvin is not unique in suggesting that God's Spirit speaks through artistic beauty. Many, in fact, both within and outside the Christian tradition, have felt that the arts are one of the sites where we are particularly liable to hear the voice of the "divine spirit." As we will see, figures as diverse as Plato, Schiller, Shelley, Tolstoy, Santayana, and Gadamer have all suggested that there is some sort of affinity between art and the realm of the spirit—admittedly, often in ways vastly different from one another. Likewise, in the broader culture and among the general public there is the intuition that there is something "spiritual" about the arts. Hints of this sort of association can be discerned in contemporary worship services as well, where "worship" has come to be almost wholly synonymous with the musical portions of the service. Outside the church, it is this intuition that stands behind the cliché that "Museums are the New Churches."[2]

Is it the case, then, that the Holy Spirit is specially active and articulate in the creative arts? And if so, what sort of testimony does the Spirit offer in these instances? We will consider several different answers that have been offered to these questions—both from within and outside the Christian tradition.[3]

Art and Spirit Possession

One historically significant proposal draws a clear and uninterrupted line between art and spirit. Perhaps, this tradition suggests, the divine spirit speaks very directly through the arts. Perhaps the artist is nothing but the pathway, the conduit, through which the Spirit travels. When the artist opens her mouth, it is the voice of God we hear. In fact, we gesture toward this tradition each time we describe a work as "inspired." The artist, the etymology of the term suggests, is one who is "breathed into"—"en-spirited."

---

2. Justin Farago, "Why Museums Are the New Churches" (July 16, 2015). *BBC Culture* website. http://www.bbc.com/culture/story/20150716-why-museums-are-the-new-churches. Accessed October 19, 2015.

3. Some of the themes that follow are also developed in Steven R. Guthrie, *Creator Spirit: The Holy Spirit and the Art of Becoming Human* (Grand Rapids, MI: Baker Academic, 2011).

This conception of the poet "as a medium who reveals divinely inspired words is by far the oldest understanding [of the poet] in the Greek tradition, and many others besides."[4]

One of the clearest descriptions of this idea is found in Plato's dialogue *Ion*. The dialogue describes a meeting between Socrates and Ion, who is a *rhapsode*—a professional performer of poetry. Ion is returning from the festival of Asclepius in high spirits, as he has just won first prize for his performance. Flush with his own success, Ion gives his vanity full rein. He exclaims: "I think I speak more beautifully than anyone else about Homer ... [no one else] past or present could offer as many beautiful thoughts about Homer as I can."[5] Socrates, however, offers a different account of Ion's skill. "That's not a subject you've mastered—speaking well about Homer," Socrates declares.

> It's a divine power that moves you, as a "Magnetic" stone moves iron rings ... and the power in all of them depends on this stone. In the same way, the Muse makes some people inspired herself, and then through those who are inspired a chain of other enthusiasts is suspended. You know, none of the epic poets, if they're good, are masters of their subject; they are inspired, possessed, and that is how they utter all of those beautiful poems.[6]

According to Socrates, then, the powerful performance does not come *from* but rather *through* the rhapsode. As a piece of iron carries the electric charge of a magnet, so Ion carries the charge of the Muse. The rhapsode is the copper wire along which the divine current runs. In fact, Socrates contends, this divine possession begins even before the poem reaches Ion. The poets themselves "are inspired, possessed, and that is how they utter all of those beautiful poems." Indeed, Socrates could easily be referring to the opening lines of *The Odyssey*: "*Sing in me*, Muse, and *through me* tell the

4. Darrin McMahon, *Divine Fury: A History of Genius* (New York: Basic Books, 2013), p. 10. Both Hesiod and Homer point to the "pneumatic source of poetic revelations, which are blown directly into the mind by the Muse. When we consider that poetry itself comes from the verb *poeien*, [*sic*.: *poiein*] to create, it follows clearly enough that poems are the creation of the gods, realized through their human artisans and agents" (McMahon, *Divine Fury*, p. 11).

5. Plato, *Two Comic Dialogues: Ion and Hippias Major*, trans. Paul Woodruff (Indianapolis: Hackett, 1983), p. 21.

6. Plato, *Ion*, p. 25.

story."[7] If Homer's prayer is answered, then neither Homer nor Ion can claim ownership of their words. When Homer opens his mouth, the voice singing in him is that of the Muse. And when Ion's listeners respond to his recitation, it is the power of the Muse that moves them.

Socrates draws out a further implication of this picture of divine inspiration. If the power of the poem derives from the Muse, then any active contribution from the human artist actually jeopardizes the work of art. To be effective, the Muse's activity must be matched by the artist's passivity. "That's why the god takes [the poets'] intellect away from them when he uses them as his servants, as he does prophets and godly diviners," Socrates explains. Why? "So that we who hear should know that they are not the ones who speak those verses that are of such high value, for their intellect is not in them."[8] The rhapsode speaks, but he does not speak. Homer's words are heard, but it is not Homer that we hear.

What we should notice is that Plato's dialogue advances not only a theory of artistic creativity, but also a theology. Socrates's exchange offers a picture of the relationship between divine and human activity. According to the dialogue, if the divine spirit is *active*, then the poet must be *passive*; if the divine voice is to be heard, then the human voice must be silenced. The Muse "takes possession" of the poet and "robs him of his intellect." Here then is one theology of divine involvement in the creative arts, but one that comes at a considerable cost.

Art and Spirit Gifting

The question we have been pursuing is whether we might expect to hear the voice of the Holy Spirit in human artistry. In his questioning of Ion, however, Socrates turns that inquiry inside out. Instead, he wonders whether one should claim to hear a *human* voice while attending to divinely inspired art. In *Ion* the sounding of the spirit's voice means a corresponding silencing of the human artist.

In fact, the very idea of divine inspiration has sometimes been criticized for just this reason. Such an idea, it is objected, destroys the humanity of the resulting work and negates the real agency of the human creator.

---

7. Homer, *The Odyssey*, trans. Robert Fitzgerald (New York: Vintage Classics, 1961), p. 1. My emphasis.

8. Plato, *Ion*, p. 26.

Moreover, it fails to acknowledge the historically and culturally "situated" character of artistic creation (that is, the ways in which works of art emerge from and reflect particular human cultures). The 19th-century poet Samuel Taylor Coleridge expresses just these concerns. They are concerns that arise in his discussion of the idea of the inspiration of scripture, but they would apply with equal force to *Ion*'s conception of artistic inspiration. The idea of divine inspiration, he writes,

> petrifies at once the whole body of Holy Writ with all its harmonies and symmetrical gradations.... This breathing organism, this glorious panharmonicon which I had seen stand on its feet as a man, and with a man's voice given to it, the doctrine in question turns at once into a colossal Memnon's head, a hollow passage for a voice, a voice that mocks the voices of many men, and speaks in their names, and yet is but one voice, and the same; and no man uttered it, and never in a human heart was it conceived.[9]

In considering the possibility that the Spirit speaks through the arts, then, we are met immediately with a concern: Does the assertion of divine creativity mean the annihilation of human creativity? If we say that the Holy Spirit testifies through the arts, do we make of the human artist merely "a hollow passage for a voice"?

From Possession to Gift

If Socrates inverts our initial question about creativity, then a Christian theology of the Holy Spirit likewise inverts Plato's pneumatology. The activity of Ion's muse is described as "possession." The Holy Spirit on the other hand is described as the giver of gifts. The Nicene Creed refers to the Spirit as "the Lord, *the giver* of life," and of course, many passages in both Old and New Testament speak of the gifts of the Spirit. Perhaps the best known example is 1 Corinthians 12:

> Now there are varieties of gifts, but the same Spirit ... To one is given through the Spirit the utterance of wisdom, and to another the utterance of knowledge according to the same Spirit, to another

9. Samuel Taylor Coleridge, *Letters on the Inspiration of Scripture*, Letter III. *The Complete Works of Samuel Taylor Coleridge*, Vol. 5 (New York: Harper and Brothers, 1884), p. 591.

faith by the same Spirit, to another gifts of healing by the one Spirit. (1 Cor. 12:4, 8–9, NRSV)

Or again, we might return to Exodus 31, where God fills Bezalel and Oholiab:

The LORD spoke to Moses: See, I have called by name Bezalel son of Uri son of Hur, of the tribe of Judah: and I have filled him with divine spirit, with ability, intelligence, and knowledge in every kind of craft, to devise artistic designs, to work in gold, silver, and bronze, in cutting stones for setting, and in carving wood, in every kind of craft. (Exod. 31:1–5, NRSV)

These biblical texts imagine the divine–human relation in a very different way from *Ion*. In *Ion*, the Muse lays hold of something that belonged to the human being (mind, use of one's own voice, command of one's own responses). In these passages of scripture, on the other hand, a human being comes to enjoy something that belongs to God (wisdom, knowledge, intelligence). And where the activity of the Muse is that of emptying out, the work of the Holy Spirit is described in terms of "filling."

The contrast between Christian and Platonic pneumatologies, however, is most striking when we consider the person of Jesus; Jesus, who is the Christ—the Anointed One; the Bearer of the Spirit. As the One who is fully God and fully human, Jesus reveals not only who God is truly, nor only who humanity is truly. Jesus also reveals the character of the union between God and humanity—what it looks like when God and humanity are joined together perfectly and fully. This is why the Church's confession at Chalcedon (451) is so important. Chalcedon steadfastly insists that in Jesus the divine and the human come together

in two natures, without confusion, without change, without division, without separation; the distinction of natures being in no way annulled by the union, but rather the characteristics of each nature being preserved and coming together to form one person and subsistence, not as parted or separated into two persons.[10]

---

10. Henry Bettenson and Chris Maunder (eds.), *Documents of the Christian Church*, 3rd ed. (Oxford: Oxford University Press, 1999), p. 56.

The reality of Jesus's deity, in other words, is not compromised by the full presence of his humanity. Neither is the integrity of Jesus's humanity swallowed up by the fullness of his divinity.[11] The two-natures doctrine tells us that when God and humanity are united, as they are perfectly in Jesus, the result is not the silencing or the obliteration of the human. Rather, "the distinction of natures [is] in no way annulled by the union."

Christian theology can affirm the presence and activity of the Holy Spirit in human creativity without denying the agency and activity of the human artist. Jesus's life makes actual in history the pneumatological claim that divine and human agency can coexist—in human artistry, as elsewhere.[12]

Arts in the Domain of the Spirit

As we saw earlier, Calvin urges that we must not disregard or dismiss the work of the Holy Spirit "wherever it shall appear, unless we wish to dishonor the Spirit of God."[13] Moreover, I have been arguing that there is no reason we should not expect to hear the testimony of the Holy Spirit, in and alongside the human voice of artistic creativity. If, then, we are to follow Calvin's admonition, if we resolve to be alert and attentive for the voice of the Spirit, where and how might we discern this testimony in and through the arts? Are there distinctive ways in which the Spirit may bear testimony through the arts?

---

11. This line of argument is suggested by Barth's discussion of the inspiration of scripture, which includes his treatment of the idea of the *testimonium spiritus sancti internum*. "Holy Scripture is like the unity of God and man in Jesus Christ," writes Barth. "It is neither divine only nor human only. Nor is it a mixture of the two nor a *tertium quid* between them. But in its own way and degree it is very God and very man, i. e., a witness of revelation which itself belongs to revelation, and historically a very human literary document" (Karl Barth, *Church Dogmatics*, I.2., trans. G. W. Bromiley, G. T. Thompson, and Harold Knight [London: T & T Clark, 2009], p. 45).

12. Kathryn Tanner has developed this kind of divine–human relationship in her discussions of a "non-competitive ontology:" "A non-competitive relation between creatures and God means that the creature does not decrease so that God may increase. The glorification of God does not come at the expense of creatures. The more full the creature is with gifts the more the creature should look in gratitude to the fullness of the gift-giver. The fuller the giver, the greater the bounty to others. Similarly, connection with God does not take away from the creature's own dignity as the being it is. The greater one's dependence upon God, the more one receives for one's own good" (Kathryn Tanner, *Jesus, Humanity and the Trinity: A Brief Systematic Theology* [Minneapolis: Fortress Press, 2001], pp. 2–3).

13. Calvin, *Institutes*, p. 273.

As we consider this question, it is good first to recall that *pneuma*—"spirit"—also can be translated breath or *wind*. The Holy Spirit is not only the breath that carries God's word; it is also the wind of God that blows where it pleases. Jesus draws attention to this dynamic, surprising, and uncontainable character of the Holy Spirit's work in his evening dialogue with Nicodemus (John 3:8, NRSV). The Spirit is the *pneuma* of Pentecost who "suddenly" rushes in "like a violent wind" (Acts 2:2), leaving "all . . . perplexed and amazed" (Acts 2:12). All of this should caution us against making categorical pronouncements about where and how the Spirit is at work.[14]

With this caution in place, it is nevertheless notable and striking how often the power of art is attributed to activities that Christian theology associates with the Holy Spirit. That is to say, when poets, philosophers, and theologians have tried to say something about what art is and what it does, they have often done so (as we will see in the following section) using language that Christian theology uses to speak of the work of the Spirit. The devotee of the arts seems to regularly, almost unavoidably, find herself in the domain of the Spirit. Why might this be? The remainder of this essay suggests an answer, by identifying four areas in which the arts bear their own sort of testimony, gesturing toward the kinds of ends the Spirit is pursuing. In this way we can also say that through the arts, the Spirit testifies—whether directly or indirectly—to the work and actions that are distinctive to the Spirit.

Imagine I visit a friend's house. When I arrive, the home is immaculate, having just been cleaned, freshened, and set in order. I am touched, because I know my friend has cleaned the house specially in preparation for my visit. The home actively testifies to my friend's interest in welcoming me. My friend cleaned the house *in order to* "say something." Imagine, then, another occasion. While my friend is at work, a plumber enters the house to repair the dishwasher. The plumber has never met my friend in person but is nevertheless impressed by his extraordinarily clean, orderly, and well-kept home. The home again bears testimony, though in this instance an indirect testimony. My friend did not clean his home to "say something" to the plumber; nor does the plumber even know who

---

14. Barth issues a similar caution in a famous passage, declaring that "God may speak to us through Russian communism, through a flute concerto, through a blossoming shrub, or through a dead dog. We shall do well to listen to him if he really does so" (Barth, *Church Dogmatics* I.1, p. 60).

is responsible for the well-ordered home. Nevertheless, the house bears effective testimony to the lifestyle my friend values.

Though the analogy is necessarily imperfect, the testimony of the Spirit I am imagining is something like this. In some instances, the Spirit may be actively bearing testimony through the arts, employing art and beauty to "say something"—to bear some specific message (in the same way my friend cleaned his house *in order to say* "I am glad to have you visit"). In other instances, however, the arts may bear indirect testimony to the Spirit (or, we might say, the Spirit may bear testimony indirectly, through the arts). In these instances, the testimony consists in some aspect of the Spirit's work being held up to view and celebrated— whether or not the artist or audience recognize this good as something distinctive to the Spirit. The point in identifying this as "indirect" is not to deny the Spirit's involvement in such art. Rather, the distinction simply allows us to remain agnostic about attributing to the Spirit any particular goal in some specific instance of art. It allows us to say (for instance) that this evening's concert testified to the beauty of community (which is indeed one of the goods the Spirit is at work bringing about), without asserting dogmatically that in this particular performance of the Brahms *Requiem*, the Spirit was at work attempting to bear testimony to community.

The four distinctive dimensions of the Holy Spirit's work we will consider in connection with art and beauty are restoring sight, creating community, bringing freedom, and sanctifying or perfecting.

The Spirit of Sight and Insight

The Spirit of the Lord is upon me, because he has anointed me ... to proclaim release to the captives and recovery of sight to the blind. (Luke 4:18, NRSV)

"Brother Saul, the Lord Jesus, who appeared to you on your way here, has sent me so that you may regain your sight and be filled with the Holy Spirit." And immediately something like scales fell from his eyes, and his sight was restored. (Acts 9:17–18, NRSV)

The great Romantic poet, Percy Bysshe Shelley, is a good example of the kind of recourse to pneumatological language I have described. An atheist, Shelley nevertheless characterized poetry as "divine" and poets as "ministers" and "hierophants of an unapprehended inspiration."[15] In particular, Shelley attaches much of this divine power to that gift that Christian theology calls discernment. The Old and New Testaments associate the Holy Spirit with both sight and insight. The Spirit enables men and women both to see what is there, and to see beyond what is there. Cyril of Jerusalem describes the work of the Holy Spirit by imagining "a man, who being previously in darkness ... suddenly beholds the sun, is enlightened in his bodily sight, and sees plainly things which he saw not[.] [S]o likewise he to whom the Holy Ghost is vouchsafed, is enlightened in his soul, and sees things beyond man's sight."[16]

This is the sort of power Shelley attributes to the poet in his *Defense of Poetry*. Poets, he says, "unveil the permanent analogy of things by images which participate in the life of truth."[17] Indeed, they are "capable of perceiving and teaching *the truth of things*."[18] A poem, then, is not simply another comment on some dimension of our world, but rather offers us "the very image of life expressed in its eternal truth."[19] It is for this reason that Shelley insists "poetry is indeed something divine."[20] Like the spirit who sheds a transfiguring light on a darkened landscape, the poem

> reproduces the common universe of which we are portions and percipients, and it purges from our inward sight the film of familiarity which obscures from us the wonder of our being. It compels us to feel that which we perceive, and to imagine that which we know. It creates anew the universe, after it has been annihilated in our minds by the recurrence of impressions blunted by reiteration.[21]

The artist has both keener sight and deeper insight than others. She peels from our eyes "the film of familiarity," allowing us to see (in the

---

15. Percy Bysshe Shelley, *A Defense of Poetry* (Boston: Ginn and Company, 1890), p. 46.

16. Cyril of Jerusalem, *The Catechetical Lectures of St. Cyril of Jerusalem*, XVI.16, ed. Paul A. Böer, Sr. (Veritatis Splendor Publications, 2014), p. 559.

17. Shelley, *Defense of Poetry*, p. 9.

18. Ibid., p. 10.

19. Ibid.

20. Ibid., p. 38.

21. Ibid., p. 42.

words of another Romantic) "a World in a grain of sand/and a Heaven in
a wild flower."[22] Shelley believes that by virtue of this capacity for insight,
poets were, in earlier times, the legislators and prophets of the world.
Indeed,

> a poet essentially comprises and unites both these characters. For
> he not only beholds intensely the present as it is, and discovers
> those laws according to which present things ought to be ordered,
> but he beholds the future in the present, and his thoughts are the
> germs of the flower and the fruit of latest time.[23]

Like the biblical prophet, the poet sees both how things truly are and—
for this reason—how things should truly be.

The 19th-century critic Clive Bell was likewise convinced that the making of art is a spiritual pursuit. In his work *Art*, he characterizes the work
of the visual artist in much the same way that Shelley describes the task of
poetry. The artist, he argues, like the prophet, mystic, or seer, is able to see
behind the veil of appearances. The artist perceives not just the surfaces,
but the significance of things. The artist then exercises a priestly function
with respect to the rest of us. Through the eyes of the artist others are
enabled to look at the world of sense and to see truly, to see *more*.

> [I]nstead of recognising its accidental and conditioned importance,
> we become aware of *its essential reality*, of *the God in everything*, of
> *the universal in the particular*, of the all-pervading rhythm. Call it
> by what name you will, the thing that I am talking about is that
> which lies behind the appearance of all things—that which gives to
> all things their individual significance, the thing in itself, the ulti-
> mate reality.[24]

Here we have an aesthetic model that derives its spiritual aspirations
directly and rather explicitly from the language of Christian theology. The
Holy Spirit opens eyes, bringing sight to those who do not see and insight
to those without discernment. The Spirit is the giver of wisdom and

---

22. William Blake, "Auguries of Innocence," in David V. Erdman (ed.), *The Complete Poetry
and Prose of William Blake* (Berkeley: University of California Press, 2008), p. 490.

23. Shelley, *Defense of Poetry*, p. 6.

24. Clive Bell, *Art* (BiblioBazaar, LLC, 2007), p. 47.

revelation (Eph. 1:17). By the Spirit, scales fall from our eyes, and we "re-see"—perceiving anew, and understanding the unseen reality by which we are surrounded. Those who are foolish and senseless "have eyes, but do not see [and] have ears, but do not hear" (Jer. 5:21, NRSV). By contrast, the prophet promises that when God's Spirit is poured out, "your sons and your daughters *shall prophesy,* your old men *shall dream dreams,* and your young men *shall see visions*" (Joel 2:28, NRSV; italics added).

One might be tempted to say that Shelley, Bell, and others have simply attributed to art those powers and capacities that scripture attributes to the Holy Spirit, but there is more going on here: These artists have intuited that there is something "spiritual" about this kind of transformed vision of the world, and Christian theology agrees. The artist is right, in fact, when she insists that the world has not only surfaces, but depths. The artist is correct to suggest that the form and beauty and texture of the world are not only enjoyable, but *meaningful.* The poet does well to alert us to a world that has a voice, that testifies and bears witness. Nor is Shelley mistaken to speak of the "film of familiarity" that dulls us to wonder and robs us of the delight and awe we should more readily feel in the presence of the world and one another. And again, the artist is right to intuit that there is something *Spirit*-ual—in the richest Christian sense of the word—to this work of deepening and transforming vision. To the extent that the artist invites us to a posture of attentiveness and receptivity, to the extent that the poet alerts us to the possibility of seeing more and seeing differently, to the extent that human creativity undertakes this work, it moves along the same trajectory as the work of the Holy Spirit. Elizabeth Barrett Browning raises the alarm:

> Earth's crammed with heaven,
> And every common bush afire with God;
> But only he who sees, takes off his shoes,
> The rest sit round it and pluck blackberries.[25]

It is not inappropriate to characterize the testimony of the Spirit as an invitation to take our place among those who see and remove their shoes. In many instances it is the work of the artist to echo this invitation.

---

25. Elizabeth Barrett Browning, *Aurora Leigh and Other Poems* (New York: James Miller, 1866), p. 265.

The Holy Spirit and the Creation of Community

The grace of the Lord Jesus Christ and the love of God and the fellowship of the Holy Spirit be with you all. (2 Cor. 13:14, RSV)

"We cannot fail to observe," Leo Tolstoy writes, "that art is one of the means of intercourse between man and man."

> Every work of art causes the receiver to enter into a certain kind of relationship both with him who produced, or is producing the art, and with all those who simultaneously, previously, or subsequently, receive the same artistic expression.... The activity of art is based on the fact that a man, receiving through his sense of hearing or sight another man's expression of feeling, is capable of experiencing the emotion which moved the man who expressed it.[26]

Here Tolstoy is setting out one part of his argument for the aesthetic theory known as Expressionism. We need not embrace every element of that particular theory to acknowledge the profound connection between art and community that Tolstoy identifies.

Tolstoy describes two levels at which art gives rise to community. First, through song, dance, story, I enter into "a relationship ... with him who produced or is producing the art." Through various forms of art, the horizons of my experience are broadened. I inhabit perspectives, see landscapes, experience emotions, and share burdens that would have been otherwise unknown to me. C. S. Lewis offers an eloquent exposition of this capacity of art. "Literary experience," he writes, "heals the wound, without undermining the privilege, of individuality."

> ... [I]n reading great literature I become a thousand men and yet remain myself. Like the night sky in the Greek poem, I see with a myriad eyes, but it is still I who see. Here, as in worship, in love, in moral action and in knowing, I transcend myself, and am never more myself than when I do.[27]

---

26. Leo N. Tolstoy, *What Is Art?* trans. Aylmer Maude (Indianapolis: Hackett Publishing, 1996), p. 49.

27. C. S. Lewis, *An Experiment in Criticism* (Cambridge: Cambridge University Press, 1961), pp. 140–41.

It is easiest to imagine this sym-pathetic function of art, this "feeling-together-with," in connection with literature, poetry, and drama (as Lewis does). In many instances, however, we also feel that nonverbal, nonrepresentational arts like dance and instrumental music communicate the experience of others as well. Indeed, this was precisely Plato's concerns with respect to music and poetic meter: " 'I'm no expert on the modes,' I said, 'but please leave me with a [musical] mode which properly captures the tones and variations of pitch of a brave man's voice during battle.... And leave me another mode which captures his voice when he's engaged in peaceful enterprises.' "[28] Brave, or lazy, or immoral rhythms, the *Republic* argues, produce bravery, laziness, and immorality. Again, we may hesitate over the way Plato develops this idea, but the intuition that musical materials (altogether apart from lyrics) nevertheless speak—indeed communicate—is neither idiosyncratic nor unfamiliar. As a boy of five or six, I remember sitting on the floor of my bedroom, tears in my eyes, as I listened to my older sister playing the first movement of Grieg's *Piano Sonata in E Minor.* It is a piece that (it seems to me now) moves from stern resolution, to frantic anxiety, to something like joyful serenity. As a boy I had no names for, nor any experience with, any of these attitudes. But the music met me not simply as pleasant sounds, but as something like the movements of a person's inner life, and it communicated those movements to me inwardly as well.

In addition to this meeting between creator and listener, Tolstoy refers to a relationship that emerges "with all those who simultaneously, previously, or subsequently, receive the same artistic expression." And this, too, is a valuable and undeniable insight. Artistic practices powerfully define communities, large and small. Lovers and nations alike can speak of a particular tune as "our song."

Both ancient and contemporary societies have defined themselves (at least in part) as "the people who sing these songs," "the people who are surrounded by these images," "the people who tell these stories." Jacques Barzun believes that the spiritual power of art arises precisely from this power to create community:

The affinity between religion and art, then, consists in this, that the artist, like the worshipper, gives himself over to an experience so

28. Plato, *Republic*, trans. Robin Waterfield (Oxford: Oxford University Press, 1993), p. 96.

very different from those of the ordinary self that he deems it loftier, truer and more lasting. This experience the beholder can share if he is receptive to art and has the capacity to feel as well as analyze. Two persons—and more than two—can then commune through art alone in a spiritual event divorced from creeds. This power of art to evoke the transcendent and bring about this unity is what has led artists and thinkers in the last two centuries to equate art and religion, and finally to substitute art for religion.[29]

Of course, this sort of communicative and communal power is not always benign. Again, Plato worries about music's power to communicate not only virtuous but also vicious character.[30] And the boundaries defined by art can exclude as well as include; art can be a means of staking out one's territory. In the Spike Lee movie *Do The Right Thing*, the music blaring from Radio Raheem's boom box delineates the boundary lines between different racial and ethnic communities. In one scene, Raheem and a group of Puerto Rican youths engage in a kind of musical turf war. Lee's script reads:

EXT: STREET—DAY On a stoop, a group of Puerto Ricans sits talking, drinking cerveza frío, and playing dominoes. One of their cars is parked near the stoop, and blasts salsa music.

ANGLE—RADIO RAHEEM As usual we hear the rap music of Radio Raheem, but underneath the salsa music. Radio Raheem does not like to be bested; the salsa music from the parked car is giving him competition, this is no good. Radio Raheem stands in front of the stoop and raises his decibel level.

---

29. Jacques Barzun, *The Use and Abuse of Art: The A. W. Mellon Lectures in the Fine Arts, 1973.* Bollingen Series XXXV.22 (Princeton: Princeton University Press, 1975), p. 26. See https://www.amazon.com/Abuse-Mellon-Lectures-Fine-Arts/dp/0691018049#reader_0691018049.

30. This same concern is also evident, of course, in many of the teachers of the early Church: "It is unlawful, I say, for the Christian faithful to be present; utterly unlawful even for those whom Greece, to please their ears, sends everywhere to all who have been schooled in her vain arts. One mimics the raucous, bellicose clangor of the trumpet; another forces his breath into the tibia to control its doleful sounds.... Even if these things were not consecrated to idols, faithful Christians ought not to frequent and observe them, for even if there were nothing criminal about them, they have in themselves an utter worthlessness hardly suitable for believers." Novation (d. c. 258), in James McKinnon, (ed.), *Music in Early Christian Literature* (Cambridge: Cambridge University Press, 1987), p. 48.

ANGLE—STOOP The Puerto Rican men look at him, then begin to yell at him in Spanish. There is a standoff, the rap and salsa clashing in a deafening roar. One of the men, STEVIE, gets off the stoop and goes to the car.

ANGLE—CAR Stevie turns the car radio off.

CLOSE—RADIO RAHEEM Radio Raheem smiles, nods, turns his box to a reasonable listening level, and bops down the block. Radio Raheem still the loudest. Radio Raheem still the king.[31]

Raheem's boom box in fact becomes the central character in the climactic scene of the film. Raheem and his friends defiantly plant the boom box on the restaurant counter of Sal, the white owner of Sal's Pizzeria. As the confrontation grows more and more heated, Sal produces a baseball bat from beneath the counter, and angrily demands:

SAL: Turn that JUNGLE MUSIC off. We ain't in Africa.... What ever happened to nice music with words you can understand?
RADIO RAHEEM: This is music. My music.
    . . .
    Sal grabs his Mickey Mantle bat from underneath the counter and brings it down on Radio Raheem's box, again and again and again. The music stops.
CLOSE—RADIO RAHEEM'S BOX
    Radio Raheem's pride and joy is smashed to smithereens. It's going to the junkyard quick.
ANGLE—PIZZERIA
    There is an eerie quiet as everyone is frozen, surprised by the suddenness of Sal's action, the swings of his Mickey Mantle bat. All look at Radio Raheem and realize what is about to happen.
ANGLE—RADIO RAHEEM
    Radio Raheem screams, he goes crazy.
RADIO RAHEEM: My music![32]

Lee's powerful script reminds us, again, that music and art are not in and of themselves redemptive. Even their power to create and embody a

---

31. Spike Lee, *Do The Right Thing*, Script. Second Draft. March 1, 1988. http://www.awesome-film.com/script/dotherightthing.txt. Accessed October 28, 2015.

32. Ibid.

sense of community is not in itself redemptive. What we are interested in is not the testimony of the arts per se, but the testimony of the Spirit. It is the Spirit who testifies to the central place of community—within the life of God, and within the Christian life. Nevertheless, we can say that the capacity of art to gather and build connection, to move us out beyond ourselves, is often powerfully enlisted by the Spirit. Within the church particularly it is significant that across history and cultures, Christians have almost without exception adorned their worship with some form of poetry and song.[33] Again, Plato, Tolstoy, and others are not wrong to recognize something "Spirit-ual" in art's capacity to carry us across boundaries and create connection.

The spirit, Colin Gunton writes, "is to do with the crossing of boundaries."[34] John V. Taylor characterizes the work of spirit in very similar terms. "Spirit," he says, "is that which lies between, making both separateness and conjunction real."[35] This same work of establishing both distinction and union can be seen in Paul's discussion of the work of the Spirit in the church. By the "one Spirit" we are made "one body" (1 Cor. 12:13, NRSV), but this same Spirit gives "varieties of gifts" (1 Cor. 12:4, NRSV). The work of the Spirit is to reproduce the life of God in us, not simply as individuals, but to produce a people who in their differentiated unity reflect the differentiated unity of God's own Trinitarian life.

If the Spirit testifies and calls us to community, then conversely, the character of sin is the destruction of community. The life of Jesus's followers is to be one that is extended outward—toward God and toward others. The way of life we are called from is, in Martin Luther's famous definition, the way of *homo incurvatus in se*—the person turned in upon himself.[36] Aesthetic experience, then, is one way at least by which we can be moved beyond ourselves. In this respect it is consonant indeed with the work

---

33. "Three acts, corporate prayer, public reading and corporate singing, form the basic building blocks of corporate worship in all of the traditions" (Simon Chan, *Spiritual Theology: A Systematic Study of the Christian Life* [Downers Grove, IL: InterVarsity, 1998], p. 116).

34. Colin Gunton, *The One, the Three and the Many: God, Creation and the Culture of Modernity. The Bampton Lectures 1992* (Cambridge: Cambridge University Press, 1993), p. 181. This is true of the biblical category of "spirit" generally, Gunton says in this section, not only of God's Spirit.

35. John V. Taylor, *The Go-Between God* (London: SCM Press, 2004), p. 8.

36. Martin Luther, *Lectures on Romans*, ed. and trans. Wilhelm Pauck (Philadelphia: Westminster, 1961), p. 159.

of Spirit. In song I am invited to respond to a voice outside of myself. "Through melody, harmony, and rhythm," Roger Scruton writes, "we enter a world where others exist besides the self."[37] In story I am invited to inhabit the perspective of another. In the visual arts I am encouraged to look, listen, and attend, carefully and appreciatively, and to regard objects, not with respect to their potential utility for me, but as ends in themselves.

The Spirit of Freedom

The Spirit of the Lord is upon me, because he has anointed me . . . to proclaim release to the captives . . . to let the oppressed go free, to proclaim the year of the Lord's favor. (Luke 4:18, NRSV)

Where the Spirit of the Lord is, there is freedom. (2 Cor. 3:17, NRSV)

Considering things "as ends in themselves" points us toward another important theme in aesthetics. Kant and many who have followed after him have described the distinctive sort of delight associated with beauty as "disinterested pleasure." Indeed,

few ideas in the history of aesthetics have been more pervasive than that of the disinterestedness of the aesthetic attitude. It has figured prominently, in various guises, in the writings of eighteenth-century English empiricists and of nineteenth-century German idealists, and in much twentieth-century writing.[38]

So, the picture on my wall might delight me for all sorts of reasons. Perhaps it delights me because it reminds me of a trip I once took with my family. Perhaps I like it because of the impression I hope it will make on visitors. Or it may delight me because purchasing that painting was a shrewd investment. But if what delights me is simply the painting itself— not some separate good that could be isolated from it—then I delight in it apart from my own interests and other motives. I take disinterested plea- sure in the painting, not as a means, but as an end. I value it for its own appearance, its own particular qualities and irreplaceable presence.

---

37. Roger Scruton, *The Aesthetics of Music* (Oxford: Oxford University Press, 1999), p. 502.

38. David Whewell, "Kant, Immanuel," in David E. Cooper (ed.), *A Companion to Aesthetics* (Oxford: Blackwell, 1992), p. 251.

This idea of "disinterested pleasure" has sometimes been distorted into a caricature of itself, as expressed by Oscar Wilde's glib maxim: "All art is quite useless."[39] This turns the positive criterion of "delightful-for-its-own-sake" into a negative criterion: "must-not-be-useful." Helpfully, a number of thinkers, including Nicholas Wolterstorff, have drawn attention to the problems that arise if the purpose of art is restricted solely to that of disinterested aesthetic contemplation.[40] Nevertheless, these distortions should not undermine the real insight here. One of the distinctive and valuable things about aesthetic experience is that it invites us to encounter the world as "end" rather than "means," and as "delightful" rather than only "useful."

One thinker who develops this connection between the spiritual value of art and its gratuitous, nonpurposive character is Friedrich Schiller. In his *On the Aesthetic Education of Man*[41] Schiller observes that for much of humanity's existence, we have "allowed appearance merely to serve [our] ends." But when "we discover traces of a disinterested free appreciation of pure appearance," a change takes place. We now begin "enjoying *differently*." A man then "becomes aware of the forms of the objects which satisfy his desires." By rising to this sort of disinterested appreciation, "he has not merely enhanced his enjoyment in scope and in degree, but also exalted it in kind."[42] The aesthetic, then, "takes us out of our everyday practical concerns, by providing us with objects, characters and actions with which we can play, and which we can enjoy for what they are, rather than for what they do for us."[43]

In particular, Schiller seizes on the category of "play." Play, on the one hand, best characterizes what is spiritually significant in the realm of the aesthetic: "Man is only serious with the agreeable, the good, the perfect; but with Beauty *he plays*."[44] Play, on the other hand, best describes that which completes and epitomizes human beings in their humanity: "To

---

39. Oscar Wilde, *The Picture of Dorian Gray* (London: Penguin, 1985), p. 4.

40. See, for instance, Nicholas Wolterstorff, *Art in Action: Toward a Christian Aesthetic* (Grand Rapids, MI: Eerdmans, 1980), pp. 19–61.

41. Friedrich Schiller, *On the Aesthetic Education of Man*, trans. Reginald Snell (Mineola, NY: Dover Publications, 2004).

42. Ibid., pp. 132–33. Italics in translation.

43. Roger Scruton, *Beauty* (Oxford: Oxford University Press, 2009), p. 127. Scruton is summarizing Schiller here.

44. Schiller, *On the Aesthetic Education of Man*, p. 79. My italics.

declare it once and for all, Man plays only when he is in the full sense of the word a man, and *he is only wholly Man when he is playing.*"[45] Art and beauty carry us into that realm where we are really and truly human, no longer concerned only with our most basic and primal needs, no longer engaging with the world simply as adjunct to our physical requirements.

> So long as Man in his first physical condition accepts the world of sense merely passively, merely perceives, his is still completely identified with it, and just because he himself is simply world, there is no world yet for him. Not until he sets it outside himself or contemplates it, in his aesthetic status, does his personality become distinct from it, and a world appears to him because he has ceased to identify himself with it. Contemplation (reflection) is Man's first free relation to the universe which surrounds him.[46]

In aesthetic contemplation the human is released from being "a slave of Nature,"[47] "chained . . . to the material,"[48] into the freedom of play.

More recently, Gadamer has likewise identified "play" as one of the three essential concepts necessary to a definition of art (along with "symbol" and "festival").[49] Gadamer insists that when we are speaking about a work of art we are describing "not the emergence of a product . . . not an item of equipment determined by its utility, as all such items or products of human work are."[50] The artistic creation, he says, "refuses to be used in any way." Rather, it "has something of the 'as if' character that we recognized as an essential feature of the nature of play."[51] This "as if" character of play "is so universal that even the play of animals sometimes seems animated by a touch of freedom."[52]

---

45. Ibid., p. 80. Italics in translation.

46. Ibid., pp. 119–20.

47. Ibid., p. 120.

48. Ibid., p. 132.

49. Hans-Georg Gadamer, *The Relevance of the Beautiful and Other Essays*, trans. Nicholas Walker (Cambridge: Cambridge University Press, 1996), p. 3. Thus, the subtitle of the main essay in the collection: "The Relevance of the Beautiful: Art as Play, Symbol, and Festival."

50. Ibid., p. 125.

51. Ibid., p. 126.

52. Ibid., pp. 125–26.

It is difficult to hear Gadamer's contrast between "human work" and "freedom," or Schiller's contrast between "slave" and "free," without thinking of Pauline discussions that draw a similar contrast—between slavery to works of the flesh on the one hand, and the freedom given in the Spirit on the other. Those who live by "the works of the law" (Gal. 3:2, NRSV), Paul declares, are held in slavery. But the one who has been "born according to the Spirit" (Gal. 4:29, NRSV) is "no longer a slave but a child, and if a child then also an heir" (Gal. 4:7, NRSV). The Spirit's role in this freedom is essential: "God has sent the Spirit of his Son into our hearts, crying 'Abba! Father'" (4:6, NRSV). The Spirit comes to indwell us, and likewise, takes us up into the life of God, initiating us into a familial relationship, in which we receive the benefits of God, not through our works, but as an inheritance.[53]

This relationship is no longer one of "duty and obligation," in which one "slaves" for God. Rather, by the indwelling Spirit, we relate to God in freedom, as children and heirs.[54]

> For you did not receive a spirit of slavery to fall back into fear, but you have received a spirit of adoption. When we cry, "Abba! Father!" it is that very Spirit bearing witness with our spirit that we are children of God, and if children, then heirs, heirs of God and joint heirs with Christ. (Rom. 8:15–17, NRSV)

The Spirit testifies to the primacy of grace over competition. In his essay *Theology and Joy*, Moltmann considers the question: Why did God create the world? "This," he writes, "is the question of a child who is no longer a child."[55]

> He has learned that in the adult world everything exists for a good reason.... Faith answers the unchildish childhood question in a childlike way; and the wisdom of theology ends with the liberty

---

53. See Michael J. Gorman, *Apostle of the Crucified Lord: A Theological Introduction to Paul and His Letters* (Grand Rapids, MI: Eerdmans, 2004), p. 211.

54. "Christian freedom," Richard Bauckham writes, "is constituted and formed as Christians within the human community of the church are drawn into the field of Trinitarian relationships. They do so as the Spirit enables them to share Jesus's relationship to the one he called Abba" (Richard Bauckham, *God and the Crisis of Freedom: Biblical and Contemporary Perspectives* [Louisville, KY: Westminster John Knox, 2002], p. 204).

55. Jürgen Moltmann, *Theology and Joy* (London: SCM Press, 1973), p. 39.

of the children of God.... Anyone who lays hold of the joy which embraces the creator and his own existence also gets rid of the dreadful question of existence: For what? ... He becomes immune also to a society which values and rewards men only in terms of their practical usefulness.[56]

Those who live by faith are freed from the burden of working to justify their own existence. They are freed, as Moltmann says, from the dreadful question of justifying utility; the question "what is it for?" The idea of "disinterested pleasure" recognizes the beatific character of that moment that has been liberated from the question "what is that for?"

Wherever the arts are nourished through the festive contemplation of universal realities and their sustaining reasons, there in truth something like a liberation occurs: the stepping-out into the open under an endless sky, not only for the creative artist himself but for the beholder as well, even the most humble. Such liberation, such foreshadowing for the ultimate and perfect fulfillment, is necessary for man, almost more necessary than his daily bread, which is indeed indispensable, and yet insufficient.[57]

Those things that are unnecessary we describe as "gratuitous." Beauty, then, may be one way that the Spirit testifies to a world that broadens out beyond necessity, into gratuity. In the experience of beauty we may hear the Spirit testify to a cosmos that God did not *need* but nevertheless intended, wanted, and delights in. Through the play of the artist, the Spirit bears witness to a cosmos whose deepest logic is not utility, competitive advantage, and survival of the fittest, but freedom, delight, and grace.

The Spirit of Completion

This is what was spoken through the prophet Joel: "In the last days it will be, God declares, that I will pour out my Spirit upon all flesh." (Acts 2:16–17, NRSV)

---

56. Ibid., pp. 39, 40, 430.

57. Joseph Pieper, *Only the Lover Sings: Art and Contemplation*, trans. Lothar Krauth (San Francisco: Ignatius Press, 1990), p. 27.

The apostle Peter explains the extraordinary events of Pentecost by repeating the words of the Old Testament prophet Joel. "In the last days," Joel had declared, God will pour out the Spirit on all people. And now, Jesus Christ, "exalted at the right hand of God, and having received from the Father the promise of the Holy Spirit . . . has poured out this that you both see and hear" (Acts 2:33, NRSV). There was, in other words, something even more startling and extraordinary taking place that Pentecost morning than an outburst of ecstatic, multilingual proclamation. The apostolic glossolalia pointed to the outpouring of the Spirit, and the outpouring of the Spirit in turn heralded the arrival of "the last days."

Elsewhere in the Old Testament as well, God's spirit is associated with the fulfillment of promise and the age to come.

> The fortress will be abandoned, the noisy city deserted; citadel and watchtower will become a wasteland forever, the delight of donkeys, a pasture for flocks, till the Spirit is poured on us from on high, and the desert becomes a fertile field, and the fertile field seems like a forest. (Isa. 32:14, 15, NIV)

> Do not fear, O Jacob my servant, Jeshurun whom I have chosen. For I will pour water on the thirsty land, and streams on the dry ground; I will pour my spirit upon your descendants, and my blessing on your offspring. They shall spring up like a green tamarisk, like willows by flowing streams. (Isa. 44:2–4, NRSV)

This outpouring of God's spirit is richly interwoven with other Old Testament promises as well. The giving of the Spirit is a realization, for instance, of God's pledge and intention to "come and dwell in your midst" (Zech. 2:10, NRSV; cf. Zech. 8:3, Jer. 7:7, Ezek. 37:27), and the broader hope for the joining of heaven and earth. Indeed, it is in light of the eschatological significance of this promise that Paul celebrates the fact that God's people are "being built together to become a dwelling in which God lives by his Spirit" (Eph. 2:22, NIV).

Another way that the Old Testament expresses this hope for the fullness of God's presence is by speaking of the knowledge of God. Isaiah declares, "a shoot shall come out from the stump of Jesse" (Isa. 11:1, NRSV) and the "spirit of the Lord shall rest on him" (11:2, NRSV). Through this Spirit-anointed servant, a new age will be ushered in, in which "the earth will be full of the knowledge of the LORD as the waters cover the sea" (Isa. 11:9, NRSV; cf. Hab. 2:14). Likewise, Jeremiah proclaims, the days are coming when "no longer shall they teach one another, or say to each other, 'Know the LORD,' for they shall all know me, from the least of them to the greatest, says the LORD" (Jer. 31:34, NRSV). It is in the context of announcing that "this is the last hour" (1 John 2:18, NIV), then, that John celebrates his hearers' knowledge of God. This knowledge is a fulfill-ment of God's Old Testament promise, and so, fittingly, John describes it using the spirit-language of "anointing": "But you have been anointed by the Holy One, and all of you have knowledge. . . . [T]he anointing that you received from him abides in you, and so you do not need anyone to teach you. But as his anointing teaches you about all things, and is true and is not a lie, and just as it has taught you, abide in him" (1 John 2:20, 27, NRSV). The outpouring of the Holy Spirit both heralds and initiates the last days, bringing into being the new age God has promised.

Finally, this eschatological orientation of the Spirit is evident in the close connections made between the Holy Spirit and the resurrection. It is Jesus's resurrection from the dead, Peter argues, that vindicates his claim to be *Christos*—the one anointed with the Spirit (Acts 2:22–32). In much the same way, Paul writes: "through the Spirit of holiness [Jesus] was declared to be God's Son with great power by rising from the dead" (Rom. 1:4, New Century Version). This same Spirit has now been given to the Christian as "seal" and "the pledge of our inheritance toward redemp-tion" (Eph. 1:13, 14, NRSV). The Spirit is "a first installment" (2 Cor. 1:22) of the fulfillment of God's promises (2 Cor. 1:20). And so, Paul says, "if the Spirit of him who raised Jesus from the dead dwells in you, he who raised Christ from the dead will give life to your mortal bodies also through his Spirit that dwells in you" (Rom. 8:11, NRSV).

The category of the eschatological, of course, necessarily includes the idea of completion or fulfillment, and the eschatological work of the Spirit encom-passes this dimension as well. "The Spirit," Hendrikus Berkhof writes, "is the movement from Christ to the consummation, from the first fruits to the full harvest."[58] At both an individual and a cosmic level, the Spirit is the sanc-tifier, the perfecter, the one who brings things to their true and promised end. As the Spirit dwells in the individual believer, she is "sanctified by the Spirit" (1 Pet. 1:2, NRSV; cf. Rom. 15:16; 2 Thess. 2:13), "transformed . . . from one degree of glory to another; for this comes from the Lord, the Spirit" (2 Cor.

---

58. Hendrikus Berkhof, *The Doctrine of the Holy Spirit* (Richmond, VA: John Knox Press, 1964), p. 105.

3:18, NRSV). In the same way, St. Basil writes that through the Holy Spirit, "hearts are lifted up, the infirm are held by the hand and those who progress are brought to perfection."[59] At a cosmic level, the same Old Testament passages that look ahead to the outpouring of the Spirit also anticipate a cosmic transformation, encompassing earth, sky, and sea; human, plant, and animal life. Under the rule of the One Anointed with the Spirit,

> the wolf shall live with the lamb, the leopard shall lie down with the kid, the calf and the lion and the fatling together, and a little child shall lead them. The cow and the bear shall graze, their young shall lie down together; and the lion shall eat straw like the ox. The nursing child shall play over the hole of the asp, and the weaned child shall put its hand on the adder's den. (Isa. 11:6–8, NRSV)

As seal and agent of the last days, it is the work of the Spirit to perfect, complete, and fulfill.

It is precisely in connection with this eschatological idea of perfection or completion that many have felt that art and beauty exercise a spiritual function. The American philosopher George Santayana is a good example of this line of thinking. "Beauty," he writes, "seems to be the clearest manifestation of perfection, and the best evidence of its possibility."[60] Art in particular, he believes, arises from a vision of how things should be.

> That man is unhappy indeed, who in all his life has had no glimpse of perfection, who in the ecstasy of love or in the delight of contemplation, has never been able to say: It is attained. Such moments of inspiration are the source of the arts, which have no higher function than to renew them. A work of art is indeed a monument to such a moment, the memorial to such a vision.[61]

Artistic perfection as Santayana describes it has the character of a prophetic vision about it. The beautiful object does not itself bring about the

---

59. St. Basil the Great, *On the Holy Spirit*, trans. David Anderson (Crestwood, NY: St. Vladimir's Seminary Press, 1980), p. 44.

60. George Santayana, *The Sense of Beauty: Being the Outline of Aesthetic Theory* (New York: Dover Publications, 1955), p. 269.

61. Ibid., p. 262.

renewal of the cosmos. Rather, it provides "a glimpse," a memorial to "a vision." In certain works of art we are enabled to experience for a moment some work, some object, as *complete*: lacking nothing, altogether whole, consistent with itself, entirely as it should be. The artwork then speaks to us about the "possibility" of perfection, and perhaps even of the possibility of a world characterized by this sort of completion.

Santayana contends that in each area of life and in each endeavor, whether large or small, we are necessarily guided by some sense of how things should be. We seek some sort of "harmony between our nature and our experience," aspiring toward that state of affairs in which "there is no inward standard different from the outward fact with which that outward fact may be compared."[62] Indeed, we would be altogether lost without such standards. "No atheism is so terrible," he writes, "as the absence of an ultimate ideal."[63] Whether we realize it or not, we move through life guided by "that perfection which is the implicit ideal of all our preferences and desires."[64]

The artwork, the beautiful object, may be one way that the Spirit testifies to the possibility of such a harmony of the ideal and the real. The work of art is a monument to moments when there has been a near approach to such a correspondence. Santayana, the naturalist, would not describe it this way, but the theologian might be tempted to characterize such moments as the in-breaking of the promised future. In these instances the Spirit points ahead, not to some other world, but to this world transformed and made whole. Abraham Kuyper suggests that art "has the mystical task of reminding us . . . of the beautiful that was lost and of anticipating its perfect coming luster." It uncovers "the still visible lines of the original plan, and what is even more, the splendid restoration by which the Supreme Artist and master-builder will one day renew and enhance the beauty of His original creation."[65]

Santayana's discussion of the ideals by which we make aesthetic judgments is particularly helpful. The standards he describes are not ideals in the Platonic sense, abstracted from the world of material objects and physical sensation. The beautiful objects we encounter are not approximating

---

62. Ibid., p. 269.

63. Ibid., p. 262.

64. Ibid., p. 263.

65. Abraham Kuyper, *Lectures on Calvinism* (Grand Rapids, MI: Eerdmans, 1943), p. 155.

some single and universal standard; rather, their "ideal is immanent in them."[66] "The highest aesthetic good," he writes, "is not that vague potentiality, nor that contradictory, infinite perfection so strongly desired; it is the greatest number and variety of finite perfections."[67] The perfection that Santayana suggests, then, is not homogeneity. It is not the uniform imposition of a single archetype. Instead, perfection increases and intensifies the assortment and multiplicity of beauties. "To learn to see in nature and to enshrine in the arts the typical forms of things; to recognize their variations ... that is the goal of [aesthetic] contemplation."[68] This vision of completion accords well with Colin Gunton's description of the "particularizing" work of the Holy Spirit. The perfecting work of the Spirit, "far from abolishing, rather maintains and even strengthens particularity. It is not a spirit of merging or assimilation—of homogenization—but of relation in otherness, relation which does not subvert but establishes the other in its true reality."[69] The perfection that Santayana describes, then, is truly a "fulfillment" or a "completion." It is a realization of what the object is intended to be.

Another interesting and helpful aspect of Santayana's account is that he insists that artistic perfection requires embodiment and finitude. "Wherever beauty is really seen and loved," he writes, "it has a definite embodiment."[70] The artist, therefore, must strive for greater attentiveness and clarity, "to disentangle the beauties so vaguely felt, and give each its adequate embodiment." Santayana also makes the striking claim that "perfection is a synonym of finitude. Neither in nature nor in the fancy can anything be perfect except by realizing a definite type, which excludes all variation, and contrasts sharply with every other possibility of being."[71] The finitude of each thing, he insists, is no limitation on beauty or perfection "for there is no limit to the number and variety of forms which the world may be made to wear; only, if it is to be appreciated as beautiful and not merely felt as unutterable, it must be seen as a kingdom of forms."[72]

---

66. Santayana, The Sense of Beauty, p. 262.

67. Ibid., pp. 151–52.

68. Ibid.

69. Gunton, The One, The Three and the Many, p. 182.

70. Santayana, The Sense of Beauty, p. 150.

71. Ibid., p. 147.

72. Ibid., p. 150.

At this point, too, Santayana's discussion of artistic perfection is useful in thinking about the Spirit's eschatological work of completion. As Santayana suggests and Christian theology insists, this perfection will be embodied and finite. The completion and eschatological beautification of human beings does not demand that they become other than human in their particularity, in their limitedness, or in their embodiment. Rather, the created world, perfected, completed, and whole, will remain *creature*. Nor is this a concession of some sort, as if some greater perfection were not possible, or as if to allow space for God's greater perfection. Rather, the embodiment and finitude of the perfected creation (or rather of each particular within the perfected creation) is *part* of its perfection. God intends for each thing he has created to be what it is, and not another. The resurrected glory of each creature is not found in overcoming this finite and distinctive identity, but in completing it. No one has expressed this idea more eloquently than Gerard Manley Hopkins:

> Each mortal thing does one thing and the same:
> Deals out that being indoors each one dwells;
> Selves—goes itself; *myself* it speaks and spells,
> Crying *What I do is me: for that I came.*[73]

This eschatological vision likewise casts a backward illumination on our aesthetic experience. In the light of a new creation, populated by an extraordinary diversity of finite perfections, we can think more clearly about beauty and artistic perfection in this present age. Beauty is not some single, eternal, and universal archetype, which finite beauties participate in to a greater or lesser extent, each reflecting more or less perfectly some ideal external to them. Rather, through the beauties of the created world the Spirit may bear testimony to the ways in which (in Santayana's words) "their ideal is immanent in them."

Likewise, the diverse and particular pleasures of our aesthetic experience can help us reimagine the sanctifying work of the Spirit. The perfection and completion of each creature is not found in the human pursuit of an impersonal and abstract standard. Instead it arises in a living and dynamic relationship with the Spirit who is person. Neither is it right to conceive sanctification as some inflexible divine rule, imposed from

---

73. Gerard Manley Hopkins, "As Kingfishers Catch Fire," in *Selected Poems of Gerard Manley Hopkins* (Mineola, NY: Dover, 2011), p. 46.

without. Rather, we are transformed by the *indwelling* Spirit, so that the transformation brought about by God is at the same time genuinely our own response, offered from our side of the relation.

Honoring the Spirit

Where and how does God's Holy Spirit bear witness through the arts? Reverence for the freedom of God's surprising and uncontainable *pneuma* should keep us from making dogmatic pronouncements about how the Spirit testifies in any particular instance of artistic beauty. Nevertheless, it is possible to look at some of the things that characterize the arts generally, and think about how these might be enlisted in the Spirit's testimony to Jesus Christ and his kingdom. We have also turned the question the other way around and asked why artists might use spiritual terms in their "testimony"—their attempts to speak about the creative work they produce. Here, too, as we consider the distinctive character of the Spirit's work, we can recognize a number of points at which artists are altogether correct to intuit some "spiritual" dimension to their pursuits.

To illustrate this with an example from outside the arts: Human beings regularly experience sexual intimacy as not only enjoyable but as *meaning*-full, momentous, and significant. It would not be surprising to hear someone describe lovemaking as "spiritual."[74] And, the theologian might say, this is precisely what we should expect if we are the kind of beings the Gospel says we are, and if the world has been made by the kind of God we worship. We are created in the image of a God who is love, who is an eternal community of Father, Son, and Spirit. We are created to reflect the image of this God—created for and called to community. It makes sense, then, that in moments of great intimacy, we feel ourselves close to the heart of things; that we become aware that our actions are played out against and oriented by some larger horizon of meaning.

---

74. J. Harold Ellens, psychologist and former chair of the Psychology and Biblical Studies Section of the Society of Biblical Literature, provides an example of this association: "The two most important aspects of human life are our spirituality and sexuality ... The energy that is generated by our sexual drives is the dynamic source of all the forces that shape our experience ... At the center of our selves, the life force that drives all of our vitality, or sense of being alive, is one force. It is this life force that we experience and refer to as our spirituality and sexuality" (J. Harold Ellens, *The Spirituality of Sex* [Westport, CT: Praeger Publishers, 2009], pp. xv, xvi).

This does not mean, of course, that every act of sexual union is in all its particulars a direct expression of God's word to the world. Neither does this deny the obvious fact that human sexual acts can be warped and distorted by human selfishness, or that they can bring not great joy and meaning, but deep hurt and sorrow. It is simply to say that human beings are not mistaken to experience sexual intimacy as meaningful on a transcendent horizon. It is not a mistake to characterize human love as "spiritual," because it does indeed gesture toward the Spirit's work of creating community. More than that, these experiences of meaning are one way in which the Spirit gives testimony to the kind of world God has created and the new creation God is bringing about. In the same way, when we think about the arts, there are, as we have seen, a number of points at which art points us toward the kind of work that God's Holy Spirit is about. If human beings sometimes sense that art is "spiritual"—as they doubtless have—then Christian theology is able to give a compelling explanation of this intuition.

We dishonor the Spirit, Calvin warns, if we fail to see the Spirit at work "in all that is most excellent in human life."[75] We might say that when Plato, Shelley, Schiller, and others associate creativity and aesthetic delight with spirit, they offer their own kind of testimony. If we attend to their witness, we will not be surprised—indeed we will expect—to hear the testimony of the Holy Spirit in art and beauty.

75. Calvin, *Institutes*, p. 274.

9

"Sighs Too Deep for Words"

THE HOLY SPIRIT, DESIRE, AND THE NAME
OF THE INCOMPREHENSIBLE GOD

Elizabeth T. Groppe

"THE SPIRIT," PAUL wrote to the Romans, "helps us in our weakness; for we do not know how to pray as we ought, but that very Spirit intercedes with sighs too deep for words" (Rom. 8:26). Two thousand years after Paul penned his letter to the Christian community in Rome, our weakness in prayer is painfully evident in the debates about gendered language for God that are transpiring within and across Christian denominations. An incident that occurred in a church I will call "St. Andrew's" is one case in point.

A well-educated woman who was a guest of a member of the parish felt her stomach tighten each time God was addressed as "Father." She quietly voiced alternative names for God by writing "*She*" or "*Mother*" in the worship book as the liturgy moved from the introductory to concluding rite. She was a woman with a strong sense of Christian vocation who had sacrificed prestigious career possibilities in order to dedicate her life to the service of families without access to health care. The following Sunday, a gentleman, who in his own way was deeply committed to the practice of the faith, sat in the same pew with one of his grown daughters, and when he saw what had been written in the liturgical books nested in the bracket on the back side of the wooden pew before him, he winced. "Who did such a thing?" he complained to his companion. "My sister," she replied.

In this chapter, I will probe the vexing pastoral problem of naming the Trinitarian God in ecclesial prayer through engagement with Anglican theologian Sarah Coakley's long-awaited *God, Sexuality, and the Self: An Essay "On the Trinity."* This book is the first installment of her four-volume systematic theology *On Desiring God*, which promises to be one of the most significant works of contemporary theology. Romans 8 is a crucial passage in Coakley's analysis of the development of the doctrine of the Trinity, for it is in the act of prayer that she finds the origins of the Christian pneumatological tradition. In the early church, prayer in the Spirit who intercedes for us with "sighs too deep for words" led to a profound theology of God's desire to incorporate human persons into the divine life. It is precisely this divine *eros*, Coakley suggests, that can flame through the knots of gendered theological language that have so entangled 21st-century women and men. Our exploration of Coakley's contribution begins with an exposition of her reconstruction of the origins of Christian pneumatology and the Trinitarian tradition.

Prayer in the Spirit and the Origins of Christian Pneumatology

Coakley's *God, Sexuality, and the Self* offers a fresh perspective on a wide array of interrelated questions through the exercise of a theological method that the British Anglican theologian describes as a *théologie totale*. This method, Coakley explains, is not a "totalizing" theology in a hegemonic sense. Rather, like the French Annales School's *l'histoire totale*, which probes every level of culture in the historical period under study, a *théologie totale* engages all dimensions of human life. Within a *théologie totale*, Christian thought and practice is the *cantus firmus* in contrapuntal orchestration with modern and postmodern philosophy, the sociology of religion and other social sciences, natural science, cultural theory, literature, music, and the arts. This methodology engages not only the intellect but also the human body, will, affect, imagination, and aesthetic sensibility in an approach in which theology, ethics, spirituality, and pastoral practice are inseparably intertwined.

Coakley's approach to Trinitarian theology is inflected by her knowledge of modern and postmodern philosophy, Freudian and post-Freudian psychoanalysis, feminism and gender studies, the sociology of religion, and other dimensions of our 21st-century intellectual milieu. It is also forged through a mastery of the patristic tradition and her conviction that the standard textbook accounts of Trinitarian theology that chronicle the emergence of conciliar orthodoxy from within a field of Sabellian, Arian, and Macedonian contenders is too narrowly construed. A *théologie totale* reads Origen of Alexandria's *De Principiis* (On First Principles) tethered to his *De oratione* (On Prayer), and Gregory of Nyssa's *Ad Ablabium, on "Not Three Gods"* in tandem with his ascetical treatise *On Perfection*, the mystical *Life of Moses*, and his *Commentary on the Song of Songs*. Coakley's reconstruction of the first centuries of Christian theological history elucidates pneumatology's origins in ascetical and contemplative practice as well as theology's inevitable entanglement with the complex realities of human desire, gender, and power.

In a chapter entitled "Praying the Trinity: A Neglected Patristic Tradition," Coakley responds at length to Maurice Wiles's position that there is no reasonable basis for the hypostatization of the Holy Spirit. Binitarianism, he avers, would have been a more logical outcome of the patristic period than the Trinitarianism that in fact emerged. This analysis, Coakley explains, does not give adequate consideration to texts that reflect what she terms an "incorporative" or "prayer-based" model of the Trinity in which the Holy Spirit actually catches up the created realm into the life of God and conforms it to Christ (Rom. 8:29). "When we cry 'Abba, Father,'" Paul testified, "it is the Spirit bearing witness with our spirit that we are children of God" (Rom. 8:15–16). Coakley comments:

> Note that the priority here, logically and experientially speaking, is given to the *Spirit*: the "Spirit" is that which, while being nothing less than "God," cannot quite be reduced to a metaphorical naming of the Father's outreach. It is not that the pray-er is having a conversation with some distant and undifferentiated deity, and then is being asked (rather arbitrarily) to "hypostasize" that conversation (or "relationship") into a "person" (the Spirit); but rather, that there is something, admittedly obscure, about the sustained activity of prayer that makes one want to claim that it is personally and divinely activated from within, and yet that that activation (the "Spirit") is not quite *reducible* to that from which it flows (the "Father").... [There] is a delicate ceding to something precisely not done by oneself. It is the sense (admittedly obscure) of an irreducibly dipolar divine *activity*—a call and response of divine desire—into which the pray-er is drawn and incorporated.[1]

1. Sarah Coakley, *God, Sexuality, and the Self: An Essay on the Trinity* (Cambridge: Cambridge University Press, 2013), pp. 112–13.

The "Son" into which the person in prayer is incorporated is neither the earthly Jesus nor the risen Christ (individualistically conceived) but "rather the divine life of Christ to which the whole creation, animate and inanimate, is tending, and into which it is being progressively transformed" as it "groans" toward its final telos (Rom. 8:18–25).[2] Coakley emphasizes the social, political, and cosmic scope of this transformation, as well as the language of "birth-pangs" that Paul employs to describe the cosmic gestation (Rom. 8:22–23), which " 'genders' the picture of prayer in a striking way, figuring the entire Christic event as the groanings of a woman in labour."[3] Prayer at its true heart "is God's, not ours," and the Spirit to whom Paul yields with sighs too deep for words "takes the pray-er beyond any normal human language or rationality of control."[4] Indeed, extant texts from the apostolic period attest to the ongoing association of the Spirit with ecstatic utterance, prophecy, and charismatic gifts.

That this *ecstasis* could become ecclesiastically problematic is evident in the emergence of Montanist prophets who claimed a revelation beyond that of Christ, and it is Coakley's thesis that the excesses of Montanism dampened the development of incorporative prayer-based Trinitarian theologies based on Romans 8 and fostered in their stead theologies that prioritized the Logos. In Origen's *On Prayer*, however, she finds a new enunciation of Pauline theology in a Middle Platonic key that creatively weds biblical themes with a Platonic notion of *eros*. She draws our attention to four features of Origen's text, a treatise addressed to both Ambrose and Tatiana, the latter a woman "most manly" (*andreiotatē*) who has gone beyond "womanish things" (*gynēkaia*) in the manner of Sarah (Gen. 18:11). In *On Prayer*, we find (1) an emphasis on the primacy of the Holy Spirit, who carries the person at prayer into unutterable mysteries beyond the realm of human rationality; (2) an account of a participation in the Word of God that becomes possible only through mingling with the Spirit; (3) the use of metaphors from the realms of procreation and sexual intercourse; *and*, at the same time, (4) a careful disjunction between prayer and physiological sexuality.

Origen's exegesis of Romans 8, for example, is accompanied by the reminder that women should wear modest apparel and head coverings to

---

2. Ibid., p. 113.

3. Ibid., p. 115.

4. Ibid.

protect men from loss of sexual control, and the exhortation to "pray as we ought" is accompanied by the injunction to perform the mysteries of marriage in a manner that is passionless and deliberate. "The intrinsic connections between prayer and eroticism, it seems," Coakley observes, "are too close to be avoided, but also too dangerous to be allowed free rein."[5] Origen's later commentary and homilies on the *Song of Songs* allegorize this erotic biblical text as an account of the soul's ascent to God through the embrace of Christ the Bridegroom, but the Alexandrian theologian cautions that the sexual metaphor is to be understood in relation only to the spiritual senses (not the physical body) and that the metaphor poses grave danger to the spiritually immature.

Coakley also finds evidence of the contemplative origins of the pneumatological tradition in Athanasius. In the course of his clash with a succession of emperors, the defender of Nicene orthodoxy was exiled from Alexandria no less than five times, and the displaced bishop discovered Anthony and the monastic movement in the Egyptian desert. This encounter, Coakley believes, was highly significant in the development of Athanasius's theology of the Holy Spirit. Whereas *On the Incarnation* articulates an incorporative Christology that has no explicit pneumatology, advancing from opening line to concluding doxology with only a fleeting reference to the Spirit, Athanasius's later *Letters to Serapion* emphasized that God "the Father does all things through the Word *in the Holy Spirit.*"[6] As was the case in Origen's *On Prayer*, Romans 8 is a keystone scriptural text. "It is through the Spirit," Athanasius writes in a commentary on Romans 8:29, "that we are partakers of God ... the unction and the seal that is in us belongs, not to the nature of things originate, but to the nature of the Son who, through the Spirit who is in him, joins us to the Father."[7]

The context in which Athanasius is writing, Coakley observes, is in important ways distinct from that of Origen. Yet although the two Alexandrian theologians are separated by two centuries and two doctrinally definitive church councils, both men read Romans 8 through the lens of a lifetime of ascetic struggle, moral and spiritual preparation for union with

---

5. Ibid., p. 128.

6. Athanasius, *Letters to Serapion*, 1.28, cited in Coakley, *God, Sexuality, and the Self*, p. 136.

7. Athanasius, *Letters to Serapion*, 1.24.

God, and the practice of prayer.[8] In their experience, the Holy Spirit is not a stepping stone or rung on the ladder of ascent to God but the very one in whom we are swept up into the communion of divine love. We pray, wrote Athanasius, "*in the Triad* . . . for inasmuch as we partake of the Spirit, we have the grace of the Word and, in the Word, the love of the Father."[9]

Origen and Athanasius influenced the Cappadocian theologian Gregory of Nyssa, and Coakley finds a strong resonance of their incorporative Trinitarian theology in Nyssa's *Life of Moses*, an account of Moses's climb up Mount Sinai retold in the tradition of Philo and Clement as an allegory of the soul's ascent to God. Moses beholds the light of the burning bush (representative of the light of the incarnation), passes through the clouds of the wilderness, and then enters the thick darkness on Sinai's peak in quest of an elusive perfection. As the soul progresses with ever-greater concentration toward knowledge of the truth, it

> comes to appreciate what the knowledge of truth is, so much the more does it see that the divine nature is invisible. It thus leaves all surface appearances, not only those that can be grasped by the senses, but also those which the mind itself seems to see, and it keeps on going deeper until by the operation of the Spirit it penetrates the invisible and incomprehensible, and it is there that it sees God. The true vision and true knowledge of what we seek consists precisely in not seeing, in an awareness that our goal transcends all knowledge and is everywhere cut off from us by the darkness of incomprehensibility.

The ascent climaxes within a womb-like darkness in a longing and desiring without end. In distinction from Gregory's earlier apologetic treatises in which Trinitarian terms are clearly delineated with transparent structure and order, the *Life of Moses* and Gregory's *Commentary on the Song of Songs* exercise "a remarkable poetic and erotic license. Here, archers and arrows, winds and billowing sails, and human erotic lovers become the new analogues of the freedom of inner-trinitarian relations, and of their transfiguring relation to us."[10]

---

8. Coakley, *God, Sexuality, and the* Self, pp. 137–40.

9. Ibid.

10. Ibid., p. 288.

Coakley reflects on texts of divine ascent not only as a master of patristic literature but also as a scholar whose sense of her own vocation as a Christian theologian has been transformed in the crucible of prayer. "There is a sense in which my mind has changed only once in the course of my career as a theologian," she writes, "but once instigated, this change was so dramatic and transformative as to sweep everything else uncomfortably in its wake. Like a subterranean explosion, the intellectual fallout was initially difficult to trace to its source."[11] The source of this upheaval was prayer, a daily discipline of silence and stillness, within the context of participation in the liturgical and sacramental life of the Anglican communion. Indeed, the "cracking open of the heart before God" that Coakley describes took place during the period of her formation for ordained ministry in the Anglican tradition. The consequence was painful and anxiety-provoking. Underneath the pain and fear, however, "was an extraordinary sense of spiritual and epistemic expansion—of being taken by the hand into a new world of glorious technicolor, in which all one's desires were newly magnetized toward God, all beauty sharpened and intensified."[12]

The discipline of silent prayer also sharpened Coakley's consciousness of poverty, deprivation, and injustice. She is keenly aware of myriad forms of suffering, including the way in which questions of gender and sexuality are precipitating pain, tension, and division within and between Christian communities and in society at large. I will focus in the remainder of this chapter on only one of these concerns: the struggle to find truthful, faithful, and pastorally viable ways of naming the triune God. In the section that follows, I will briefly outline some of the critiques of the Trinitarian language of "Father, Son, and Spirit" that have been raised in recent decades, note some of the alternative theological formulations that have been proposed, and indicate some of the critical responses to these proposals. I will then return in the final section to Coakley's work and consider some of the ways in which her *On Desiring God* can reframe the vexing problems posed by the gendered language that Christians employ in our worship.

11. Coakley, "Prayer as Crucible: How My Mind Has Changed," *Christian Century* (March 22, 2011): 32.

12. Ibid., p. 33.

The Holy Spirit, Gender, and the Divine Name

How, Pseudo-Dionysius ponders, is one to speak of the hidden divinity who is above and beyond speech, mind, and being itself? "'Not in the plausible words of human wisdom,'" he determines, "'but in demonstration of the power granted by the Spirit'" (1 Cor. 2:4).[13] Attributing to the writers of scripture an inspired knowledge that is superior to human wisdom, he presents a litany of biblical names for God: "I am being (Ex 3:14), life (Jn 11:25), light (Jn 8:12), God (Gn 28:13), the truth (Jn 14:6), good (Mt 19:17), beautiful (Sg 1:16), wise (Job 9:4), beloved (Isa 5:1), God of gods (Deut 10:17), Lord of Lords (Deut 10:17), Holy of Holies (Dn 9:24), eternal (Isa 40:28), existent (Ex 3:14), cause of the ages (Heb 1:2), source of life (2 Mac 1:25), wisdom (Prv 8:22-21), mind (Is 40:13), word (Jn 1:1), knower (Sus 42), possessor beforehand of all the treasures of knowledge (Col 2:3), power (Rev 19:1), powerful (1 Tim 6:15), King of Kings (Dn 7:9), ancient of days (Mal 3:6), the unaging and unchanging (Ex 15:2), salvation (1 Cor 1:30), righteousness and sanctification (1 Cor 1:30), redemption (1 Cor 30), greatest of all and yet the one in the still breeze (1 Kgs 19:12)."[14] Only one of these names is gendered male (King of Kings), but had the litany been an exhaustive list of biblical names for God it would have also included some names that are gendered female: God is "the Rock that bore you, the God who gave you birth" (Deut. 32:18), a nursing mother (Isa. 49:15), a comforting mother (Isa. 66:13), a woman in the pangs of childbirth (Isa. 42:14).

It is the biblical texts that name the relationship between Jesus Christ and God the Father that generate tensions in the pews of St. Andrew's: "This is how you are to pray: Our Father in heaven, hallowed be your name" (Matt. 6:9–13); "Go baptize in the name of the Father, the Son, and the Holy Spirit" (Matt. 28:19). Even before the 20th-century sensitivity to gendered language, there were theologians who carefully qualified the interpretation of these biblical terms. Gregory of Nazianzus, for example, ridiculed opponents who thought that God is male because he is called "Father."[15] Thomas Aquinas believed that God is properly called "Father" rather than "Mother" because God is pure act, and under the influence of

---

13. Pseudo-Dionysius, *The Complete Works*, trans. Colm Luibheid (New York: Paulist, 1987), p. 49.

14. Ibid., p. 55.

15. Gregory of Nazianzus, Oration 31.8.

Aristotelian biology he considered the male to be the sole active principle in the process of begetting.[16] At the same time, however, he emphasized that even words like "Father" that are properly predicated of God are used analogically. They are affirmed at one level, but their creaturely connotations are then negated, and they ultimately point in a supereminent way to a reality that transcends the limits of human words.

The emergence of theological feminism brought a new kind of scrutiny to Trinitarian language. Mary Daly was trained in Thomistic theology but was not persuaded that the careful qualifications of the analogical method were sufficient to protect male theological language from abuse. Regardless of how a theologian might qualify a reference to "God the Father," this language has sociological consequences: "If God in 'his' heaven is a father ruling 'his' people, then it is in the nature of things and according to divine plan and the order of the universe that society be male-dominated."[17] Indeed, Elizabeth Johnson observes, sociologist of religion Clifford Geertz found a correlation between the symbols of a religious system and the character of the social order in which a religion is embedded, and Paul Tillich noted that when an earthly reality is used as a symbol for the divine, there is a transference of a divine aura to a finite reality:

> If God is symbolized as "Father," he is brought down to the human relationship of father and child. But, at the same time, this human relationship is consecrated into a pattern of the divine-human relationship. If "Father" is employed as a symbol for God, fatherhood is seen in its theonomous, sacramental depth.[18]

"Male images [of God]," Johnson reflects, "allow men to participate fully in [the divine ground], while women can do so only by abstracting themselves from their concrete, bodily identity as women." This is a "subtle conditioning that operates to debilitate women's sense of dignity, power, and self-esteem."[19]

---

16. Thomas Aquinas, *Summa Contra Gentiles*, trans. Charles J. O'Neil (Notre Dame, IN: University of Notre Dame Press, 1957), 4.11.19.

17. Mary Daly, *Beyond God the Father: Toward a Philosophy of Women's Liberation* (Boston: Beacon Press, 1973), p. 13.

18. Paul Tillich, *Systematic Theology* (Chicago: University of Chicago Press, 1951), p. 140.

19. Elizabeth Johnson, *She Who Is: The Mystery of God in Feminist Theological Discourse* (New York: Crossroad, 1993), pp. 37–38.

Moreover, Johnson continues, if God is exclusively named in masculine terms in the public prayer of the church, this language can easily be interpreted univocally, as if God were actually a biologically male being. Many Christians would share the unease of the gentleman at St. Andrew's who winced at the language of "God, the Mother" that had been written into the worship book. If we do not experience any dissonance when we speak of God the Father, however, it is possible that at some subconscious or unconscious level we have actually gendered God as male. Language that should lead us deeper into the mystery of God then becomes an obstacle to true theological knowledge. When the difference between human language and the divine reality is collapsed, "then an idol comes into being. Then the comprehensible image, rather than disclosing mystery, is taken for the reality."[20]

As an alternative to the Trinitarian language of "Father, Son, and Holy Spirit," the gender-neutral language of "Creator, Redeemer, and Sustainer" won sufficient favor in some ecclesial communities to gain incorporation in worship services. As Catherine Mowry LaCugna has observed, however, there are a number of theological problems with this approach. The language of "Creator, Redeemer, and Sustainer" implies that each of the divine *hypostases* has an exclusive function in the economy of creation and redemption, whereas scripture attests that God creates *through* the Son (Col. 1:16, Heb. 11:3, John 1:1–3) and the Spirit (Gen. 1:1–2), and that God redeems creation *through* Christ (2 Cor. 5:19, Eph. 1:7, Col. 1:14). The triune *hypostases* are not discrete individuals in the modern sense that the term "person" typically conveys. Moreover, prayer that addresses God in the economic terms of "Creator" and "Redeemer" is functional rather than metaphysical.[21]

Another alternative construction maintains the biblical language of "Father" and "Son" but retrieves sources from the tradition that name the Holy Spirit with female pronouns and imagery. This language is particularly prominent in the early Syriac tradition. The *Odes of Solomon*, dated between the first and early third centuries, compare the Dove-Spirit to a mother who gives milk to her children, and a Syriac hymn describes the Spirit as a merciful mother.[22] Drawing on these and other

---

20. Ibid., p. 39.

21. Catherine Mowry LaCugna, "The Trinitarian Mystery of God," in Francis Schüssler Fiorenza and John P. Galvin (eds.), *Systematic Theology: Roman Catholic Perspectives* (Minneapolis: Fortress, 1991), 1, p. 182.

22. Emmanuel-Pataq Siman, *L'Expérience de L'Esprit par L'Eglise d'après la tradition syrienne d'Antioche*, Theol. Hist. no. 15 (Beauchesne: Paris, 1971), p. 155.

historical sources, Yves Congar devotes a chapter to "The Motherhood in God and the Femininity of the Holy Spirit" in his *I Believe in the Holy Spirit*.[23] The maternal character of the Holy Spirit, he observes, is evident in the brooding of God's *ruach* over the primordial waters of creation (Gen. 1:2), the hovering presence of the Spirit over the baptismal waters in which Jesus is named as God's Son, the Spirit's role in the glorification of Christ, and the birthing of the Church through the Spirit at Pentecost. Theologians who have developed more fully a theology of a feminine Spirit include Leonardo Boff and Donald Gelpi, both of whom employ qualified versions of Jung's theory of gender archetypes in their Trinitarian reflections.[24] But these well-intentioned efforts to redress the problems of gendered theological language are not without their own difficulties. The designation of the Holy Spirit as a feminine counterpart to the Father and the Son may give the impression that God is two parts male and one part female. And, in a Western tradition in which the Holy Spirit has been described as a "faceless" divine person,[25] the feminine *hypostasis* of the Trinity may appear marginal or subordinate to the Father and the Son.

Rather than adopting feminine language only for the Holy Spirit, Elizabeth Johnson's *She Who Is: The Mystery of God in Feminist Theological Discourse* names God using female symbolism. Johnson's theological ideal is the use in equal measure of male and female terminology. Because of the degree to which male language has dominated the tradition, however, *She Who Is* prioritizes female imagery drawn from scripture, tradition, and the lived experience of women. "Unless a strong measure of undervalued female symbolism is introduced and used with ease," she explains, "equivalent imaging of God male and female, which I myself have advocated and still hold to be a goal, remains an abstraction, expressive of an ideal but unrealizable in actual life."[26] Exegeting biblical texts from the wisdom traditions, she explains that the feminine biblical figure of Wisdom (*hokmah* in Hebrew and *Sophia* in Greek) is engaged in activities

---

23. Yves Congar, *I Believe in the Holy Spirit*, 3 vols., trans. David Smith (New York: Seabury, 1983).

24. Leonardo Boff, *The Maternal Face of God: The Feminine and Its Religious Expressions*, trans. Robert Barr and John Diercksmeier (Maryknoll, NY: Orbis, 1987); Donald Gelpi, *The Divine Mother: A Trinitarian Theology of the Holy Spirit* (Lanham, MD: University Press of America, 1984).

25. Walter Kasper, *The God of Jesus Christ* (New York: Crossroad, 1984), p. 223.

26. Johnson, *She Who Is*, p. 57.

that are functionally equivalent to the activities of the biblical God,[27] and she develops a full Trinitarian theology of Spirit-Sophia, Jesus-Sophia, and Mother-Sophia.

In response to these developments, some theologians have affirmed that the triune God must be named only in the New Testament language of "Father, Son, and Spirit." It is epistemologically axiomatic, writes Protestant theologian Thomas Torrance, that God is unknowable and unnamable by finite human beings. "No one can know God except God, and so no one can know God except through God—that is, only through sharing in some way in the knowledge which God has of himself."[28] Without the participation in God's own knowing that the Holy Spirit enables, discourse about God is nothing but projection or mythology. Scripture testifies to God's triadic movement of self-communication in which "*God* reveals *himself* through *himself*" and "*names himself as Father, Son, and Holy Spirit.*"[29] Torrance does not intend these terms to be interpreted in a univocal sense. God cannot be conceived or represented in visual or sensual images, and theological terms are not descriptions of the divine but transparent and open analogies. Although God has named himself as "Father," we must hear this language in the Spirit and not project creaturely fatherhood or gender onto God, who is beyond imagining.[30] Others who have affirmed the singular theological significance of the scriptural language "Father, Son, and Spirit" include Dominican theologian J. A. DiNoia and Orthodox theologian Thomas Hopko.[31]

Yet another approach retains the biblical and creedal language of Father, Son, and Holy Spirit but combines this with feminine terms that complexify theological signification and nudge our imagination away from the temptation to hear the words "Father" and "Son" in a univocal sense. There is precedent for this in the tradition. Catherine Mowry LaCugna observes, for example, that in 675 CE the Eleventh Council of Toledo affirmed that

---

27. Ibid., pp. 87 and 91.

28. Thomas F. Torrance, "The Christian Apprehension of God the Father," in Alvin F. Kimel, Jr. (ed.), *Speaking the Christian God: The Holy Trinity and the Challenge of Feminism* (Grand Rapids, MI: Eerdmans, 1992), p. 120.

29. Ibid., p. 121.

30. Ibid., p. 137.

31. Thomas Hopko, "Apophatic Theology and the Naming of God in Eastern Orthodox Tradition," in *Speaking the Christian God*, pp. 144–61; J. A. DiNoia, "Knowing and Naming the Triune God: The Grammar of Trinitarian Confession," in *Speaking the Christian God*, pp. 162–87.

the Son is begotten *"de utero Patris* [from the womb of the Father]."[32] In the 14th century, Julian of Norwich wrote of "our precious Mother Jesus," who "can feed us with himself, and does, most courteously and most tenderly, with the blessed sacrament, which is the precious food of true life."[33]

On Desiring God

Those who probe the way in which our human proclivity to idolatry can distort theological and liturgical language do so with good reason. Theological language is embedded in the human psyche, relationships, and culture, and bears the mark of our fallen condition. Overtly or subliminally, the naming of God as "Father"—or as "Mother"—may project a human longing onto the divine, reinforce a social system, or bolster a human ego. "No trinitarian language," writes Coakley, "is innocent of sexual, political, and ecclesiastical overtones and implications, and ... it is a primary task of a *théologie totale* to ferret out these implications, and to bring them to greater critical consciousness."[34] The scrutiny of theological language's potential to obfuscate true knowledge of God is a perpetually necessary discipline that must be practiced with respect to theologies composed by both men and women. "Feminist theology's abiding significance," Coakley affirms, "abides in its attention to the perennial spiritual temptation of idolatry" to which it may itself fall prey.[35]

At the same time, Coakley emphasizes, "such suspicion can never have the last word."[36] If our theological work is no more than an elucidation of the psychological, social, ecclesiastical, and political abuses of theological language, we reduce theology to an enterprise of social critique and lose the *theo*logical moorings that alone can chasten and reorient the fallen desires that result in the domination, control, subservience, and violence that are characteristic of the gender disorders of our day. Freud, Feuerbach, Geertz, Foucault, and others are important contrapuntal voices in a *théologie totale*, but staying true to theology's *cantus firmus* requires

---

32. LaCugna, "The Trinitarian Mystery of God," 1, p. 183.

33. Julian of Norwich, *Showings*, trans. and intro. by Edmund Colledge and James Walsh (New York: Paulist, 1978), p. 398.

34. Coakley, *God, Sexuality, and the Self,* p. 308.

35. Ibid., p. 68.

36. Ibid., p. 267.

much more than a hermeneutic of suspicion and a critique of projection and power; it requires immersion in Christian practice and an openness of the heart to the Holy Spirit who "always blows afresh to purge, enlighten, and inflame."[37] This purgation and illumination is a necessary precursor to the reordering of human relationships, including relations between the genders. It is only in the grace of the Spirit that "the fallen political and ecclesiastical structures can be reformed, transformed."[38] And it is in the grace of the Spirit that we may find a deep propulsion to "the true goal of human longing."

In our modern and postmodern context, however, it may be difficult to name and recognize this longing for what it truly is. So thoroughly has our secular culture individualized, commodified, physicalized, and sexualized desire that to speak of a "desire for God" may strike us as puzzling or odd.[39] The *telos* of desire has shrunk from an eschatological goal to a fleeting moment of pleasure and gratification. This problem, Coakley observes, has no "quick fix." But we may begin what will be a lifelong endeavor of repair by asking questions such as: What is desire? What is its ultimate meaning and purpose? What is the relation between gendered sexual desire and desire for God? How do we adjudicate between the variety of desires we experience? How are our desires shaped by our culture and the subconscious levels of our psyche? Why do we desire domination, power, possession, subservience, or control? How can we open our hearts to the healing of corrupted desire made possible through the Spirit of Christ?

To adequately address these questions, Coakley emphasizes, a renewed understanding and practice of asceticism is necessary. In *The New Asceticism: Sexuality, Gender, and the Quest for God*, she observes that the meaning of the term "asceticism," like that of "desire," has been so obscured by its modern associations that it must be rehabilitated before it can be put to good theological use. True asceticism is neither repression nor authoritarianism, but a habit and practice of spiritual formation that through grace bears fruit in freedom, agency, self-knowledge, and humility. Asceticism does not repress desire but chastens, purifies, refines, and intensifies it within the crucible of divine love. Spiritual discipline is a

---

37. Ibid.

38. Ibid., p. 84.

39. Sarah Coakley, *The New Asceticism: Sexuality, Gender, and the Quest for God* (London: Bloomsbury Continuum, 2015), p. 4.

yielding not to ecclesiastical power but "to that subtle but ecstatic plenti-
tude of divine desire freely outpoured in the life of Christ," and its "test
and measure is an extension of that transforming love to the world."[40]
Authentic obedience is not an infantile or slave mentality, but the freedom
to desire with the very desire of God.[41] It is in this sense that God has given
the Holy Spirit "to those who obey him" (Acts 5:32).

Coakley finds some support for her retrieval of ascetical practice in
Sigmund Freud, the founder of psychoanalysis. In popular culture, Freud
is often associated with the position that a thwarting of one's sexual desires
is repressive and psychologically unhealthy. This, however, is an over-
simplified and bowdlerized version of the 19th-century Austrian thinker,
who revised his theories repeatedly over the course of his lifetime. In his
late *Civilization and Its Discontents* and *Why War?*, Freud aligns Eros and
Libido as a single drive that includes not just the biological sexual impulse
but also the Ego's instinct for life and self-preservation, which exists in
psychic tension with its binary opposite, Thanatos. In a remarkable correspondence with Albert Einstein that the physicist initiated in 1933, Freud
expresses his hope that Eros can triumph over Thanatos not by suppress-
ing our inclinations to aggression and war but by diverting and "rechan-
neling" the energies of hate. His reflections on the channeling of the love
instinct, Coakley observes, are reminiscent of Plato's *Symposium*.

At the same time, there is one very important difference between Freud
and Plato: The ladder of ascent that Freud begins to mount leads nowhere.
It culminates neither in a transcendent world of forms nor in a personal
God. In Freud, "'Eros' lacks eschatological, or *divine*, direction."[42] Without
this telos, Coakley hypothesizes, there is no lodestar to channel our love
instinct on its course: "Unless we have some sense of the implications of
the trinitarian God's 'proto-erotic' desire for us, then we can hardly begin
to get rightly ordered our own desires at the human level."[43]

---

40. Ibid., pp. 27–28.

41. Jean-Claude Sagne puts it thus: "[I]t is the function of the Holy Spirit to be the desire of
God in God himself and also the desire of God in us. The Spirit forms, deepens, expands
and adjusts our desire to the desire of God by giving it the same object. The Spirit makes our
desire live from the heart of God himself, to the point where God himself comes to desire
at the heart of our own desire" (Jean-Claude Sagne, "L'Esprit-Saint ou le désir de Dieu,"
Concilium 99 [French edition] [1974]: 94).

42. Coakley, *New Asceticism*, p. 45.

43. Ibid., p. 96.

Coakley is convinced by her own discipline of prayer that we truly can have a sense of God's desire for us. At the heart of her theology is the ascetic and liturgical practice of contemplation, a bodily and spiritual discipline of wordless waiting upon God that has the potential to purify the mind, will, and senses of the idolatries that we absorb from our culture and forge by our own projections and desires. This painful and discomforting purgation is a lifelong and ethically demanding journey of epistemic stripping, submission to mystery, sweat and perseverance in the face of the bombardments of the unconscious that require vigilance against self-deception. It is an apophatic negation not only of all of our language for God but also of our very will to grasp at the divine and to cast God in our own image and likeness.

"What is blanked out," Coakley explains, "in the regular, patient attempt to attend to God in prayer is *any* sense of human grasp; and what comes to replace such an ambition, over time, is the elusive, but nonetheless ineluctable, sense of *being grasped,* of the Spirit's simultaneous erasure of human idolatry and subtle reconstitution of human selfhood in God."[44] If we allow the Holy Spirit to cleanse and reorder our desires, a way is opened for a "new and deeper knowledge-beyond-knowledge."[45] All of this is humanly impossible. It is, in the end, the Holy Spirit who prays *in* us, for we ourselves do not know how to pray as we ought. This grace capacitates a distinctive kind of knowing in which reason is "stretched and changed beyond its normal, secular reach."[46] Orthodoxy is not merely the assent of the will to cerebral propositions or doctrines, but "a demanding, and ongoing, spiritual *project,* in which the language of the creeds is personally and progressively assimilated."[47]

What, then, of the father and daughter sitting on alternate Sundays in the pew of St. Andrew's? How are we to name the Trinitarian God in Christian liturgical practice and worship? Coakley's work may lead us beyond some of the impasses that our struggles with gendered theological language have occasioned. We can distill from her most recent work the following five insights that can contribute constructively to theological and pastoral discussions of the naming of the triune God.

---

44. Coakley, *God, Sexuality, and the Self,* p. 23.

45. Ibid., p. 43.

46. Ibid., p. 25.

47. Ibid., p. 5.

1. Desire Is More Fundamental than Gender

Coakley's careful reading of the tradition and her own experience of the purgative process of prayer led her to the theological realization that desire is more fundamental than either sex or gender. This is so because *eros* or desire is an ontological category that belongs primarily and preeminently to God, and only secondarily to humans created in the divine image.[48] Neither sex nor gender, in contrast, can be properly predicated of a God who does not have a biologically sexed body and does not beget through sexual intercourse. A substantial corpus of theological literature probes the potential for idolatry in language for God that is exclusively male in its *ratio nominis*.[49] And yet, in Coakley's analysis, it is not simply maleness (and femaleness) that can become idolatrous, but the very conception of gender itself. If gender becomes our utmost or ultimate concern, it assumes a place of importance in our human identities and theological imaginations that belongs only to God.

This is not to say, Coakley emphasizes, that gender and sexuality are unimportant; to the contrary, they matter profoundly. Gender, which she defines as "differentiated, embodied relationship," is a profound aspect of human experience and a crucial dimension of theological anthropology, and sexual desire is a "precious clue woven into our created being reminding us of our rootedness in God."[50] But if we are "to bring this desire into *right* alignment with God's purposes, purified from sin and possessiveness, something profoundly transformative has to happen."[51]

2. Reframing Theological Inquiry in the Primacy of Divine Desire

Our heightened awareness of gender has generated important theological questions over the course of the last 50 years. Theologians have probed the psychological, sociological, and spiritual implications of gendered language for God and revisited classic questions about the character of

---

48. Ibid., p. 10.

49. For a helpful summary of Aquinas's distinctions of the *ratio nominis*, *res significata*, and *modus significandi* that are fundamental to analogical language, see J. A. DiNoia, "Knowing and Naming the Triune God," pp. 162–87.

50. Coakley, *God, Sexuality, and the Self*, p. 309.

51. Ibid., pp. 309–10.

theological language. These inquiries are essential to the responsible exercise of the theological discipline, but they will bear limited fruit if they are not contextualized within a theological framework that grapples with the meaning of desire. What do we intend to express when we call God "Father"? Can the community at St. Andrew's also call God "Mother"? Is God a "He" or a "She"? These are significant questions. But we can address them more adequately if we ask also these more fundamental questions: What is the origin and meaning of the desire that is embedded in human gender and sexuality? What is its ultimate purpose and telos? What is the relationship between our various forms of desire (for food, wealth, power, love, and God)? How can we discriminate between the desire for love and the desire for domination, possession, power, or control? How and why does desire become distorted? How can a corrupted desire be healed?

3. Practicing a New Asceticism

Responding adequately and honestly to questions about desire will require a retrieval of the ascetical traditions of Christian spirituality. A daily practice of prayer within the context of an active sacramental life is essential to the process of learning to discriminate distorted desires from the true *eros* of God. Only with wisdom gained from this ascetic crucible can we navigate pressing pastoral questions about gender and the naming of the triune God. There is validity, for example, to the concern that the liturgical language of "God the Father" can subliminally legitimate relationships that subordinate women to men. And yet, Coakley cautions, if we simply replace terms and imagery that are male with language that is female, "the purgative process of renewal in the Spirit is short-changed."[52] Freud, she notes, knew well that "to kill the Father is to remain with and reaffirm the rule of the Father."[53]

To undo patriarchy at its root requires something deeper: the "kneeling work" that can purify our imaginations in the crucible of divine desire: "It is the Holy Spirit that thereby causes me to see God no longer as patriarchal threat but as infinite tenderness; but it is also the Holy Spirit who first painfully darkens my prior certainties, enflames and checks my own desires, and so invites me ever more deeply into the life of redemption

52. Ibid., p. 323.
53. Ibid., p. 326.

in Christ."[54] Living exemplars of people who practice the kneeling work of the Spirit have always been important in ecclesial life, and in an era in which asceticism is disdained or misunderstood, the need for these models and mentors is more acute than ever. Gregory of Nyssa wrote of the "indispensable spiritual power of a person from whom one may *mimetically* 'catch the halo,' as he puts it, of rightly ordered desire."[55] She or he can witness to the reality that the fruits of the discipline of prayer are neither instantaneous nor commodifiable and that asceticism is accompanied by both sacrifice and joy. We may behold in such mentors the transparency to the divine that follows the progressive purification of the self.[56]

4. Dionysian Profusion and Analogical Awareness

Does Coakley's ascetical approach then leave "everything as it is" in the prevailing liturgical patterns of naming the triune God? "Yes," Coakley responds, "and no (*but above all no*)." No, first and foremost, "because in the mysterious ongoing contemplative surrender to Dionysius' 'ray of divine darkness' the psychic bag and baggage which we bring to our prayer ... is by slow degrees retrieved, sorted, and held up for healing."[57] And *no*, because this approach does allow for a Dionysian profusion of metaphors for God that remind us that "*God* is beyond all positive and negative attributes," and careful liturgical reformers can use these metaphors in deliberately illogical conjunctions "with delicacy and power to bounce us out of our unconscious ongoing idolatries."[58] To be sure, she continues:

> the free poetic use of maternal language, especially if conjoined paradoxically with paternal language, can in some circumstances have an exhilaratingly releasing effect on the imagination, as long as it is not allowed to harden into its own dogmatism. But we have seen enough of the complexity of this issue by now to know that the question of naming God "appropriately" (*proprie*) is not resolvable by any one isolable strategy, nor indeed at any one distinguishable

---

54. Ibid., p. 56.

55. Coakley, *New Asceticism*, p. 51.

56. Ibid., p. 112.

57. Coakley, *God, Sexuality, and the Self*, p. 323.

58. Ibid., p. 324.

level of engagement. The strategy of metaphorical profusion (or visual indeterminacy or movement in the artistic realm) at one—culturally accessible—level of imaginative engagement needs to be *conjoined* with rigorous, nuanced theological and philosophical understanding of the precise semantic character of creedal *trinitarian* naming, at another. Both strategies are needed; but even they do not exhaust what is underlyingly an invitation to engage a Reality that is itself triune. And what is at stake here, at base, is a slow but steady assault on idolatry which only the patient practices of prayer can allow God to do *in* us: in the purgative kneeling before the blankness of the darkness which nonetheless dazzles, the Spirit is at work in this very noetic slippage, drawing all things into Christ and recasting our whole sense of how language for God *works.*[59]

It is in this context that Coakley notes that the name of God as Trinity differs in important ways from the many terms we can rightly use in a profuse array of metaphors. It is here that she articulates a *yes* to the traditional form of the triune name. "Father," she explains, with reference to Aquinas, is used appropriately (*proprie*) of God when the word is used of inner-Trinitarian relations in a sense qualitatively distinct from the way in which the term is used of human men. Her own practice throughout *God, Sexuality, and the Self* is to enclose the terms "Father" and "Son" in quotation marks that serve to remind the reader that these words are not being used in a sense univocal with the meanings that they have in other contexts.

5. The Social Character of Desire

The gentleman at St. Andrew's was understandably disturbed by the marking up of liturgical books. But his daughter who preceded him in the parish pew is also justified in her desire to make her concerns about the language of worship public in some small way. The ecclesial conflicts about gendered language for God cannot be resolved by private prayer practices in which everyone worships God on his or her own terms. Although our culture construes desires individually, this is a reductive approach that fails to account for the social construction of desire and the social consequences of the manner in which each of us responds (or fails to respond)

---

59. Ibid., p. 325.

to the divine *eros*. Commenting on the Rule of Saint Benedict, Coakley observes that it is through the endurance of community living "and not through virtuosity in private prayer (on which Benedict has remarkably little to say) that the 'heart' comes to be 'enlarged' 'with unspeakable sweetness of love.' "[60]

---

60. Coakley, *New Asceticism*, p. 116.

10

The Spirit and the Bride Say "Come"

APOLOGETICS AND THE WITNESS OF THE HOLY SPIRIT

Kevin Kinghorn and Jerry L. Walls

IN A WORD, Christian apologetics is a *defense* of Christian theism. The Greek word *apologia* may refer to the kind of reasoned case a lawyer provides in defending the innocence of an accused person. Or, more broadly, the word may refer to any line of argument showing the truth of some position. 1 Peter 3:15 contains the instruction to Christians: "Always be prepared to give an answer [*apologia*] to everyone who asks you to give the reason for the hope that you have."[1]

Testimony: Human and Divine

Within the four Gospels one finds a heavy emphasis on human testimony in helping others come to beliefs about Christ. For example, St. Luke opens his Gospel by explaining to its recipient, Theophilus, that he is writing "an orderly account" of the life of Jesus "so that you may know the certainty of the things you have been taught." Luke describes himself as drawing together a written account of things "just as they were handed down to us by those who from the first were eyewitnesses and servants of the Word."[2] As Richard Swinburne remarks, "it is hard to read the Gospels, Acts of the Apostles, and 1 Corinthians without seeing them as claiming that various

---

1. All quotations from the Bible taken from NIV.

2. Luke 1:1–4.

historical events (above all, the Resurrection) occurred and that others can know these things on the testimony of the apostles to have seen them."[3]

This passing down of apostolic testimony continued through the next generations of the early Christian Church. Ignatius, in contending for the bodily resurrection of Jesus, emphasized that the disciples "touched him and believed."[4] Later Church fathers frequently appealed to Ignatius and to such other early fathers as Clement of Rome and Polycarp, who also were reputed to have been taught directly by the apostles. So, for example, Irenaeus appeals to the teachings of Polycarp, whose word can be trusted because he was "instructed by the apostles, and conversed with many who had seen Christ."[5]

Alongside this eyewitness testimony preserved and proclaimed by the Church, the Christian tradition affirms a complementary form of testimony that is essential for bringing people to faith in Christ, namely the testimony of the Holy Spirit. The Gospel of John, while recording Jesus's prayer "for those who will believe in me through their [the disciples'] message,"[6] also contains Jesus's promise that the Father will send the Holy Spirit, who "will teach you all things" and who will "guide you into all the truth."[7] Likewise, the writer of Hebrews, in corroborating his own summation of Jesus's teaching, remarks that "the Holy Spirit also testifies to us about this."[8]

So God's plan for helping people form beliefs about Jesus Christ involves dual streams of testimony—human and divine. Jesus expressly indicated this when he told his disciples that the Holy Spirit "will testify about me. And you must also testify, for you have been with me from the beginning."[9] We also see this dual witness invoked in early Christian

---

3. Richard Swinburne, "Natural Theology, Its 'Dwindling Probabilities' and 'Lack of Rapport'." *Faith and Philosophy* 21(4): 536–37.

4. Ignatius, *Epistle of Ignatius to the Smyrnaeans*, trans. A. Roberts and J. Donaldson, in A. Roberts, J. Donaldson, and A. Coxe (eds.), *Ante-Nicene Fathers*, vol. 1 (Grand Rapids, MI: Eerdmans. 1950), §3.

5. Irenaeus, *Against Heresies*, trans. A. and W. Rambaut, in A. Roberts, J. Donaldson, and A. Coxe (eds.), *Ante-Nicene Fathers*, vol. 1 (Grand Rapids, MI: Eerdmans, 1950), 3.3.4. Irenaeus in both 3.3.3 and 3.3.4 traces chains of testimonial succession involving Polycarp, Clement of Rome, and others.

6. John 17:20.

7. John 14:26, 16:13.

8. Heb. 10:15.

9. John 15:26–27.

preaching. When the apostles were called before the Jewish leaders to account for their actions as they continued to proclaim Christ despite being ordered not to do so, they appealed to the resurrection of Christ and to the demands God had placed on them as witnesses of that signal event: "We are witnesses of these things, and so is the Holy Spirit, whom God has given to those who obey him."[10]

There are important theological reasons why God would include his followers in his outreach to others. Not only did God reveal himself most dramatically and decisively by entering the stream of human history in the Incarnation and Resurrection of Christ, but this revelation is the supreme ground of Christian *fellowship*, as we together join Christ in his work of reconciling the world to God. The author of 1 John testifies to this fellowship: "We proclaim to you what we have seen and heard, so that you also may have fellowship with us. And our fellowship is with the Father and with his Son, Jesus Christ."[11] As we faithfully pass on this testimony ourselves, we participate in bringing others into this eternal fellowship of love: "My command is this: Love each other as I have loved you."[12]

All this is not to say that the Holy Spirit will in *every* case utilize human testimony in communicating to an individual. A person need not have heard the Gospel message from other humans in order to receive a private revelation from God. Further, even where a person *has* received human testimony, this testimony may be incidental to the testimony of the Holy Spirit. That is, the Holy Spirit may not *utilize* this human testimony when himself testifying. Even so, our concern in this chapter—discussing the role of apologetics—will be cases in which the Holy Spirit does in some way utilize, ratify, or confirm human testimony.

In one sense, Christians will affirm the work of the Holy Spirit as always *preceding* any human work. The Second Council of Orange (529 AD) established as Christian orthodoxy that any movement humans make toward God is in fact *initiated* by God, who endeavors to draw people to himself. This includes the Christian's efforts—which are prompted by the Holy Spirit—to help lead others to Christ.

---

10. Acts 5:32. It is worth noting that the book of Acts is pervaded by references both to the witness of the Holy Spirit to the gospel and to the human witness, which sometimes takes the form of arguing, giving persuasive reasons, and so on. See Acts 1:8, 22; 4:31–33; 6:10; 17:2–4, 17; 18:4; 19:8–10; 24:25.

11. I John 1:3.

12. John 15:12. Consider the implications of this command in light of John 17:24 and 15:9.

Still, if God is to afford his followers a role in jointly testifying to others who are still outside the faith, it does seem appropriate to speak in terms of the Holy Spirit *joining* his testimony to the testimony of his followers. Perhaps an analogy is instructive. Consider a case where a teenage girl has a strained relationship with her parents, and even doubts their love. The father, in an effort to repair their relationship, takes her to a movie in which the lead character is a mother who loves her children sacrificially. As the lead character attests to the joys and sorrows of loving others deeply, her heart tends to soften as she and her father share the emotion of the story. Later, over dinner, as they discuss the film, its message and emotional impact are enlarged when he notes that the mother in the film depicted the very sort of affection that he and her mother feel for her.

Given that the Holy Spirit does not have physical vocal cords like the parent from our example, what does the Holy Spirit *do* as a way of joining his own testimony to the testimony of humans? Most straightforwardly, the Holy Spirit may "speak" in a "still, small voice" that a person recognizes as in fact the voice of the Holy Spirit.[13] A person "hears" an inner voice that resembles an audible voice, that is almost as if one has heard a vocal utterance. Origen remarked that "if anyone ponders over the prophetic sayings . . . it is certain that in the very act of reading and diligently studying them his mind and feelings will be touched by a divine breath and he will recognize that the words he is reading are not the utterances of men but the language of God."[14] One interpretation of this depiction is that hearing the voice of the Holy Spirit has a unique phenomenology, akin perhaps to recognizing the tenor of a friend's voice. Such recognition may be because the perceived tone of voice resembles the voice one has already come to believe is the voice of the Holy Spirit. And perhaps one's prior beliefs about the voice of the Holy Spirit and how it might be discerned were due to evidential considerations that the prophetic and apostolic writings were inspired by the Holy Spirit. Or, one may simply find herself believing that the voice she is hearing is the voice of God—without being able to offer any reasons why she should have this belief.

Alternatively, the Holy Spirit may causally influence a person's belief, without the person recognizing that the Holy Spirit has in any way communicated or otherwise acted. Perhaps a person hears a Christian proclaim

---

13. Cf. Elijah's encounter with the voice of God in 1 Kings 19:11–13.

14. Origen, *De Principiis*, trans. F. Crombie, in A. Roberts, J. Donaldson, and A. Coxe (eds.), *Ante-Nicene Fathers*, vol. 4 (Buffalo, NY: Christian Literature Publishing Co., 1885), 4.6.

that Jesus died for the sins of the world. Following Alvin Plantinga, the person may find that "what is said simply seems right; it seems compelling; one finds oneself saying, 'Yes, that's right, that's the truth of the matter.' "[15] In this case, the person need not have any idea that the Holy Spirit is causally influencing her belief. But it certainly would be within the power of the Holy Spirit to exert this causal influence.

The details of such causal influence may vary. If a person hears human testimony about God, the Holy Spirit could directly incline the person to believe that testimony. More indirectly, the Holy Spirit may remove obstacles that would otherwise prevent the person from believing. For example, the Holy Spirit may provide healing of damaged *emotions*, stemming from an abusive earthly father, so that the proclaimed Good News that Jesus reconciles us to our heavenly Father is recognized as in fact good news. The Holy Spirit may exert causal influence on a person's *will* by prompting the person to attend more closely to the human testimony she has heard. The Holy Spirit may cause the person to have a *new desire*, say, for the Gospel message about Jesus to be true (leading more readily to the belief that it *is* true).[16] Or, the Holy Spirit may help cause the person to see some truth in a new light, with the person's *existing* desires being roused.[17]

This last point about seeing truths in a new light raises the further point that doxastic changes may result from the Holy Spirit's activity, even if these changes do not amount to a change in beliefs about specific, propositional statements. Human testimony about God has often come in the form of art: paintings, literature, film, even architecture. These forms of communication have a distinctive power to produce changes in our doxastic *orientation* even if these changes cannot readily be reduced to a list of new propositional statements that are now believed.

---

15. Alvin Plantinga, *Warranted Christian Belief* (New York: Oxford University Press, 2000), p. 250.

16. Francis Bacon observed that "in innumerable ways, and those sometimes imperceptible, the affection tinges and infects the Intellect" (Bacon, *Novum Organon*, trans. G. W. Kitchin [Oxford: Oxford University Press, 1855], Bk I, §xlix). While Bacon's concern was primarily how affections can *negatively* affect one's belief formation, we will note later how some truths can only be seen if affection is already present.

17. Think of how a daughter might announce her engagement to her father, who then views his future son-in-law as the person with whom his daughter wants to share his life. The father may now find he has deep affection for, and a desire to help and protect, his son-in-law—with this new desire being a kind of extension of his existing desire to help and protect his daughter.

Having noted how the Holy Spirit's causal influence on people's beliefs, will, desires, and emotions may serve to complement and build upon human testimony, it is difficult to offer more details of this causal story. It remains a mystery *how* it is that the Holy Spirit can cause people to attend, or can cause people to have desires, or can present himself to people so as to cause feelings of peace. Yet, the mysterious nature of this causal story is no more mysterious than any other story about how an immaterial God can cause physical or mental events in our world.

Testimony and Apologetics

An interesting question, though not to be pursued here, is how much of the above work of the Holy Spirit should be thought of as genuine instances of *testimony*. Must testimony always come in some linguistic form? Must it be expressible in propositional form? However one answers such questions, it seems clear that the previously described work of the Holy Spirit will extend well beyond what would naturally be called testimony. All the same, this variety of causal influence is understandably needed as the Holy Spirit engages the whole person, as part of God's work of drawing people to himself.

Likewise, human testimony about Jesus is narrower than the project of apologetics—though there is also a sense in which human testimony is broader. It is broader in the sense that only select kinds of testimony may be relevant to apologetic efforts. Maturing Christians may share with one another their experiences of God as encouragement or as part of Christian accountability; but testimony here is not intended as a reasoned defense of the Christian faith. At the same time, testimony remains narrower than apologetics in that a Christian's testimony may represent only one part of her apologetic arsenal.

A Christian apologist may, for example, employ fictional stories as a means of pointing others to truths about God—following Jesus's use of parables. Or an apologist may ask probing questions of others, or share a piece of art that kindles benevolent sentiments, or simply stand with others during their times of crisis. It would again stretch the concept to say that the apologist is offering *testimony* in all these cases.

The Scope of Apologetics

The wide range of activity of the Holy Spirit and of the apologist, in leading people to God, also brings up the point that their shared, ultimate purpose is not merely that a person might come to hold *beliefs* about God—at least, as this term is used in the modern sense of intellectual assent. Christians affirm that God draws us toward a *relationship* with him in which we find our ultimate fulfillment. However the distinction is to be drawn between "belief" and a relational commitment marked by "faith," the latter is obviously the final aim of the Holy Spirit's work in a person's life.

Equally, it is the final aim of the apologist. With the instruction in 1 Peter 3:15 to "always be prepared to give an answer [*apologia*]," we are told to "do this with gentleness and respect." The wider context here is the goal to "live such good lives among the pagans" that they "may see your good deeds and glorify God on the day he visits us."[18] The goal of the apologist is thus the unbeliever's standing before God, or relationship with God. The cognitive element of belief may play an essential role in this relational dynamic, but the goal of the apologist is not mere belief; it is rather a relationship, which Christians historically have described as a relationship marked by faith.

The goal of the apologist is close to, yet distinguishable from, the goal of the evangelist. Evangelists extend in Christ's name the invitation to follow him, to relate to him as lord. Apologists work to clear obstacles that would impede a positive response to this invitation. Apologists defend the coherence and truth of Christian theism; and they work to correct misunderstandings. They commend the Christian life to others. And they perform the important work of translating the Gospel message into a vocabulary and conceptual framework that others will understand.

Jesus compared his kingdom to a great feast.[19] The Christian evangelist proclaims that Jesus Christ says to all, "Come and eat," urging hearers to respond. The apologist, again, prepares people for this invitation. As Alister McGrath puts it, in the example of the feast "apologetics can be thought of as explaining to people that there really is going to be a feast. It invites them to reflect on what they might find there—the food and drink. How wonderful it would be to be invited!"[20]

Pascal's Stages of the Apologetic Process

If the Christian apologist, then, joins in the work of the Holy Spirit in preparing others to respond positively to God's invitation to a relationship,

---

18. 1 Pet. 2:12.

19. Matt. 22:1–14, Luke 14:15–24.

20. Alister McGrath, *Mere Apologetics* (Grand Rapids, MI: Baker Books, 2012), p. 23.

how might we categorize this work? That is, what are the more immediate goals that the apologist should adopt, as a means of realizing this ultimate goal of apologetics? The apologist again is simply joining the ongoing work of the Holy Spirit in others' lives. And so insight into the work to which the apologist is called will give us insight into the kinds of work the Holy Spirit is already doing to draw unbelievers to God.

Blaise Pascal is often a favorite voice among Christian apologists, and for good reason. Pascal's collection of thoughts—or *Pensées*—offers profound insight into the human condition and into the work that God must do to draw people to himself. One well-known passage offers a succinct summation of the task of the apologist in helping move others toward Christian faith: "make good men wish it were true, and then show that it is."[21] Three elements can be found in this short instruction. There is the directive to endeavor to show that Christianity is true. Before that, there is the condition that others should wish it were true. And before that, a contextual qualification is given that this process requires that others be in some sense good.

We can note here that some theologians reject in principle the apologetic method of finding points of common ground with unbelievers and then moving with them through inductive reasoning to conclusions about the truth of Christian theism. Concerns about this methodology include the following: that we end up with a picture of God (a "god of the philosophers") removed from the biblical picture; that we undermine God's sovereign choice to reveal himself to those he chooses; that any evidence not grounded in personal, religious experience will simply not lead to a change in belief; and that reason improperly becomes the "higher court" in which we creatures assess with hubris the merits of God's self-disclosure to us.[22]

While space does not allow us to respond to these concerns, we do note that the bulk of the Christian tradition clearly has thought it a worthwhile enterprise to find common starting points with unbelievers and then to lead them through inferential reasoning to the conclusion that Jesus is truly who he claimed to be. Indeed, this method is seen in scripture itself. The writer of the Gospel of John recorded the miraculous signs of Jesus

---

21. Blaise Pascal, *Pensées*, trans. A. J. Krailsheimer (Harmondsworth: Penguin Books, 1966), p. 187.

22. Karl Barth, *Church Dogmatics: I.1 The Doctrine of the Word of God*, trans. G. Bromiley, G. Thomson, and H. Knight (London: T & T Clark, 2010), p. 10. Barth in fact seems to have all these concerns.

so "that you may believe that Jesus is the Messiah, the Son of God."[23] And Peter begins his speech at Pentecost by commending Jesus as one who was "accredited by God to you by miracles."[24] The appeal here is clearly to inductive reasoning: that the divinity of Jesus is the best explanation for the data we have of his life among us.

Turning now to a fuller discussion of the three segments of Pascal's apologetic process, a few preliminary points are worth noting. In each of the three segments there are further distinctions we might make in cataloging the work of the Holy Spirit. Certain works of the Holy Spirit might be described as "negative" work in the sense of mitigating *against* the following: a growing orientation toward the bad, an increase of desires toward that which competes with God, and a confidence that there is evidence that points decisively away from Christian theism. Correspondingly, there is "positive" work in orienting a person *toward* the good, in cultivating desires *for* God, and in giving clarity of vision to appreciate the evidence in Christian theism's favor. In each of the three apologetic segments there are also *cognitive* effects from the Holy Spirit's activity, as well as *noncognitive* effects.

Orienting Toward the Good
Mitigating Work

Jonathan Edwards, following John Calvin and others, maintained that the structure of our world attests clearly to being the workmanship of God; and an understanding of many divine, eternal things is implanted within us. So why does not everyone form beliefs about the truth of theism in general, and even Christian doctrines in particular? Edwards's answer is that "if men have not respect to them as real and certain things, it cannot be for want of sufficient evidence of their truth."[25] Instead, the reason involves the corrupt state from which one views this evidence: "The mind of man is naturally full of enmity against the doctrines of the gospel; which is a disadvantage to those arguments that prove their truth, and causes them to lose their force upon the mind."[26]

---

23. John 20:30–31.

24. Acts 2:22.

25. Jonathan Edwards, *Works of Jonathan Edwards* (3 vols.), ed. J. Smith (New Haven, CT: Yale University Press, 1970), III, p. 157.

26. Edwards, *Works*, II, p. 307. Cf. John Calvin's remarks: "How can the idea of God enter your mind without instantly giving rise to the thought, that since you are his workmanship,

Edwards's statement here is far too sweeping in that *all* instances of unbelief, even when one is clearly presented with the Gospel message, cannot simply be assumed to be the result of *motivated* errors in reasoning.[27] Rational people seeking truth can come to different conclusions. And even when a belief is irrationally held, a person can be open to the truth and make an (unmotivated) error in reasoning. Still, Edwards is right to draw our attention to the possibility of being willfully *blind*, unable to see the truth of Christian theism even if the evidence for it lies plainly for those with eyes to see it.

If this state of spiritual blindness is indeed to be *willful*, then seemingly it will have been the result of some sort of active self-deception. It is questionable whether a person can literally deceive herself—as this requires a person (as deceiver) to believe one thing, while at the same time to fail (as deceived) to believe that same thing. However, it is clear that people can actively avoid uncomfortable truths, with this active avoidance affecting what a person does or does not come to believe.[28] When this process prevents a person from holding beliefs about God's existence and one's standing before him, then the process can rightly be called a case of willful spiritual blindness.

Modern psychologists have shown that humans have devised a variety of overt and subtle ways to avoid truths about themselves. They can remind themselves and others that their behavior really does not hurt anyone, or that their peccadillos are not among the more serious ones, or that everyone has some such faults, or that their own failures are temporary and uncharacteristic lapses. The list goes and on. People can sabotage the efforts of friends so that their own behavior appears good by comparison. They may seek to avoid conclusions about their own behavior and motives by taking performance-inhibiting drugs such as alcohol so as to handicap their own performances and thereby create a ready-made, external explanation for their moral failings. They may even in certain cases embrace the diagnosis of a mental or physical illness because

---

you are bound, by the very law of creation, to submit to his authority?—that your life is due to him?—that whatever you do ought to have reference to him? If so, it undoubtedly follows that your life is sadly corrupted" (Calvin, *Institutes of the Christian Religion*, trans. H. Beveridge [Albany, OR: Sage Software, 1996], I.2.2).

27. Edwards's claim is grounded in his theology, which offers a very pessimistic account of the moral dispositions of fallen humanity.

28. See Alfred Mele, *Irrationality* (New York: Oxford University Press, 1987), Chapter 9, as to why this process merits the description "self-deception."

the conclusion "I'm unwell" is more comfortable than the conclusion "I'm willfully engaged in unacceptable behavior." If these strategies fail, there is always the option simply to *pretend* to have the moral character that sits well with one's conscience. Sadly, modern psychology has also documented that humans are remarkably adept at (very quickly) coming to believe that they possess the character and dispositions that they were once merely pretending to have.[29]

Pascal saw how the desire to avoid uncomfortable truths blinds us to certain truths about ourselves:

We are not satisfied with the life we have in ourselves and our own being. We want to lead an imaginary life in the eyes of others, and so we try to make an impression. We strive constantly to embellish and preserve our imaginary being, and neglect the real one.[30]

Accordingly, we will be attracted to false beliefs—about others, about the world, about God—that reinforce our own favored views of ourselves.

Equally, as William Wood puts it, "we are unlikely to be attracted to beliefs—like the belief in God—that threaten to destabilize our false self-understanding. According to Pascal, such is our situation."[31] The previous discussion on the reframing strategies of humans, while by no means an exhaustive taxonomy, nevertheless provides some indication of the multipart task the Holy Spirit may undertake in helping a person face up to the truth that "no, I'm not the person I've been picturing myself as being." While the apologist, following Pascal, may draw others' attention to this human condition, it remains the role of the Holy Spirit, Jesus made plain, to convict the world of sin.[32]

The effects of the Holy Spirit's communication here may be cognitive or noncognitive. Cognitively, a person may find herself with the belief that she indeed stands guilty of wrongdoing, that she has sought to justify her

29. For a summary of psychological literature on these strategies, as well as their potential connection to theistic beliefs, see Kevin Kinghorn, "Spiritual Blindness, Self-Deception and Morally Culpable Nonbelief," *Heythrop Journal* 48(4) (2007): 527–545.

30. Pascal, *Pensées*, p. 806.

31. William Wood, "Reason's Rapport: Pascalian Reflections on the Persuasiveness of Natural Theology," *Faith and Philosophy* 21(4) (2004): 525. Cf. Pascal: "Man is ... nothing but disguise, falsehood and hypocrisy, both in himself and with regard to others. He does not want to be told the truth" (*Pensées*, p. 978).

32. John 16:8.

bad choices, that she has sought to understand the world in a way that amounts to a kind of "curving in on oneself."[33] The apologist may perhaps point these things out, attesting to the common human condition. But in keeping with Christian doctrine, it is again the Holy Spirit who convicts here—that is, who causally influences in some way the person's coming to believe that all this is so.

Noncognitive effects of the Holy Spirit's influence can also be noted. Humans often attest to feeling shame, even if they cannot articulate precisely what has gone wrong with their lives and why they should feel shame about it. To be sure, feelings associated with shame or guilt or dishonor can be illegitimate—as when a person is scapegoated by other people in their own attempts to deflect blame. Still, these kinds of feelings may at times be a (noncognitive) prompt from the Holy Spirit, impeding the continued, self-deceptive pattern of justifying oneself as one is.

Positive Work

Along with this "negative" work of the Holy Spirit in helping turn a person *from* an orientation unduly toward self, there are varieties of influence possible from the Holy Spirit—again both cognitive and noncognitive—in orienting a person *toward* the good. Given the Christian affirmation that God is the source of life, love, and all that is good, becoming oriented toward the good involves moving toward the dispositions and commitments that reflect the loving, self-giving relationships within the Trinity. The more our characters are formed in this manner, the more we will be disposed to embrace Jesus's call to follow him as lord, surrendering all aspects of our lives to God.

The Holy Spirit may enable a person to form beliefs that help move him toward self-giving patterns of action. For example, a person may find himself believing that it is right to respect his neighbor's wishes, or that it is his duty to care for his sick aunt, or that he is obliged to keep a promise to his colleague. The Christian scriptures contain references to God's "law being written" on the human heart.[34] Plausibly, we can unpack this notion partly in terms of moral beliefs the Holy Spirit prompts people to have that help orient them toward the good.

---

33. Cf. Pascal, "The nature of self-love and of this human self is to love only self and consider only self" (*Pensées*, p. 978).

34. Jer. 31:33, Rom. 2:14–15, Heb. 10:16.

An affective element also exists within this prompting from the Holy Spirit. Calvin emphasized that, apart from the activity of the Holy Spirit, any *beliefs* a person might form about God will not motivate him to *obey* God.[35] In moving a person toward a pattern of self-giving actions, the Holy Spirit must rouse our desires: for that which helps others, for that which is noble, for that which is good and right.

The noncognitive effects of the Holy Spirit, orienting one toward the good, may not require any new beliefs at all about God or about specific people. For example, upon reading the substitutionary act of Sydney Carton at the end of *A Tale of Two Cities*—the "far better thing" that he is doing—a person may find herself with new feelings we associate with nobleness or open-handedness. Although the person cannot readily identify any specific person she should address, or any specific behavior she should now change, her new generosity of spirit may affect upcoming decisions when she does face choices about how to relate to others. The feelings she has—whether we think of them as emotions or as desires with no specific objects—are serving to orient her toward the good, toward the life of God (which is characterized by self-giving love) into which the Holy Spirit draws us.

The apologist may facilitate these kinds of noncognitive influences. Christians can communicate elements of God's character through works of fiction, through poetry, through music, through paintings, and so forth. Christians are not alone in identifying a connection between beauty and goodness.[36] And even while Christian art may only point suggestively at that which answers fully to our aesthetic inspirations and longings, it is again not always necessary that a change in specific beliefs accompany an instance of being oriented in some way toward that which is good.

Desiring Christianity to Be True
Mitigating Work

The second segment of Pascal's apologetic process is that we should "make good men *wish* that it is true." The first segment had to do with orienting others toward the good in some way. We see the importance of this when we reflect on the nature of the offer Jesus extends to us, and why a person might be attracted to it. An eternal relationship with God in heaven is not

---

35. "Even if [Scripture] wins reverence for itself by its own majesty, it seriously affects us only when it is sealed upon our hearts through the Spirit" (Calvin, *Institutes*, I.7.5).

36. Cf. the way Plato links the Beautiful with the Good in his *Republic* and *Symposium*.

the kind of opportunity that would be attractive to just anyone. The relationships among the redeemed in heaven mirror the loving, *self-giving* relationships among the Trinity. The invitation to an eternal relationship with God and others is an invitation to *serve* others in love. Of course, the great paradox of the Christian religion is that when we "lose" our lives in service to God and others, we actually *gain* a life of ever-deepening relationships in which our ultimate well-being is alone found.

But an eternity of sharing the joys of mutual love will not be attractive to someone who is oriented fully toward self. And so the discussion in the previous section emphasized the work of the Holy Spirit—and of the apologist—in orienting others in some way toward the good, which is realized through self-giving love. How might this work then move to focus on cultivating specifically a desire for Christian theism (including the "great truths of the Gospel," as Jonathan Edwards and others have put it) to be true?

As with the previous segment, there is "negative" work that the Holy Spirit can do in cultivating this desire. The Christian scriptures reference God as sometimes frustrating people's desires, undermining their projects, in an effort to turn their hopes and plans toward him.[37] Interestingly, the scriptures also reference God in some contexts giving people what they want, while knowing that the satisfaction of their wants will not in fact bring lasting joy and peace. The familiar adages "Be careful what you wish for" and "It's not what it's cracked up to be" attest to the frequent gap between what people *think* will make them happy and what will actually make them happy.

So as a way of prompting people to set their hopes and desires on God, the Holy Spirit may at times frustrate people's attempts to realize their desires, as a way of prompting them to put their hope in God. Or, the Holy Spirit may at times actually work to advance people's existing desires, as a way of enabling them to realize the diminishing returns of projects that do not involve God—again as a means of communicating to them the folly of trusting one's existing desires as a guide to where one's ultimate flourishing lies.

Although the apologist may need careful discernment from the Holy Spirit before knowing which approach is the more effective tactic in a particular situation, the apologist is at all times still able to join in the work of the Holy Spirit by adding another human voice to Augustine's testimony: "Thou madest us for Thyself, and our heart is restless, until

---

37. Cf. Gen. 11:1–9, Ps. 33:10, Job 5:12.

it repose in Thee."[38] Alister McGrath on this point finds an apologetic resource in the writings of existential thinkers such as Heidegger and Sartre, who explored the various aspects of *angst*, a "deeply rooted fear of meaninglessness and pointlessness, a sense of the utter futility of life, even sheer despair at the bewildering things that threaten to reduce us to nothing more than a statistic—ultimately a mortality statistic."[39] As the witness of the Holy Spirit is added to the apologist's testimony that God alone satisfies the deepest desires we have, the influence on the unbeliever will (typically at least) include a cognitive element: a belief that what the apologist says is true. But whether any specific belief is formed, the ultimate work of the Holy Spirit here is to weaken those desires an unbeliever has that lead her away from a pursuit of God.

Positive Work

In addition to this negative work of moderating a person's desires (for ends apart from God), we can also note positive work the Holy Spirit may do in cultivating a desire *for* God. As Augustine stated, the reason the pursuits of this world never finally satisfy is that we were made for fellowship with the one who transcends our world. As the Holy Spirit arouses a person's innate desire for God, the effects on an unbeliever might again fall into both cognitive and noncognitive categories.

Especially in recent times, Christian apologists have emphasized an approach toward unbelievers that is neither clearly a cognitive nor clearly a noncognitive one. Specifically, they have emphasized engaging an unbeliever's *imagination*. We humans already spend a great deal of time imagining, as part of our ongoing quest to make sense of the world and of our role in it. We also employ imagination as a means of decision making: imagining what life would be like if we attended this university, or worked at this job, or married that person. So an appeal to unbelievers'

---

38. Augustine, *Confessions*, trans. E. Pusey (Rockville, MD: Arc Manor, 2008), bk. I, 7. Cf. Aquinas: "God only satisfies and infinitely exceeds man's desires; and, therefore, perfect satiety is found in God alone" (Aquinas, "Explanation of the Apostles' Creed," *The Catechetical Instructions of St. Thomas Aquinas*, trans. J. Collins [New York: J. F. Wagner, 1939], art. 12, p. 74); and the *Catechism of the Catholic Church*: "The Beatitudes respond to the natural desire for happiness. This desire is of divine origin: God has placed it in the human heart in order to draw man to the One who alone can fulfill it" (pt. III, sect. I, chpt. I, art. II, II, §1718).

39. Alister McGrath, *Intellectuals Don't Need God and Other Modern Myths* (Grand Rapids, MI: Zondervan, 1993), p. 43.

imagination seems on the surface a promising way of engaging them. Further, in Pascal's apologetic approach the apologist is seeking to stir a person's desire for God *before* that person has any settled beliefs about God. Helpfully, it remains within an unbeliever's voluntary control—even for those with settled beliefs *against* God's existence—to imagine what life might look like if Christian theism is true.

C. S. Lewis (following George MacDonald) did much to rekindle Christian apologists' interest in the area of imagination. While Lewis's fiction books are well known, he also commented on the way in which poetry has the potential to give people insight into the nature of experiences they themselves have never had. Lewis remarked,

> This is the most remarkable of the powers of Poetic language: to convey to us the quality of experiences which we have not had. . . . Many of us have never had an experience like that which Wordsworth records near the end of *Prelude* XIII; but when he speaks of "the visionary dreariness," I think we get an inkling of it.[40]

Lewis in his own life attested to the power of poetic words to stir a desire for something one does not yet understand. In his spiritual autobiography, he reflects on an early reading of Longfellow's *Saga of King Olaf*:

> I idly turned the pages of the book . . . and read
>
> > *I heard a voice that cried,*
> > *Balder the beautiful*
> > *Is dead, is dead—*
>
> I knew nothing of Balder; but instantly I was uplifted into huge regions of northern sky, I desired with almost sickening intensity something never to be described (except that it is cold, spacious, severe, pale, and remote) and then . . . found myself at the very same moment already falling out of that desire and wishing I were back in it.[41]

Lewis later was able to name the object of his long-felt desires. In reflecting on his initial encounter with George MacDonald's *Phantastes*, Lewis remarked,

---

40. C. S. Lewis, "The Language of Religion," in *Christian Reflections* (Grand Rapids, MI: Eerdmans, 2014), pp. 164–65.

41. C. S. Lewis, *Surprised by Joy* (Orlando: Harcourt, 1966), p. 17.

"I should have been shocked in my teens if anyone had told me that what I learned to love in *Phantastes* was goodness."[42] And in another reflection on MacDonald's works, "I had tried not to see that the true quality which first met me in his books is Holiness."[43] What Lewis's comments point up is that even when our imagination leads us to objects and experiences we do not yet understand, our desires for such things can be powerfully stirred.

Interestingly, scripture records that a common avenue for the Holy Spirit to communicate to people is through *dreams*. Within at least some of our dreams are heavy elements of imagination and of suggestive language or imagery, which may in the case of unbelievers serve to stir their desires for God—even if they cannot yet identify the object of their desires as in fact God. The apologist can of course join in offering suggestive language and imagery, perhaps adding at key times an articulation of the Christian view that such desires both are from God and can only be satisfied by God.

A more tangible Christian witness to unbelievers involves the witness of the *Church*, which is intended by Christ to serve as his "body" in the world. By reflecting the Trinitarian relationships of love, and by exhibiting spiritual fruit such as peace and joy as it does so, the Church stands as witness that the things of God are indeed desirable.

Showing Christianity to Be True
Mitigating Work

The final segment of Pascal's apologetic strategy—showing others that Christianity is true—follows only after an unbeliever's desire for God has in some way been stirred. A Christian epistemology will not view subsequent Christian belief as the result of irresponsibly wishful thinking. Rather, certain truths about God can only be seen through the eyes of love for God. We recognize this phenomenon in art: Certain qualities of a painting can only be seen by one who loves that painting. After all, a knowledge of art history or brush techniques does not by itself prompt a person to stare at the same painting day after day after day. Similarly, we recognize that certain qualities of another person can only be appreciated by a spouse or parent or someone else who truly sees that person through the eyes of love. Knowledge of God is ultimately *personal* knowledge, an

---

42. C. S. Lewis, Introduction to George MacDonald, *Phantastes and Lilith* (Grand Rapids, MI: Eerdmans, 1964), p. 12.

43. C. S. Lewis, *The Great Divorce* (New York: HarperOne, 2015), pp. 66–67.

awareness of God's *self*-disclosure to us. The apologist may offer supporting evidence that God exists and became incarnate in the person of Jesus,
but this evidence will have limited value, in terms of helping lead to knowledge of God, unless an unbeliever has some affective attitude toward God
(or at least toward the possibility that God exists).[44]

Turning now to the kinds of evidence that the apologist might offer,
arguments that undermine the position of atheism (and of non-Christian
theism) are well rehearsed in the Christian tradition. Often, such arguments amount to *reductio ad absurdum* arguments. For example, if we suppose that God does not exist as a necessary being, then this contingent
world of ours could never have come to exist; or if we suppose that God did
not create us and give us our moral intuitions, then we lose any plausible
explanation for our clear sense that we do have obligations that do not
depend on any human structures; or if we suppose that the resurrection of
Christ did not occur, then we are left with no plausible explanation of the
behavior of his disciples. If the Christian apologist's "negative" arguments
intended to undermine atheistic conclusions do not take this form, they
will probably take the form of showing that positive atheist arguments—
from the presence of evil, from religious diversity, and so forth—are not so
forceful as one might initially think.

Positive Work

Also well rehearsed are positive arguments for Christian theism: the teleologi-
cal argument for God's existence, historical evidence for Christ's resurrection,
arguments from miracles or religious experience, and so forth. Following
Alvin Plantinga and other so-called Reformed Epistemologists, we might
view such arguments as not always (or even usually) serving as *evidence* for an
unbeliever, but instead serving (in the way that preaching or scripture reading
does) as the *occasion* on which the Holy Spirit prompts a person to form various beliefs about God. The claim here, drawn from Calvin, is that, typically,
Christian beliefs are (rationally) formed under the influence of the Holy Spirit
in a way that does not involve inferential reasoning from evidence.

But Pascal and the majority of apologists historically have understood their positive arguments for Christian theism indeed to serve as

---

44. Cf. 1 John 4:8: "Whoever does not love does not know God, because God is love."

evidence for the unbeliever. This role for reason by no means renders the influence of the Holy Spirit unnecessary. Hence, while Richard Swinburne meticulously lays out inductive arguments for Christian theism according to Bayesian probability assessments,[45] he nevertheless appeals to the enabling power of the Holy Spirit: "we may need grace to help us to see that the arguments work."[46] Thus, the Holy Spirit may exert causal influence in helping a person attend to, and understand, the apologist's argument. Or the Holy Spirit may help a person overcome an unwillingness to admit that a certain conclusion does indeed follow from the argument.

How probable a conclusion should the apologist expect to reach, reasoning alongside the unbeliever? Pascal's estimation is that "The prophecies, even the miracles and proofs of our religion, are not of such a kind that they can be said to be absolutely convincing. . . . But the evidence is such as to exceed, or at least equal, the evidence to the contrary, so that it cannot be reason that decides us against following it."[47] The implication is that the Holy Spirit's witness will not run contrary to human reason properly functioning. Also, the limited goal identified by Pascal frees the apologist from an undue pressure of needing to establish very high probabilities for Christian theism, if the confirming testimony of the Holy Spirit is to operate in harmony with the apologist's work.

One *action* the Holy Spirit and the apologist may encourage an unbeliever to take, as a way of showing Christian theism to be true, is to take up aspects of the Christian way of life. This was Pascal's encouragement to those who found the evidence for Christianity ambiguous and did not yet believe. Here again Christ's body, the Church, may play a vital role in that, as an unbeliever participates within the community of Christians, she comes to see that the feast God has been described as offering is not only desirable but is indeed *here* and available. Pascal's vision of how an unbeliever might form Christian beliefs *after* participating in the Christian life allows us to see very clearly how the dual streams of human and divine testimony can work together as witness to the world.

---

45. See Richard Swinburne, *The Resurrection of God Incarnate* (Oxford: Clarendon Press, 2003); Richard Swinburne, *The Existence of God*, 2nd ed. (Oxford: Clarendon Press, 2004).

46. Swinburne, "Natural Theology," p. 538.

47. Pascal, *Pensées*, p. 835.

Grace: Resistible, Prevenient, and Synergistic

Having noted the need for divine grace in enabling belief either through or outside inferential reasoning, two final, related matters might be considered, if only briefly for present purposes: (1) the extent to which the enabling, prompting work of the Holy Spirit is *irresistible*, and (2) the kinds of influence from the Holy Spirit that are prevenient versus synergistic. On the first matter, Augustine was a key figure in shifting the majority view in the Western Church—until at least the time of Duns Scotus—to one of the irresistible nature of God's grace, if we fallen humans are to be moved to embrace God. Prominent Reformers in the Protestant tradition followed Augustine on this point, and this pattern continues today in some of these traditions.[48]

Within the Eastern Church, God's grace has rarely been viewed in this way. And the Roman Catholic position, seemingly before Augustine and certainly sometime after Duns Scotus and continuing today, is summed up by the Council of Trent. While affirming that humans cannot escape their sinful state without being "aroused and assisted by divine grace,"[49] the Council also affirmed that a person can respond to this grace "by agreeing to, and cooperating with His grace, which he could resist."[50] John Wesley, for one, is representative of those in the Protestant tradition who insist that God *enables* us to embrace him, but does not *causally necessitate* our doing so. Against the idea of God irresistibly moving (elect) people to turn to him, Wesley insisted on an account of God's mercy in which God is "offering salvation to every creature, actually saving all that consent thereto, and doing for the rest all that infinite wisdom, almighty power, and boundless love can do, without forcing them to be saved, which would be to destroy the very nature that he had given them."[51]

Wesley also offered a rich account of God's *prevenient grace*, understood as God's communication and enabling power extended to all people, even those who are actively resisting him. In contrast to this witness of the Holy

---

48. Against Chrysostom and the other "Greek fathers," Calvin described the prompting of God's grace as "one which affects us efficaciously"—in contrast to "a movement which thereafter leaves us the choice to obey or resist it" (*Institutes*, II.3.10).

49. *Enchiridion Symbolorum* (1957), p. 798.

50. *Enchiridion Symbolorum* (1957), p. 1791.

51. John Wesley, "Predestination Calmly Considered." *Works of John Wesley* (Grand Rapids, MI: Baker, 1979), 10, p. 235.

Spirit that precedes any positive human response, there also are influences from the Holy Spirit that can only come about as we accept the ongoing work of the Spirit in our lives. Tracing the previous discussions of this chapter with an eye toward how the variety of works of the Spirit in an unbeliever's life may expand or shift focus, as one cooperates with the promptings of the Spirit, would be an interesting (though complex!) exploration. Such a study would have to take account of the real differences between the traditions just outlined.

Conclusion

The dual witness we have been discussing, and the various aspects of that witness, underscore the vital point that biblical apologetics is a holistic enterprise. While some recoil from anything labeled apologetics because they see it as a one-dimensional activity that reduces faith to intellectual assent, relying sometimes on weak arguments and exaggerated claims to certainty, others are equally leery of talk about the witness of the Holy Spirit, suspecting it is an attempt to do an end run around our rational faculties. The account of apologetics we have sketched here is one in which the Holy Spirit is the primary witness to the truth of the gospel, but that witness is addressed to, and works in concert with, the full range of our rational faculties and the testimony of human witnesses.

It is worth emphasizing again that the objective of apologetics is nothing less than persuading human beings to enter into a relationship with the Supreme Lover, a relationship that constitutes the highest possible good for them. As such, it elicits from us a loving response that encompasses our whole heart, soul, mind, and strength. The biblical model of apologetics, then, far from being a narrowly intellectual engagement, is a highly personal encounter in which God himself witnesses to the truth about his Son, his love for us, and the eternal life he offers us. Our part in the encounter, though secondary, is a vital ministry of love.

II

The Role of the Church in Discerning the Testimony of the Spirit

Angus Ritchie

Introduction

In one sense, the Holy Spirit is essential to all human knowledge. All human beings owe their rationality, indeed every moment of their existence, to his sustaining work. In most areas of human knowledge that does not lead us to make appeal to the "testimony of the Spirit" in order to justify our beliefs. For (as I have argued elsewhere[1]) it is usually possible to make a sharp distinction between the *justification* of a true belief and the full *explanation* of how human beings arrive at that belief.

This chapter is going to assume the truth of orthodox Christianity: the faith revealed in Holy Scripture, and expressed in the Nicene Creed.[2] From within such a Christian worldview, a full *explanation* of any true belief will need to make reference to the work of the Holy Spirit in creating and sustaining human beings, and endowing them with the power to reason.

One of the many things that distinguish particle physics from theology is that, while the work of the Spirit is part of the full *explanation* of our knowledge of particle physics, an appeal to the testimony of the Spirit is

---

1. Angus Ritchie, *From Morality to Metaphysics* (Oxford: Oxford University Press, 2012), pp. 43f.

2. I have chosen to focus on this because it is the creedal statement affirmed by the widest body of churches—having an authoritative status within Roman Catholicism and both Eastern and Oriental Orthodoxy, and being affirmed by most Protestants (whether they accord it any particular authority or simply believe that the assertions it makes are true).

not part of the *justification* of scientific beliefs. By contrast, we justify the claims we make in theology in part by showing we have reason to believe they are the fruit of the testimony of the Spirit. The central claims of orthodox Christianity are not things we could have worked out about God by reason alone. We know them because God has revealed them to us.

I am going to use the term "revealed truth" to refer to all knowledge where the process of justification as well as that of full explanation involves reference to the work of the Holy Spirit. In this chapter, I will explore the extent to which there needs to be a social aspect to the discernment of such revealed truths.

Discerning the Testimony of the Spirit
The Need for Objectivity

A central challenge for all Christian accounts of the Spirit's work of revelation is to provide a plausible answer to the following: How are we to distinguish what is genuinely inspired by the Holy Spirit and what is simply the product of the interests and desires, conscious and unconscious, of the believer and her surrounding culture? After all, the two are notoriously hard to separate. The history of Christianity is one of deep disagreement between believers who were equally convinced that the Spirit was inspiring them. If we are to avoid epistemic anarchy, there will need to be some objective method—something independent from individual believers and their surrounding culture—for judging when a purported revelation is indeed the "testimony of the Spirit" and when it is simply a reflection of the unconscious biases of them as individuals, or of their surrounding culture.

The testimony of the Spirit does not float free of the individuals and cultures that receive it. In weighing up a purported revelation, we should not assume *either* that the Spirit has guided us without any influence from these preferences, desires, and biases *or* that a purported revelation is wholly erroneous. There is an obvious analogy here with ethics, where it is plausible to think that our sensitivity to moral values can be clouded but is not completely obscured by our own interests and desires. The account of moral knowledge given by St. Paul (in Rom. 1:19f.)[3] is a case in point: He clearly

3. All biblical quotations in this essay are from the *New Revised Standard Version: Anglicised Edition with Apocrypha* (Oxford: Oxford University Press, 1995). Qur'anic citations are from *The Holy Qur'an: Translation and Commentary* (Lahore: The Holy Qur'an Publishing House, 1934).

takes certain moral truths to be knowable by nonbelievers, but he also offers an account of how their interests and desires then distort their beliefs.

The Purpose of the Spirit's Work

It is important to ground any discussion of what the Spirit might or might not reveal in an understanding of the purpose of the Spirit's action in the world. The testimony of Scripture leaves us with no grounds for thinking God's primary purpose is to fill our minds with true propositions (cf. James 2:19). Nonetheless, our acceptance of certain propositional truths is necessary if God is to draw us into the kind of loving relationship for which he made us (Rom. 10:5f.). Our understanding of the work of the Spirit in *revealing truths to us* depends at least in part on how we understand this wider work of the Spirit, in drawing us into a loving relationship with the Father through Jesus Christ.

This loving relationship is not a purely personal one: The Old and New Testaments emphasize repeatedly that the relationship between believers and God is social as well as individual. As Walter Brueggemann observes, "[t]he invitation of the Biblical God is that persons may enter into covenant with God ... There is no solitary covenant with the Lord; it is always a covenant *in a community* of people who have made like commitments and received parallel promises to God." To be "in Christ," in the understanding of the New Testament, is "to be in the community of the Lord's covenant."[4] In 1 Corinthians 12, perhaps the best-known of the many New Testament passages on this theme, St. Paul makes a clear connection between the social aspect of Christian discipleship and the work of the Spirit in the individual believer. Through the Holy Spirit, Christians are being called into one Body in Christ (verses 12, 13) and "to each is given the manifestation of the Spirit for the common good" (verse 7).

Our increasingly individualistic culture has often been forgetful of this social dimension of the work of the Spirit. As Kenneth Leech observes, the Western church is

in the midst today of a long-overdue renewal of belief in, and stress upon, the role of the Spirit of God in the Christian community.

---

4. Walter Brueggemann, *The Bible Makes Sense* (Louisville, KY: Westminster John Knox Press, 2001), p. 75.

Much earlier reflection on the doctrine of the Holy Spirit in both Catholic and Protestant traditions was heavily dominated by interest in personal piety. But in order to make sense of the place of the Holy Spirit in the Christian understanding of God, we need to widen the perspective. It is necessary to place our doctrine of the Spirit within the context of the empowering of the Christian community. The subsequent history of Christian thought has seen a deterioration in understanding of the Spirit so that the Spirit has come to be seen as an impersonal force, an "it," a power of presence, but not the personal power and presence of God.[5]

The testimony of the Spirit is therefore not simply a matter of implanting propositional truths in the mind of an individual believer. What we have reason to believe about the way the Spirit guides believers toward propositional truths will depend upon our wider understanding of the work of Spirit in the life of the individual believer and the community of the church.

From the perspective of orthodox Christianity, the work of the Spirit is to draw us—both individually and corporately—into the life and love of the Triune God. Because we are creatures who are created to come to judgment partly in propositional form, that includes coming to true judgments in that form. In any discussion of religious epistemology, and of the different texts and institutions through which the testimony of the Spirit may be discerned, we must not lose sight of this wider perspective.

What would it mean to have a less proposition-focused understanding of the testimony of the Spirit? There is at least a partial analogy here with ethics. On the account of ethics I developed elsewhere—drawing on the work of contemporary moral philosophers such as Philippa Foot, John McDowell, and Martha Nussbaum—moral truths can be stated propositionally, and are objectively true. But the process by which we come to know them is not one of pure ratiocination. Part of the way in which we come to know such moral truths is through affective engagement.

We have even more reason to believe this to be true in the case of theology. The foundation of all revealed theology is an encounter with God. To divorce theology from spirituality, or to divorce moral philosophy from affective engagement, leaves each party impoverished. Theology and moral philosophy are deprived of their fundamental sources, and spirituality and

5. Kenneth Leech, *True God* (London: Sheldon Press/SPCK, 1985), p. 199.

our affective responses become excessively subjective. Leszcek Kolakowski observes that

> Religion is not a set of propositions, it is the realm of worship wherein understanding, knowledge, the feeling of participation in the ultimate reality and moral commitment [all] appear within a single act, whose subsequent segregation into separate classes of metaphysical, moral and other assertions might be useful but is bound to distort the sense of the original act of worship.[6]

Kolakowski's observation is carefully worded: It is not that propositions are dispensable, but that what he calls the process of "segregating" the objective and the affective is fraught with danger. It leads to a mutual impoverishment: Not only does theology need the affective and "subjective" elements of spirituality, but Christian prayer and spirituality need to be rooted in an orthodox theology. Andrew Louth makes the same point, warning that theology must never be "cut off from the movement of the heart towards God":

> Cut off from theology, prayer loses its objectivity, its concern with reality. For Christian prayer ... is engagement with the object of our faith, an object which is in some way apprehended or known; and in such cognitive engagement the *mind* is involved. Faith is, to use the traditional phrase, *cum assensione cogitare*, to *think* with assent. We do not just feel something in prayer, we know something.[7]

In theology, as in ethics, the objective is disclosed through subjective engagement and personal experience. The testimony of the Spirit is not a matter of an impersonal force, an "it" introducing propositions into the believer's mind in a way that bypasses her natural reason, affections, and other psychological attributes. Rather, the Spirit *is* "the personal power and presence of God," and from that living encounter, believers come to knowledge of the One they have encountered.

---

6. Leszek Kolakowski, *Religion* (South Bend, IN: St. Augustine's Press, 2001), cited in John Cottingham, *The Spiritual Dimension: Religion, Philosophy, and Human Value* (Cambridge: Cambridge University Press, 2005), pp. 1–2.

7. Andrew Louth, *Discerning the Mystery: An Essay on the Nature of Theology* (Oxford: Oxford University Press, 1989), pp. 2–3.

Scripture, Reason, and Church in the Process of Discernment

This means we cannot accept a completely experience-based account of the testimony of the Spirit. Precisely because theology is a matter of objective truth, and because our own subjectivity is vulnerable to wish fulfillment and other kinds of delusion, we need some method for discerning when the propositional beliefs that arise from what we take to be our personal experience of God genuinely are part of the "testimony of the Spirit."

There are three obvious candidates for enabling us to make such discernment. The first candidate is scripture, which all orthodox Christians hold to have a distinctive kind of authority. The testimony of the Spirit through scripture is, of course, a huge topic in itself, and this chapter will only consider such issues to the extent that they relate to our main theme—the social aspects of discerning and receiving the testimony of the Spirit.

The second candidate is the process of rational argument. All purported testimony of the Spirit can be judged against what is already known about God. Moreover, there may on particular occasions be specific reasons for skepticism about a purported revelation—as there may be an obvious psychological or sociological explanation for the belief's attractiveness that may undermine any claim it has to truth.

These first two candidates should be uncontroversial. All orthodox Christians hold the Bible to be inspired by the Spirit, and one cannot credibly dispute that processes of rational argument or inference need to be invoked at some point in the process of discerning what is and is not genuinely the Spirit's testimony. The relative priority of scripture and reason may be a matter of dispute, but both are needed, for it is necessary to use rational argument and inference to work out what the text of scripture is actually *saying*. Someone who thought that rational argument had no role in the interpretation of scripture would have removed all constraints on what could be deemed to be a legitimate interpretation of scripture. All the work would be done by the testimony of the Spirit to the individual or community reading the text. For if God simply transmits the meaning of each passage of scripture into the individual believer's soul (with no rational constraints on what can count as a valid interpretation of the text) we are in the same position epistemologically as if God only ever transmitted "words of knowledge" into the individual believer's soul. Scripture would not be something one could test such "words of knowledge" against, because the sole arbiter of both the "words" and the interpretation of Scripture would be the promptings of the Spirit in the individual believer. Paradoxically, then, the revealed text can play a more, not less, significant role in the process of revelation if there is a distinct role for reason in constraining the range of legitimate textual interpretations.

The third and most controversial candidate for enabling our discernment of the Spirit is the community of the Church. While all Christians will use both their powers of reasoning and the Bible in the process of discerning what is and is not genuinely the testimony of the Spirit, not all accept that the Church has an important role in the process. In this chapter, I will argue that the Church has an important and indeed authoritative role in the discernment process. I shall leave open the question of whether this role is simply about developing the implications of the teaching in scripture, or whether the Spirit is also revealing truths that are not contained within (though not incompatible with) its teaching.

Against Individualism
The Chicago Declaration on Biblical Inerrancy

The claim that the Church has an authoritative role in the discernment process is uncontroversial for Roman Catholic and Orthodox theology, and for the Anglican Catholic tradition. The argument I want to make here is that Protestants also have reason to give a significant role to the Church in discerning the testimony of the Spirit, even if they understand the nature and extent of the Church rather differently from their Catholic and Orthodox colleagues.

A reason some Protestants might resist giving an authoritative role to the Church in discerning the testimony of the Spirit is that they believe a proper account of scriptural authority involves Biblical inerrancy, and that belief in Biblical inerrancy precludes any such role for the Church. My aim is to show that *even if you hold the highest possible doctrine of the authority and inerrancy of the Bible*, you nonetheless have reason to agree that the Church has an authoritative role in discerning the testimony of the Spirit. In this chapter, I am going to focus on the Chicago Statement of Biblical Inerrancy—both because it contains the strongest possible affirmation of the verbal authority of scripture, and because it is neutral on the question at the heart of this chapter, offering no particular doctrine of the authority that the Church might (or might not) have beyond asserting that any such authority must be subordinate to scripture.

The Chicago Statement on Biblical Inerrancy is the touchstone of a form of Protestantism concerned to maintain orthodox doctrine against a perceived erosion of belief in the authority and accuracy of the Bible. It was adopted in 1978 by over 300 leading evangelical theologians. The Statement affirms that "inspiration was the work in which God by His Spirit, through human writers, gave us His Word. The origin of Scripture is divine" (Article VII). This statement in Article VII is agnostic as to the manner of this inspiration, which (it says) "remains largely a mystery to us."

The Statement makes reference to the Church, arguing that the doctrine of inerrancy is not a new one: "We affirm that the doctrine of inerrancy has been integral to the Church's faith throughout its history. We deny that inerrancy is a doctrine invented by scholastic Protestantism, or is a reactionary position postulated in response to negative higher criticism" (Article XVI). According to the Statement, a key part of the ongoing testimony of the Spirit is his work of "assuring believers of the truthfulness of God's written Word" (Article XVII).

The Need for an Internally Coherent Account

How might we evaluate the claims of the Chicago Statement? We might start by asking whether the account of revelation that is being advanced is *internally coherent.*

The accounts of revelation offered by the Catholic and Orthodox churches certainly do seem coherent. That is to say, the statements they make about the way the testimony of the Spirit is discerned would (if true) vindicate those statements. For example, the account of the teaching authority of the Roman Catholic Church given in the Documents of the Second Vatican Council (most notably *Lumen Gentium*) would, if true, give us reason to believe that the teaching of the Council was itself inspired by the Holy Spirit.[8] To say that this teaching is *internally coherent* is, of course, very different from saying that it is *compelling*—a matter that lies beyond the remit of this chapter. What is important for our purposes is to note that coherence is a necessary but not a sufficient condition for a tenable account of revelation.

I will argue that the Chicago Statement requires an account of the authority of the Church for its own coherence. If *all* revelatory authority

---

8. See Austin Flannery (ed.), *The Basic Sixteen Documents of Vatican II: A Completely Revised Translation in Inclusive Language* (New York: Costello Publishing Company, 1995), pp. 1–96.

is invested in the written text of scripture, and no room is left for any ecclesiastical authority, the Chicago Statement will find it very difficult to make sense of its own epistemic status. Although we are considering the Chicago Statement in particular, this difficulty will arise for *any* account that seeks to combine a very high doctrine of the reliability of revelation with an exclusive focus of all authority in scripture. If you believe that scripture is the *sole* authority for Christians, and you think that scripture is infallible, on what authority do you make the latter claim?

The Chicago Statement is compatible with a range of different views about the authority of the Church. It denies that "Scriptures receive their authority from the Church, tradition, or any other human source" and that "church creeds, councils, or declarations have authority greater than or equal to the authority of the Bible." This still leaves considerable latitude for either a very individualistic or a very social view of how scripture is interpreted, and how the testimony of the Spirit in our own time is to be discerned.

The Statement offers two arguments for the doctrine of the inerrancy of scripture. One focuses on the text itself, claiming that "the doctrine of inerrancy is grounded in the teaching of the Bible about inspiration" (Article XV). The second appeals to the way the text has been received down through history by the community of the Church. The final section of the Statement says that "In our affirmation of the authority of Scripture as involving its total truth, we are consciously standing with Christ and His apostles, indeed with the whole Bible and with the main stream of Church history from the first days until very recently."

Corresponding with these two lines of argument in the Statement are two possible ways of accounting for its own epistemic status. There is a highly individualistic line of argument, which places most weight on the first of these arguments (i.e., that scripture teaches its own inerrancy, and this insight is available to individuals through their own private reading of scripture), where the appeal to Church history is relatively peripheral to the argument. I will examine this argument later in the next section of this chapter. Alternatively, adherents to the Statement could place much more weight on the social argument, in which case the conviction of Christians in "the main stream of Church history from the first days until very recently" would have some distinct authority, and provide additional grounds for believing scripture to be authoritative. My argument is that it is only the latter reading that is internally consistent—and, therefore, that even Protestants who make the strongest possible affirmation of the verbal authority of scripture have good reason to ascribe an authoritative role to the Church in discerning the testimony of the Spirit.

The Defense from Biblical Teaching on Inerrancy

What exactly *is* the teaching of the Bible about its inspiration? Does the text of scripture (considered independently of the way the Church has treated it across the centuries) provide grounds for the claim that it is inerrant?

One point that is often overlooked, but seems hard to deny, is that the Christian Bible makes no explicit statements about its *composition, extent,* or *authority.* The New Testament texts cited most often in debates on biblical authority (most notably Matt. 5.17–18, 2 Tim. 3:16–17, and 2 Pet. 1:20–21) are clearly not, in their plain sense, about the authority of the Christian Bible *as a whole.* In Matthew 5, Jesus is explicitly referring to "the Law and the Prophets." Likewise, the plain sense of the passages in the Second Letter to Timothy and the Second Letter of Peter can only be referring to the "sacred writings" and "scripture" that their readership would have recognized—that is to say, the Jewish scriptures. Moreover, they do not say that these texts are "inerrant" or "infallible." In Paul's Second Letter to Timothy, we are told that these scriptures are "inspired by God and . . . useful for teaching, for reproof, for correction and for training in righteousness" (2 Tim. 3:16).

The Second Letter of Peter is perhaps the most significant of these passages for our discussion. While the Chicago Statement only quotes the clause that emphasizes the inspiration of the Biblical *text,* the wider context of the passage makes clear that the passage (1) is in fact referring only to Scriptural *prophecies* and (2) is primarily about the importance of the *communal discernment* of the meaning of such prophecies: "First of all, you must understand this, that no prophecy of scripture is a matter of one's own interpretation, because no prophecy ever came by human will, but men and women moved by the Holy Spirit spoke from God" (2 Pet. 1.20–21). In this chapter, unlike the Second Letter to Timothy, a parallel is being made between the authority of the Jewish scriptures and the authority of the writer's testimony, but it would involve a considerable amount of eisegesis to interpret this passage as bestowing the same authority on a specific collection of texts (some of which would not have existed at the time this letter was written) that now form the canon of the New Testament. Indeed, the concept of a canon of *Christian* scripture—that is, of a collection of divinely inspired texts that includes both Old and New Testament—is completely absent from the texts that make up the Christian Bible.

The fact that the Christian Bible lacks any explicit account of its com- position, extent, and authority is so obvious that it can sometimes pass unremarked. But if scripture is the sole source of authoritative Christian revelation, this is a very puzzling omission. According to the Chicago Statement, the Bible is "wholly and verbally God-given, [and] without error or fault in all its teaching," the Holy Spirit being the "divine Author" of its every word. Yet the Spirit has failed to ensure the text contains these three pieces of information that are necessary for its correct reception. (Indeed, there continues to be disagreement within what I have called "orthodox Christianity" about the extent of the canonical texts of scripture.)

It is instructive to compare the Christian Bible's silence on this subject with the teaching of the Koran. The Koran contains clear statements on all three issues: the manner of its composition, the extent of the text, and its authority (e.g., Sura 3:7, 6:92). The Koran contains a clear doctrine of its own authority, so someone holding *this* text to be infallible and inerrant is making a claim that passes the test of internal coherence.

John Barton began his 1988 Bampton Lectures by citing the Koran:

> In a saying which seems to promise a degree of religious toleration much needed in the modern world both East and West, the Qur'an urges the Muslim: "Do not dispute with the People of the Book: say, we believe in what has been sent down to us and what has been sent down to you; our God and your God is one" (Sura 29:45).

But, as Barton went on to observe, the phrase "People of the Book" can serve to obscure the quite fundamental differences between the self- description of the Koran and the self-understanding of Christianity.[9]

First, and most obviously, the Bible does not present itself as the cen- ter of the Christian revelation—which is, of course, the person of Jesus. Second, the genre of the Bible is fundamentally different from that of the Koran. Indeed, the Bible lacks any single genre. It is a collection of very different books, with a multiplicity of earthly authors. (This is not to make a point for or against a doctrine of inerrancy. Even if all the books are inspired, as the Chicago Statement teaches, the tone and temperament of

---

9. John Barton, *People of the Book? The Authority of the Bible in Christianity* (London: SPCK, 1988), p. 1.

the individual authors clearly shines through.) Third, as we have seen, the Koran contains an account of its composition, extent, and authority in a manner strikingly absent from the Christian Bible.

To respect the authority of God's revelation—to sit under it with humility and obedience—is a central concern of the Chicago Statement. Its authors are motivated by the fear that an excessive theological liberalism risks reshaping Christian teaching to fit the preoccupations and interests of the age, so that instead of heeding the testimony of the Spirit, Christians will simply do as they please. That is an understandable concern, and a continuing risk. However, as N. T. Wright argues, we do not respect the Biblical revelation by forcing it into categories that are fundamentally alien:

> It seems, when we get close up to [the Bible], as though, if we grant for a moment that in some sense or other God has indeed inspired this book, he has not wanted to give us an abstract set of truths unrelated to space and time. He has wanted to give us something rather different, which is not (in our post-enlightenment world) nearly so easy to handle as such a set of truths might seem to be.[10]

Wright's reference to the Enlightenment, and the way it may have warped our expectations of the Biblical text, is worth exploring further.

Motivations for Individualism

It is perhaps the influence of Cartesianism in secular philosophy that has moved so many Christians in the direction of an excessively individualistic understanding of the work of the Spirit. An individualistic interpretation of the Chicago Statement involves an ideal of human knowledge that has striking echoes of the one held by René Descartes as he wrote the *Meditations*.[11] Reflecting alone in his study, Descartes wanted to be able to reason from unshakeable foundations through a chain of watertight inferences to an equally certain conclusion. One of the many dangers of the Cartesian approach, and one of its baleful

---

10. N. T. Wright, "How Can The Bible Be Authoritative?" The Laing Lecture (1989), http://ntwrightpage.com/Wright_Bible_Authoritative.htm (accessed August 28, 2015).

11. René Descartes, *Meditations on First Philosophy with Selections from the Objections and Replies*, translated by John Cottingham (Cambridge: Cambridge University Press, 1986), pp. 17f.

influences on subsequent debates in epistemology, is its assumption that, unless this putatively highly secure form of knowledge is available, we are left only with doubt.

Within secular philosophy, the centuries following Descartes have seen a variety of unsuccessful defenses of this kind of foundationalism, followed by a flirtation with various kinds of anti-realism about knowledge in general—a flirtation that gained much of its energy from the all-or-nothing rhetoric of the foundationalists. It is relatively recently that we have seen the re-emergence of positions that are confidently realist about knowledge, and yet more sanguine about the fact that epistemology is usually more a matter of arriving at a "reflective equilibrium" than about building up knowledge from infallible foundations through a series of incontrovertible steps. The work of T. M. Scanlon and Robert Audi on moral epistemology is a good example of this approach.[12]

An approach that stresses reflective equilibrium rather than infallible deductions is necessarily less individualistic. As Scanlon observes:

> Substantive conclusions [in ethics] ... seem "subjective" only if they are assumed to be isolated individual responses, like the occurrence of a desire. But the judgments about reasons which survive [a reflective] equilibrium process are not like this. They too have undergone careful reflection and re-examination. Perhaps it will be said that the process of reflection through which we arrive at an overall view of reasons for action [i.e., ethical reasoning] is not an *intellectual* process in the relevant sense. But this seems to me a mere prejudice.[13]

Scanlon's work on moral epistemology is deeply significant for our discussion because he has challenged two prejudices that often seem to be at work in such debates. The first, which we discussed earlier in the section entitled "The Purpose of the Spirit's Work," is the view that all reflection must be ratiocination. But we can see (from the debates in moral epistemology cited in that section) that this is far from true. Our sentiments are part of the process by which we come to know a set of truths that are

---

12. See Ritchie, *From Morality to Metaphysics*, pp. 16–18 and 107–108; T. M. Scanlon, *The John Locke Lectures 2009: Being Realistic About Reasons*, http://www.philosophy.ox.ac.uk/lectures/john_locke_lectures/past_lectures (accessed September 8, 2015), Lecture IV; and Robert Audi, "Moderate Intuitionism and the Epistemology of Moral Judgment," *Ethical Theory and Moral Practice* 1(1) (1998): 15–44.

13. Scanlon, 2009, p. 26.

nonetheless objective. The second, which is not unrelated, is the view that all knowledge must be built up from infallible foundations by a series of incontrovertible steps. (In some forms of conservative Protestantism, that is accomplished by an initial, Spirit-inspired "leap of faith" to accept the inerrancy of scripture, and then by a watertight process of deductions once that leap has been made.)

In *Love's Knowledge*, Martha Nussbaum writes of an "affective equilibrium" being reached as moral agents develop more nuanced affective responses, in dialogue with both rational arguments and the educated sensibilities of other agents.[14]

In the work of Scanlon and Nussbaum, we are seeing secular Anglo-American philosophy—and in particular moral epistemology—recovering a set of insights that would seem unsurprising to an older tradition of Christian theology. This tradition, which is defended so forcefully by Andrew Louth, sees the correct formation of the sentiments as central to ethical and theological knowledge and recognizes that affective engagement is a source of knowledge. Indeed, as Louth points out, Patristic writers used the same word (*theologia*) for a discourse we have now separated into the disciplines of "theology" and "spirituality."[15] Precisely because of the ways in which self-interest and wishful thinking can act on our sentiments, this tradition of Christian theology has a much stronger sense of the social dimensions of discerning what is and is not the genuine testimony of the Spirit.

Does Individualism Distort Scripture?

The great irony is that the self-image of individualistic Protestantism (that it is about receiving and obeying God's Word, unmediated by corruptible human institutions) is at odds with the historical reality. As Wright suggests, its highly individualistic view of scripture (which is deeply alien to many of the original Reformers) has had to force God's revelation into a shape that comes from secular individualism, and not from any scriptural teaching. The vision of a revelation that is given to the individual with

---

14. Martha Nussbaum, *Love's Knowledge: Essays on Philosophy and Literature* (Oxford: Oxford University Press, 1992), pp. 173–83. See also Martha Nussbaum, *Upheavals of Thought: The Intelligence of the Emotions* (Cambridge: Cambridge University Press, 2001) for a more comprehensive statement of the argument.

15. Louth, *Discerning the Mystery*, p. 3.

certainty (guaranteed by the work of the Spirit inspiring every word of the text, convincing each individual that the text is inspired, and showing each individual its plain meaning) does not come from anything the *Bible* has to say about the process of revelation, or anything we might legitimately infer from the nature of the Bible.

The charge here is a very serious one: that the individualistic epistemology of much Evangelical Protestantism in fact *distorts* the Bible. Precisely because it seeks to force it into a fundamentally alien mold, it has to stretch the text beyond breaking point. The interpretations of 2 Timothy 3 and of 2 Peter 1 we considered above are, in fact, a case in point. The irony is that, as I argued above, in seeking to use them as proof texts for Biblical inerrancy, individualistic defenders of the Chicago Statement have to read something into them that their authors cannot possibly have meant. But this point stands much more generally. If the very plurality of scripture is part of God's intention, then we distort his revelation by making it into a different kind of document. In our efforts to sit only under the authority of the text God *has* given us, we end up making it into a text he has *not* given us.

As Wright observes, this means the very abuses the Reformers criticized in the excessive use of allegory in scriptural interpretation resurface in this individualistic, text-focused Protestantism: "If we are not careful, the appeal to "timeless truths" not only distorts the Bible itself, making it into the sort of book it manifestly is not, but also creeps back, behind the Reformers' polemic against allegory, into a neo-allegorization which is all the more dangerous for being unrecognised."[16] Rowan Williams makes a related point in an essay entitled "The Discipline of Scripture."[17] Like Wright, Williams argues that we must allow our doctrine of revelation to be shaped appropriately by the genre and circumstances of the revelation, rather than attempting to force it into a mold that we have decided upon independently of that divine disclosure.

Williams draws our attention to the fact that the biblical texts are the texts of a living community. Quite unlike the Koran (which tells us that it has been revealed to a single individual), the Bible declares itself to have many different human authors. These authors are evidently engaged in a dialogue with one another. As Williams observes, this is most obvious

---

16. Wright, "How Can The Bible Be Authoritative?"

17. In Rowan Williams, *On Christian Theology* (Oxford: Basil Blackwell, 2000), pp. 44–60.

in the relationship between New and Old Testaments: "To read the New Testament with any understanding at all is to see it in part as an attempt to claim and re-order the existing texts and traditions of a community from which the producers of these new texts seek to distance themselves even as they seek to present themselves as its true heirs." But, as he goes on to argue, this process of dialogue is already present in the Hebrew Scriptures:

> Ruth not only tells the story of a "mixed marriage" such as the policy of Ezra and Nehemiah disallowed, it also presents this disreputable event as a crucial moment in the working out of the covenant, since David is presented as Ruth's descendant; while Jonah wittily contrasts the disobedience and stubbornness of a Hebrew prophet of impeccable credentials with the ready obedience of everybody and everything else ... In both Ruth and Jonah, the integrity of the covenant, which Ezra's circle seek to preserve by an enforcement of "purity," separateness, is made to rest primarily on God's single-minded will to show mercy and to raise up new things, rather than on a narrow interpretation of human single-mindedness. Yet Ezra is not written out of the story as a whole: without the zeal for renewal, the very sense of covenanted identity of God's people, symbolised in the rebuilt Temple, would be eroded, and the history of divine faithfulness that is taken for granted in Ruth and Jonah would be in danger of oblivion.[18]

The recognition that there is a dialogue going on within the scriptures is not (as the authors of the Chicago Statement might fear) the first step on a very slippery slope to theological liberalism. Rather, such recognition of the kind of text the Bible actually is must be part of any serious attempt to sit under its authority. The significance of Williams' argument is that the Bible speaks to us of a truth *discerned in community*—that the way the Spirit seems to have chosen to disclose the truth to us in scripture is not simply by putting words into the minds of individuals, but by enabling a canon of texts to emerge and enabling each generation of the community to interpret it.

At several different stages in this process, the discernment of the testimony of the Spirit is social, not purely individualistic. First, as we have

---

18. Ibid., pp. 53–54.

seen, the biblical writers are engaged in a communal dialogue. Second, it was the community of the Church that discerned the extent and authority of the scriptures. Third, because of the plural and dialogic nature of the biblical texts, the Church has an ongoing role in interpreting them today (whether or not one also grants the Church a role in revealing truths that are not contained within—though not incompatible with—its teaching). Far from being the first step on the slippery slope to liberalism, it is only an account of the role of the Church in discerning the meaning of scripture and the subsequent testimony of the Spirit that will in the end preserve us from the liberalism the authors of the Chicago Statement fear. For in fact Christian orthodoxy is most likely to be undermined when it is based on an account of the Bible that is at odds with the evident nature of the text.

The dispute here is not one about what authority scripture should have relative to reason and the Church. Rather, the question is whether the account of scripture in an individualistic understanding of the testimony of the Spirit is faithful to the kind of document God has actually given us—or whether it is forced to "make the Bible into something which it basically is not." If the evidence of scripture is that (both in the composition of the scriptures, and—as we saw in the section "The Purpose of the Spirit's Work"—the content of its message) the Spirit's testimony and work involves the community as well as the individual believer, then an excessively individualistic Protestantism contradicts the very document it takes to be solely authoritative.

Conclusion

The argument of this chapter has been that the authority of scripture and the authority of the Christian community go together. Far from pulling in opposite theological directions, the nature and content of the Christian scriptures demand an authoritative community of interpretation—and the testimony of the Church over the centuries has consistently affirmed the authority of scripture.

As well as offering a positive account of the role of the Christian community in discerning the testimony of the Spirit, I have claimed that there is an incoherence involved in asserting the supreme authority of the Christian scriptures while denying any authority to the Christian community. I have supported this claim by examining the Chicago Statement, the most prominent Protestant affirmation of biblical inerrancy. My argument has been that the only coherent reading of the Chicago Statement is one that gives some authority to the Christian community, and therefore to the social discernment of the testimony of the Holy Spirit.

As well as arguing for a communal reading of the Chicago Statement, I have sought to explain the continuing attraction of a more individualistic Protestantism. I have suggested that its appeal comes not from within the Bible, but from a Cartesian epistemology, in which it is assumed that beliefs can only be justified if they proceed from unshakeable foundations through a chain of watertight inferences to a therefore equally certain conclusion. As I have argued, this is an untenable approach—a fact increasingly recognized by secular as well as religious epistemologists. Indeed, secular epistemology is now recovering a set of insights that should be familiar to Christian thinkers who have not fallen into Cartesianism. In its new appreciation of the role of affect, and in particular of the correct formation of the sentiments in ethical knowledge, secular epistemology is moving in the very direction writers such as Louth and Kolakowski are arguing for in theology. These writers would (in my view, rightly) argue that this involves the recovery of an earlier understanding of theological knowledge, rather than any kind of new departure.

All of these considerations serve to reinforce the central theses of this chapter: (1) the discernment of the testimony of the Holy Spirit has a social dimension and (2) a proper recognition of this does not compete with the authority of scripture. Rather, it is a consequence of taking the nature and content of the Christian scriptures seriously.[19]

---

19. I am very grateful to the Rev. Dr. Philip Krinks and to Andy Walton for their comments on the text.

Bibliography on the Testimony
of the Spirit

Abraham, William J. 1990. "The Epistemological Significance of the Inner Witness of the Holy Spirit." *Faith and Philosophy* 7: 434–50.

Aloisi, John. 2004. "The Paraclete's Ministry of Conviction: Another look at John 16:8–11." *Journal of the Evangelical Theological Society* 47: 55–69.

Aquinas, Thomas. 1998. *Light of Faith: Compendium of Theology*, rev. ed. Bedford, NH: Sophia Institute Press.

Averbeck, Richard E. 2005. "God, People, and the Bible: The Relationship between Illumination and Biblical Scholarship." In Daniel B. Wallace and M. James Sawyer (eds.), *Who's Afraid of the Holy Spirit? An Investigation into the Ministry of the Spirit of God Today*, pp. 137–66. Dallas, TX: Biblical Studies Press.

Badcock, F. J. 1933–34. "'The Spirit' and Spirit in the New Testament." *Expository Times* 45: 218–22.

Baillie, John. 1939. *Our Knowledge of God*. New York: Charles Scribner's Sons.

Baillie, John. 1962. *The Sense of the Presence of God*. New York: Charles Scribner's Sons.

Begbie, Jeremy. 1992. "Who Is This God? Biblical Inspiration Revisited." *Tyndale Bulletin* 43: 259–82.

Berkhof, Hendrikus. 1964. *The Doctrine of the Holy Spirit*. Richmond, VA: John Knox Press.

Berkouwer, G. C. 1975. "The Testimony of the Spirit." In G. C. Berkouwer (ed.), *Studies in Dogmatics: Holy Scripture*, trans. J. B. Rogers, pp. 39–66. Grand Rapids, MI: Eerdmans.

Bondi, Roberta C. 1986. "The Role of the Holy Spirit from a United Methodist Perspective." *Greek Orthodox Theological Review* 31: 351–60.

Bruner, F. D. 1970. *A Theology of the Holy Spirit*. Grand Rapids, MI: Eerdmans.

Brunner, Emil. 1962. *Dogmatics, Vol. III: The Christian Doctrine of the Church, Faith, and the Consummation*, trans. David Cairns. London: Lutterworth Press.

Burke, Trevor J., and Keith Warrington (eds.). 2014. *A Biblical Theology of the Holy Spirit*. Eugene, OR: Cascade Books.

Carrell, William. 2008. "The Inner Testimony of the Spirit: Locating the Coherent Center of E.Y. Mullins's Theology." *Baptist History and Heritage* 43: 35–48.

Carson, D. A., and John D. Woodbridge (eds.). 1992. *Scripture and Truth*. Grand Rapids, MI: Baker Academic.

Chung, Paul. 2002. "Calvin and the Holy Spirit: A Reconsideration in Light of Spirituality and Social Ethics." *Pneuma* 24: 40–55.

Congar, Yves. 1983. *I Believe in the Holy Spirit, Vol. 1: The Experience of the Spirit*, trans. David Smith. London: Geoffrey Chapman.

Cosgrove, Charles. 1989. *The Cross and the Spirit*. Macon, GA: Mercer University Press.

Del Colle, Ralph. 2001. "The Holy Spirit: Presence, Power, Person." *Theological Studies* 62: 322–40.

Dewar, Lindsay. 1959. *The Holy Spirit and Modern Thought*. New York: Harper.

Dickie, Edward P. 1954. *God Is Light*. New York: Charles Scribner's Sons.

Dillistone, F. W. 1946. *The Holy Spirit in the Life of Today*. London: Canterbury.

Dragas, George D. 2011. "The Seal of the Gift of the Holy Spirit: The Sacrament of Chrismation." *Greek Orthodox Theological Review* 56: 143–59.

Duggan, Michael. 1985. "The Cross and the Holy Spirit in Paul: Implications for Baptism in the Holy Spirit." *Pneuma* 7: 135–46.

Dunn, James D. G. 1970. *Baptism in the Holy Spirit*. London: SCM Press.

Dunn, James D. G. 1975. *Jesus and the Spirit: A Study of the Religious and Charismatic Experience of Jesus and the First Christians as Reflected in the New Testament*. Grand Rapids, MI: Eerdmans.

Dunn, James D. G. 1998. *The Christ and the Spirit, Vol. 2: Pneumatology*. Grand Rapids, MI: Eerdmans.

Dunn, James D. G. 2009. *The Living Word*, 2d ed. Minneapolis: Fortress Press.

Durwell, François. 1980. "Christian Witness: A Theological Study." *International Review of Mission* 69: 121–34.

Eckman, David. 2005. "The Holy Spirit and Our Emotions." In Daniel B. Wallace and M. James Sawyer (eds.), *Who's Afraid of the Holy Spirit? An Investigation into the Ministry of the Spirit of God Today*, pp. 203–20. Dallas, TX: Biblical Studies Press.

Edwards, Jonathan. 1984 [1741]. *The Distinguishing Marks of a Work of the Spirit of God*. Edinburgh: Banner of Truth Trust.

Elbert, Paul. 2009. "Contextual Analysis and Interpretation with Sensitivity to the Spirit as Interactive Person: Editor's Explanation and Welcome to JBPR." *Journal of Biblical and Pneumatological Research* 1: 1–14.

Fea, John. 1994. "Power from on High in an Age of Ecclesiastical Impotence: The 'Enduement of the Holy Spirit' in American Fundamentalist Thought, 1880–1936." *Fides et Historia* 26: 23–35.

Fee, Gordon D. 1994. *God's Empowering Presence: The Holy Spirit in the Letters of Paul*. Peabody, MA: Hendrickson Publishers.

Fee, Gordon D. 1996. *Paul, the Spirit, and the People of God.* Grand Rapids, MI: Baker.

Ferre, Nels. 1969. *The Universal Word.* Philadelphia: Westminster Press.

Fitzgerald, Michael L. 1997. "Witness and Dialogue." *International Review of Mission* 86: 340–41, 113–17.

Foster, Frank Hugh. 1900. *Christian Life and Theology.* Chicago: Fleming Revell.

Foster, Frank Hugh. 1903. "Review: Where May Christian Certainty Be Found?" *American Journal of Theology* 7: 730–33.

Grant, Reg. 2005. "The Holy Spirit and the Arts." In Daniel B. Wallace and M. James Sawyer (eds.), *Who's Afraid of the Holy Spirit? An Investigation into the Ministry of the Spirit of God Today*, pp. 167–82. Dallas, TX: Biblical Studies Press.

Guillaume, Alfred. 1938. *Prophecy and Divination.* London: Hodder and Stoughton.

Gunkel, Hermann. 1979 [1888]. *The Influence of the Holy Spirit*, trans. R. A. Harrisville and P. A. Quanbeck. Philadelphia: Fortress Press.

Helm, Paul. 1998. "John Calvin, the Sensus Divinitatis, and the Noetic Effects of Sin." *International Journal for Philosophy of Religion* 43: 87–107.

Helm, Paul. 2004. "Natural Theology and the Sensus Divinitatis." In Paul Helm (ed.), *John Calvin's Ideas*, pp. 209–45. Oxford: Oxford University Press.

Hendry, G. S. 1957. *The Holy Spirit in Christian Theology.* London: SCM Press.

Hepp, V. 1914. *Het Testimonium Spiritus Sancti.* Kampen: J. H. Kok.

Hermann, Wilhelm. 1906. *The Communion of the Christian with God*, trans. J. Sandys Stanyon. Minneapolis: Fortress Press, 1971.

Hilderbrandt, Wilf. 1995. *An Old Testament Theology of the Spirit of God.* Peabody, MA: Hendrickson Publishers.

Hoeck, Andreas. 2012. "The Johannine Paraclete: Herald of the Eschaton." *Journal of Biblical and Pneumatological Research* 4: 23–37.

Hoyle, R. B. 1927. *The Holy Spirit in St. Paul.* London: Hodder and Stoughton.

Hübner, Hans. 1989. "The Holy Spirit in Holy Scripture." *Ecumenical Review* 41: 324–38.

Humphries, A. L. 1917. *The Holy Spirit in Faith and Experience.* London: SCM Press.

Jeffreys, Derek S. 1997. "How Reformed Is Reformed Epistemology? Alvin Plantinga and Calvin's Sensus Divinitatis." *Religious Studies* 33: 419–31.

Jenkins, John I. 1997. *Knowledge and Faith in Thomas Aquinas.* Cambridge: Cambridge University Press.

Jerseld, Paul. 2000. *Spirit Ethics.* Minneapolis: Fortress Press.

Kaftan, Julius. 1894. *The Truth of the Christian Religion.* Edinburgh: T & T Clark.

Kärkäinen, Veli-Matti. 2004. "The Working of the Spirit of God in Creation and in the People of God: The Pneumatology of Wolfhart Pannenberg." *Journal of the Society for Pentecostal Studies* 26: 17–35.

Kärkäinen, Veli-Matti (ed.). 2010. *Holy Spirit and Salvation: The Sources of Christian Theology.* Louisville, KY: Westminster Press.

Klooster, F. H. 1984. "Internal Testimony of the Spirit." In Walter Elwell (ed.), *Evangelical Dictionary of Theology*, pp. 564–65. Grand Rapids, MI: Baker.

Kooi, Cornelis van der. 1994. "Within Proper Limits: Basic Features of John Calvin's Theological Epistemology." *Calvin Theological Journal* 29: 364–87.

Kooi, Cornelis van der. 2008. "The Appeal to the Inner Testimony of the Spirit, Especially in H. Bavinck." *Journal of Reformed Theology* 2: 103–12.

Kuruvilla, Abraham. 1989. "The Holy Spirit in the Mar Thoma Tradition." *Ecumenical Review* 41: 436–45.

Kuyper, Abraham. 1941. *The Work of the Holy Spirit*. Grand Rapids, MI: Eerdmans.

Lampe, G. W. H. 1951. *The Seal of the Spirit*. London: Longmans, Green.

Lampe, G. W. H. 1955. "The Holy Spirit in the Writings of St. Luke." In D. E. Nineham (ed.), *Studies in the Gospels*, pp. 159–200. Oxford: Blackwell.

Lampe, G. W. H. 1972. "The Holy Spirit and the Person of Christ." In S. W. Sykes and J. P. Clayton (eds.), *Christ, Faith and History: Cambridge Studies in Christology*, pp. 111–30. Cambridge: Cambridge University Press.

Lampe, G. W. H. 1977. *God as Spirit*. Oxford: Oxford University Press.

McDonnell, Kilian. 1985. "A Trinitarian Theology of the Holy Spirit." *Theological Studies* 46: 191–227.

Menzies, Robert P. 2006. "A Fitting Tribute: A Review Essay of The Holy Spirit and Christian Origins: Essays in Honor of James D. G. Dunn." *Pneuma* 28: 131–40.

Moller, Philip. 2013. "What Should They Be Saying About Biblical Inspiration? A Note on the State of the Question." *Theological Studies* 74: 605–31.

Moltmann, Jürgen. 1977. *The Church in the Power of the Spirit*. London: SCM Press.

Moltmann, Jürgen. 1993. *God in Creation: A New Theology of Creation and the Spirit of God*. Minneapolis: Fortress Press.

Montgomery, John Warwick. 1997. "The Holy Spirit and the Defense of the Faith." *Bibliotheca Sacra* 154: 387–95.

Morgan-Wynne, John E. 1984. "The Holy Spirit and Christian Experience in Justin Martyr." *Vigiliae Christianae* 38: 172–77.

Moser, Paul K. 2008. *The Elusive God*. Cambridge: Cambridge University Press.

Moser, Paul K. 2017. *The God Relationship*. Cambridge: Cambridge University Press.

Moule, C. F. D. *The Holy Spirit*. Oxford: Mowbray.

Nessan, Craig L. 1994. "Allergic to the Spirit No More: Rethinking Pneumatology." *Currents in Theology and Mission* 21: 183–96.

Novenson, Matthew V. 2010. "'God Is Witness': A Classical Rhetorical Idiom in Its Pauline Usage." *Novum Testamentum* 52: 355–75.

Packer, J. I. 2005. "The Ministry of the Spirit in Discerning the Will of God." In Daniel B. Wallace and M. James Sawyer (eds.), *Who's Afraid of the Holy Spirit? An Investigation into the Ministry of the Spirit of God Today*, pp. 95–110. Dallas, TX: Biblical Studies Press.

Pannenberg, Wolfhart. 1977. *Theology and the Kingdom of God*. Philadelphia: Westminster Press.

Pannenberg, Wolfhart. 1993. *Toward a Theology of Nature: Essays on Science and Faith*. Louisville, KY: Westminster John Knox Press.

Pannenberg, Wolfhart. 2001. "God as Spirit—and Natural Science." *Zygon: Journal of Religion and Science* 36: 783–94.

Plantinga, Alvin. 2000. *Warranted Christian Belief.* New York: Oxford University Press.

Polkinghorne, John. 2001. "Field Theories and Theology: A Response to Wolfhart Pannenberg." *Zygon: Journal of Religion and Science* 36: 796.

Polkinghorne, John. 2007. *One World: The Interaction of Science and Theology.* Philadelphia: Temple Foundation Press.

Rabens, Volker. 2013. *The Holy Spirit and Ethics in Paul,* 2d ed. Minneapolis: Fortress Press.

Ramm, Bernard. 1960. *The Witness of the Spirit.* Grand Rapids, MI: Eerdmans.

Robinson, H. Wheeler. 1928. *The Christian Experience of the Holy Spirit.* London: Nisbet.

Sabatier, Auguste. 1904. *Religions of Authority and the Religion of the Spirit.* New York: Hodder and Stoughton.

Sawyer, M. James. 2005. "The Witness of the Spirit in the Protestant Tradition." In Daniel B. Wallace and M. James Sawyer (eds.), *Who's Afraid of the Holy Spirit? An Investigation into the Ministry of the Spirit of God Today,* pp. 71–94. Dallas, TX: Biblical Studies Press.

Schweizer, Eduard. 1980. *The Holy Spirit,* trans. R. H. and Ilse Fuller. Philadelphia: Fortress Press.

Scott, E. F. 1923. *The Spirit in the New Testament.* New York: Hodder and Stoughton.

Smeaton, George. 1882. *The Doctrine of the Holy Spirit.* Edinburgh: T & T Clark.

Stanton, Graham, Bruce Longenecker, and Stephen Barton, eds. 2004. *The Holy Spirit and Christian Origins.* Grand Rapids, MI: Eerdmans.

Stearns, Lewis French. 1911. *The Evidence of Christian Experience.* The Ely Lectures for 1890. New York: Charles Scribner's Sons.

Stortz, Martha. 2005. "Purpose-Driven or Spirit-Led?" *Word & World* 25: 403–12.

Streeter, B. F. 1922. *The Spirit: The Relation of God and Man, Considered from the Standpoint of Recent Philosophy and Science.* New York: Macmillan.

Swete, Henry. 1910. *The Holy Spirit in the New Testament.* London: Macmillan.

Taylor, John V. 1972. *The Go-Between God.* London: SCM Press.

Thielicke, Helmut. 1974. *The Evangelical Faith, Vol. 1: Prolegomena,* trans. G. W. Bromiley, Chaps. 7–10. Grand Rapids, MI: Eerdmans.

Thielicke, Helmut. 1982. *The Evangelical Faith, Vol. 3: Theology of the Spirit,* trans. G. W. Bromiley. Grand Rapids, MI: Eerdmans.

Thiselton, Anthony C. 2013. *The Holy Spirit—In Biblical Teaching, Through the Centuries, and Today.* Grand Rapids, MI: Eerdmans.

Trites, Allison. 1977. *The New Testament Concept of Witness.* Cambridge: Cambridge University Press.

Turner, Max. 1996. *Power from on High.* Sheffield: Sheffield Academic.

Turner, Max. 1997. *The Holy Spirit and Spiritual Gifts.* Peabody, MA: Hendrickson.

Van Pelt, J. R. 1908. "Witness." In James Hastings (ed.), *Dictionary of Christ and the Gospels,* Volume 2, pp. 830–32. Edinburgh: T & T Clark.

Wallace, Daniel B., and M. James Sawyer (eds.). *Who's Afraid of the Holy Spirit? An Investigation into the Ministry of the Spirit of God Today.* Dallas, TX: Biblical Studies Press.

Welker, Michael. 1989. "The Holy Spirit." *Theology Today* 46: 5–20.

Welker, Michael. 2004. *God the Spirit.* Minneapolis: Fortress Press.

Welker, Michael. 2007. "The Holy Spirit." In Kathryn Tanner, John Webster, and Iaian Torrence (eds.), *The Oxford Handbook of Systematic Theology*, pp. 236–48. Oxford: Oxford University Press.

Wesley, John. 1836. "The Witness of the Spirit." In Wesley, *Sermons on Several Occasions*, 2 vols. New York: Waugh and Mason.

Whapham, Theodore James. 2014. "Spirit as Field of Force." *Scottish Journal of Theology* 67: 15–32.

Wilder, William. 2001. *Echoes of the Exodus Narrative in the Context and Background of Galatians 5:18.* New York: Peter Lang.

Winstanley, Edward W. 1908. *Spirit in the New Testament.* Cambridge: Cambridge University Press.

Wright, Christopher. 2006. *Knowing the Holy Spirit Through the Old Testament.* Downers Grove, IL: InterVarsity Press.

Yates, John C. 1993. "How Does God Speak to Us Today: Biblical Anthropology and the Witness of the Holy Spirit." *Churchman* 107: 102–29.

Index

Scripture Index